D1446617

ISLAMIC BRANDING AND MARKETING

CREATING A GLOBAL ISLAMIC BUSINESS

ISLAMIC BRANDING AND MARKETING
CREATING A GLOBAL ISLAMIC BUSINESS

PAUL TEMPORAL

WILEY

John Wiley & Sons (Asia) Pte. Ltd.

Copyright © 2011 John Wiley & Sons (Asia) Pte. Ltd.
Published in 2011 by John Wiley & Sons (Asia) Pte. Ltd.
1 Fusionopolis Walk, #07-01, Solaris South Tower, Singapore 138628

Other Wiley Editorial Offices

John Wiley & Sons, 111 River Street, Hoboken, NJ 07030, USA

John Wiley & Sons, The Atrium, Southern Gate, Chichester, West Sussex, P019 8SQ,
    United Kingdom

John Wiley & Sons (Canada) Ltd., 5353 Dundas Street West, Suite 400, Toronto, Ontario,
    M9B 6HB, Canada

John Wiley & Sons Australia Ltd., 42 McDougall Street, Milton, Queensland 4064, Australia

Wiley-VCH, Boschstrasse 12, D-69469 Weinheim, Germany

Library of Congress Cataloging-in-Publication Data

ISBN 978-0-470-82539-6 (Hardcover)

ISBN 978-0-470-82847-2 (e-PDF)

ISBN 978-0-470-82846-5 (e-Mobi)

ISBN 978-0-470-82848-9 (e-Pub)

Typeset in 10.5/13.5 Berkeley Medium by MPS Limited, a Macmillan Company

Printed in Singapore by Toppan Security Printing Pte. Ltd.

10 9 8 7 6 5 4 3 2 1

Contents

Preface

Very little has been written to date about how Islamic branding and marketing, or "marketing to Muslims," differs from or is similar to traditional branding and marketing, which is based on Western corporate development. The lack of literature on the topic is surprising, given the extent of the world's Muslim population and the prominence of Islam. This gap in our knowledge gave rise to The Oxford Research and Education Project on Islamic Branding and Marketing, which is being conducted at Oxford University's Saïd Business School and which I am directing. A brief description of this project is given in Appendix 1. Much of the findings of this research work have been incorporated into this text.

A second reason for writing this book is that many of my clients, as well as professional people whom I have met in Islamic countries, have commented to me on the need for a body of thought on this subject area. The extent of this interest, and the impact of the extremely rapid development of Islamic countries on the aspirations of Muslims in a branded world, leave me in no doubt that the next wave of global branding will come from Islamic economies and companies.

A third reason is that global brands from Western countries are becoming very interested in Muslim markets. Some have already started to build their brands across the Islamic world and are seeking to achieve a complete global presence by entering the last remaining and biggest significant segment of the world's population.

Around 23 percent of the world's population is Islamic, with varying degrees of affiliation and implementation of that religion. While some businesses, academics, and people living in the West often think of the Islamic population as being concentrated in a handful of nations, especially in the Middle East and Southeast Asia, the truth is that there are significant Muslim-minority populations around the world—from India to China, and from France to Japan.

In Islamic-majority and minority countries throughout the Middle East, Asia, Africa, and Europe, there is a massive amount of business activity, with

Islamic trade currently assessed as being worth trillions of dollars. In terms of global economic power and commercial success, it is becoming clear that Islamic countries are gaining ground on their Western counterparts.

The rising prosperity and spreading population of Islam is, however, only part of the story. Muslim consumers are no different to non-Muslims in their love of brands. From a marketing perspective, just as the Western world has done, the Muslim world would dearly like to develop an array of leading global brands of its own.

Muslim countries would also like to see their local brands going global, because they have seen how powerful brands can be in making an economic contribution and shaping a country's national image. In particular, they have noticed that the cultivation of intangible assets such as strong brands is seen as an essential feature of a mature, stable national economy. Finally, many Muslim countries want to diversify their business interests in order to achieve greater economic well-being and to rely less on narrow resource-based industries such as energy.

Since the late 1980s, there has been a substantial increase in the number and success of Western-held brands. During the 1990s, we saw a competitive response beginning in Asia, with brands from countries such as Singapore, South Korea, India, and China making considerable progress in regional and global markets.

It is perhaps not surprising, therefore, that early signs of branding success from Islamic countries, such as those in the Middle East and Asia, are emerging. At the same time, the vast potential represented by large Muslim populations everywhere has caught the eye of the Western multinationals.

However, it is only recently that the potential of the global Islamic market has been fully understood. Principally, the impetus for doing more business in Islamic-majority and minority markets has come from three sources:

- the rapid expansion of Western brands to penetrate these markets in order to gain a global presence;
- the response from Islamic companies, and the need to rely less on finite resources such as oil production; and
- the rise of industries that conform to Islamic practice, such as Islamic financial services.

By way of response, Islamic audiences love Western brands, but there are three main reasons why they wish to have their own.

1. Western brands are often not compliant with Islamic values (or their ethical base)—for instance, in hospitality, food and beverage, pharmaceutical and medical products, and services markets.
2. Islamic countries want to create their own global brands, which they see as strategic business assets and national brand ambassadors.
3. The growth of the educated middle class in Muslim-minority and majority cultures and countries has created an impetus for developing businesses, products, and services that are competitive with the long-established and accepted brands.

As a consequence of the above, there is now a considerable surge in demand within Islamic countries and companies to master the branding and marketing techniques and skills so ably demonstrated by the West in order to address international perceptions not just of Islamic products, services, and businesses, but also of the countries and cultures of their origin.

What Is "Islamic Branding and Marketing"?

When I use the phrase "Islamic branding and marketing," I am not referring just to brands that originate from Islamic countries, although they would of course come under such a definition. Rather, I am referring to *any brands that seek to address the needs of Muslim markets*. I include in this definition any activity related to the branding and marketing of countries, products, and services to Islamic audiences, regardless of whether or not they derive from a Muslim-majority or Muslim-minority country or have Muslim ownership. This rather broad definition thus encompasses not just Islamic branding and marketing to Muslim-owned businesses, but also companies that don't have Islamic owners but which are reaching out to Muslim consumers. Thus, non-Muslim brands would also come under this heading if they were looking to build their brands and market share in any

Muslim-majority or minority market; brands such as Nestlé, for example. Indeed, many of the first-mover brands that are meeting the needs of global Muslim audiences are owned by non-Muslim companies.

I also use the terms "Islamic" and "Muslim" interchangeably on occasion. Muslims are people who are followers of Islam, and so one can refer to "Islamic markets" and "Muslim markets" and mean the same thing.

Branding and Religion

No doubt, there will be some observers who will comment that it is not appropriate to mix branding and marketing with religion, but I would disagree on this point. From a marketing perspective, it is always good to give consumers what they really want, and Muslims are a significant market segment that hasn't yet been studied and understood. It would be foolish to think that Islam as a religion doesn't influence the needs and wants of its followers. Western brands and marketers fully understand the main markets they are dealing with, but Islam as a market has not yet been properly addressed, either in Muslim-majority or minority markets. The opening up of these markets, and the increased immigration of Muslims to Western countries as significant minorities, can no longer be ignored.

The question of segmenting markets based on religion is always a thorny one. Most of the brand managers I have met while conducting my research have emphasized that they are not selling a religion; they are giving a large market products and services they have long wanted but which have never before been tailored to them.

From this wider definition it follows that I am writing not about building religious brands, but about building brands that appeal to a global religious population; a global audience who are bound together by common values and practices.

Another reason for taking a wider stance is that, although Muslims have a set of shared values and principles, as markets they can behave very differently. There are, in fact, a number of variables—the industry category, the brand positioning, the country of origin, and the varying cultures and degrees of religiosity—that make "Islamic branding and marketing" very difficult to pin down in terms of consumer behavior. These issues, and many more, will be discussed throughout the book. Nevertheless, there are a great many opportunities for brand and marketing managers when looking at the needs of the Muslim world.

The Oxford Research and Education Project on Islamic Branding and Marketing (see Appendix 1) was instituted in 2008 after I began to question why there were not more brands emanating from, and addressing the needs of, Islamic countries and their populations. The project is ongoing, and involves working with a variety of partners.

A Large and Disparate Market

The Muslim market is huge and disparate. One of the interesting findings of the research that I have been involved in is that, despite the huge numbers and—in the case of Muslim-majority countries—concentrations, there is no one homogeneous Islamic or Muslim market. As we will see, Muslims account for a quarter of the world's population, and yet within this huge global segment there are many different forms of consumer behavior that are dependent on a wide array of variables, many of which have not yet been researched properly. Thus, this book is groundbreaking in its attempt to understand one of the largest single markets in the world, and to provide advice on how to reach that market to brand and marketing professionals.

It should be noted that I have not taken into account the five different schools of Islamic thought—Shia, Hanafi, Maliki, Hanbali, and Shafi'i—in writing this book. They are highly technical; and although they account for issues that may impinge on marketing, a discussion of them would not add substantial value to the principles and strategies discussed. They are all consistent in following the fundamental thinking of Islam, but they can interpret various concepts in different ways. This can affect whether or not some products and services developed under one school of thought are accepted by scholars from another school, and thus be allowed or not allowed to be sold in certain countries. This book doesn't attempt to probe these different schools, but it would be advisable for those involved in new product development in, say, Islamic finance, to take them into consideration.

Overview of the Book ━━━━━━━━━━━━

This book describes what is happening in Muslim markets, contrasts Western and Muslim branding and marketing activities, and looks at what the future holds for both Western and Islamic brands in global markets.

Chapter 1 introduces some of the concepts underlying Islamic economics and business, and examines why branding and marketing are gaining in importance within this framework.

Chapter 2 underlines how serious branding and marketing activities are in terms of their potential impact on national prosperity. In particular, it looks at the need for branding to be carried out at the national, sector, industry, and corporate levels if its full impact is to be realized.

In Chapter 3, I will look more specifically at the structure of Muslim-majority and minority markets, describe their similarities, and give an overview of the latest research on the Muslim market worldwide. We will see that this research is giving marketers not only more precise information, but also some clues as to how Muslim markets can behave differently and how they might be segmented.

Chapter 4 looks at the sources of brands in Islamic markets, and gives a typology with examples that reveal the many opportunities that can be explored by aspiring businesses.

Chapter 5 deals with the principles of branding and explains how these can be adapted by Islamic brands, especially with regard to the use of universally appealing values.

Chapter 6 looks at the variety of strategic opportunities for Islamic branding and marketing, including options for brand creation and business development across many categories, including *halal* food, finance, cosmetics, pharmaceuticals, health care, hospitality, and more lifestyle products and services, with case studies to illustrate these.

Chapter 7 discusses the future in terms of digital branding and marketing, and looks at the specific opportunities offered within this fast-growing category.

Chapter 8 summarizes the challenges faced by Islamic companies in building and marketing international brands. Chapter 9 follows with a comprehensive exposition of the key factors and branding and marketing strategies that will be of use to all aspiring Islamic companies in order to be successful in overcoming these challenges in global markets.

Chapter 10 looks at the challenges and strategies for non-Muslim brands in reaching out to Muslim markets, while Chapter 11 summarizes the lessons to be learned and makes some strategic business recommendations for Islamic and non-Islamic brands.

Finally, as we shall also see in this book, non-Muslims can also be attracted to Islamic products intended for Muslims, a fact that offers both challenges and opportunities for brand managers and marketers.

Paul Temporal, 2011

Acknowledgments

Many people, organizations and governments have kindly offered advice, information and content that has been included in the writing of this book, and I am grateful to them all, including:

Chicken Cottage Ltd., DinarStandard, Dubai Aluminium (DUBAL), EMEL, EuropeArab Bank, Gallup, Government of Brunei Darussalam, Government of Malaysia, HSBC, Islam Channel, Islamic Bank of Britain, Johor Corporation, J. Walter Thompson (JWT), MDUK Media, MoneyGram International, Muxlim Inc, Nestlé, Ogilvy & Mather Worldwide, Ogilvy Noor, OnePure Beauty, Opus, Petronas, Pew Research Center, Standard Chartered Bank and Standard Chartered Saadiq, State Government of Sarawak, The Muslim Council of Britain, Ummah Foods.

Allen Lai, Amjid Ali, Azrulnizam Abd Aziz, Firoz Abdul Hamid, John Goodman, Kazi Hussain, Khalid Sharif, Lau Kong Cheen, Layla Mandi, M. Fahad Mehboob, Michael Maedel, Miles Young, Mohamed El-Fatatry, Muhammad Ali Hashim, Naeem Dar, Nazia Hussain, Noel Shield, Riaz Hassan, Riaz Ramzan, Rafi-uddin Shikoh, Roy Haddad, Roziah Abu Bakar, Sarah Joseph , Stephen Lee, Steven Amos, Suhaimi Halim, Tariq Ramadan, Tunku Siti Raudzoh Tunku Ibrahim.

I would particularly like to thank the Saïd Business School, University of Oxford, and all of my colleagues there for their support, encouragement, and assistance, and in allowing research and forum material to be published. However, the views and opinions expressed in this book are mine and do not necessarily reflect those of the University of Oxford.

1 Introduction

Islam: The Religion and the Brand ━━━━━━

Islam has a huge following, as befits a religion that is around 14 centuries old. Islam is based on a belief in one God, Allah. The primary sources of Islamic law that believers follow are the *Qur'an*, a book believed to have been given by Allah to the Prophet Muhammad, and the *Sunnah*, a body of Islamic law based on the Prophet Muhammad's words and deeds. Followers of Islam are known as Muslims. The word "Muslim" means "those who accept and submit to the will of God."

Islam, as with any other well-known name, has an image. It can be considered to be a brand in its own right, with its own brand image; and like any global brand, this image is viewed differently by different people in different places. However, Islam is a very complex brand, and the differences in religious affiliation to Islam enhance this complexity; for example, the Sunni and Shia sects interpret some of the principles of Islam in different ways. And Islam, like any brand, may be perceived either positively or negatively. When left uncontrolled or unmanaged, such positive and negative perceptions will affect attitudes toward the brand.

For instance, in the West, some negative connotations of the word "Islam" stem principally from associations with extremist forms of behavior. While the purpose of this book is not to look at this issue, the lack of education and understanding about the religion is one reason for such perceptual differences, and this affects the acceptability of Islamic businesses globally if they choose to use their religious affiliation as a part of their brand identity. But if we take a broader view, we can see another reason for concern about Islamic businesses: that in any areas of the world where poverty is rife, more extremes of behavior occur, and this is so in the Muslim world. The fact that the majority of Muslims come from poor backgrounds can and does impact the image of Islam.

From a marketing perspective, the fact that some Muslim markets are poorer than others needs to be borne in mind by Western companies keen to offer products and services to those markets. In the next chapter, we will look at how marketers can improve their understanding and decision making in this regard.

Adding to the complexity with respect to Islam and Muslim markets is the impact of the culture of each country, whether it contains a Muslim-majority or minority population, on the behavior of Muslim companies and consumers. Culture impacts how people view the religion, and how strongly they express their beliefs. For example, Turkey is Muslim but very secular, while Iran falls more toward the other end of the religious conformity scale. Governments, businesses, and consumers in these two countries act in very different ways.

Another misperception in many people's minds is the strong association of Islam and Muslim markets with Arabian countries. In fact, the Middle East countries don't make up the majority of the global Muslim population, as we shall see in Chapter 2 when we look at the latest figures available for Muslim populations.

All of the above facts mean that any marketer or brand manager, whether from a Muslim or a non-Muslim company, must try to understand the structure and behavior of these markets if they are to be successful in doing business in them. But before I move on to discuss Muslim markets in detail, I would like to address a question that is uppermost in many people's minds.

Is Islamic Branding a Myth or a Reality?

This is an interesting question, and it is one that I was required to address in public at the 6th World Islamic Economic Forum, 2010, held in Kuala Lumpur.

My answer to the question is that Islamic branding is a reality and not a myth. My reason for stating this is that there are substantial markets that want products, services, brands, and communications that are *Shariah* compliant, or demonstrate that they understand Islamic values and principles and are prepared to become *Shariah* friendly. Muslims the world over look for what is "*halal*," as opposed to what is "*haram*," and so there is substantial demand for *halal* or *Shariah*-compliant products and services. The Muslim population represents around 23 percent of the world's population and thus is a significant market. While this huge market is not homogeneous in behavior, it is—as we shall see later—bound by certain values that all Muslims share.

This fact raises related questions, such as: "Is it worthwhile or proper to carry out branding based on religion?" and "Is it a good thing to discriminate in branding on the basis of religion?" The most important thing that marketers need to bear in mind is that Islam is a way of life. The values and principles of Islam are taken much more seriously in terms of influencing the everyday way of life of Muslims than are the values and principles of other religions. In other words, from a marketing perspective, we are dealing with a huge number of people who have shared values, and therefore who share similar wants and needs, and branding is all about addressing consumers' shared values, wants, and needs.

The major difference between other religions and Islam is that the practice of Islam influences all Muslims to a larger or lesser extent on an everyday basis, and this means that brand owners and marketers who wish to gain a strong foothold in a market of 1.57 billion people must cater to their needs—and with Islam, this means Islamic values, principles, and practices. This indisputable fact brings up the question of what information is available to assist marketers in understanding Islamic markets, because not all Muslims behave as one homogeneous group and there are many Muslim markets that vary in size and behavior.

Until very recently, there has been little data available to help with such understanding, but recent studies do give an insight into some of the questions marketers are asking, particularly about where Muslim populations are located and what size they are. A summary of some of this recent work will be provided in Chapter 3. However, having an understanding of the global spread of the Muslim population, and of the size of that population in various countries, doesn't give marketers enough information, on its own, to enable them to create and manage their brands properly. Questions about how Muslim populations can be reached, and how their behavior differs or remains similar from place to place, remain largely unanswered, and much more work remain to be done to gain a proper understanding of consumer behavior in Muslim-majority and minority markets. Fortunately, some major research is now being carried out to elicit more information on these issues, as will be seen later in the book.

Despite the differences in Muslim markets around the world, we can safely say that Islam has certain principles and values upon which business is based, and these are briefly discussed below.

The Five Pillars of Islam

Islam is what is called a monotheistic faith; that is, it is based on the belief that there is only one God. As an Abrahamic-based religion, Islam—as opposed to, say, Christianity—makes no allowance for the plurality of God.

The most important Muslim practices are the Five Pillars of Islam, the five obligations that every Muslim must satisfy in order to live a good and responsible life, according to Islam. The Five Pillars of Islam consist of:

1. *Shahadah:* a declaration of faith that there is no god but God, and that the Prophet Muhammad is the messenger of God.
2. *Salat:* an obligation to perform ritual prayers five times every day in the proper way.
3. *Zakat:* a regular (usually annual) welfare contribution to the poor in society.
4. *Sawm:* the observation of fasting during the holy month of Ramadan.
5. *Hajj:* the undertaking of a pilgrimage journey to Mecca, at least once in a person's lifetime (if that person has the means and is physically able to do so).

Carrying out these obligations provides the framework of a Muslim's life, and weaves his or her everyday activities and beliefs into a single cloth of religious devotion. No matter how sincerely a person may believe, Islam regards it as pointless to live life without putting that faith into action and practice, and so it ensures that it is a way of life if practised properly.

When duly carried out, the Five Pillars demonstrate that Muslims put their faith first, and do not just try to fit it in around their secular lives.[1]

This is an important fact for marketers to bear in mind: that, for most Muslims, Islam is not just a component or part of one's life; it *is* a way of life.

The Principles of Islamic Trade and Commerce

Islamic Law

If Islam is a way of life, then it could be liberally described as a lifestyle as well as a religion. The Islamic system of governance is based on *Shariah*, or Islamic law. In Arabic, *Shariah* means "the clear, well-trodden path to water," and is regarded by Muslims as God's guide to human behavior. Life is a journey that presents to everyone many paths, but only one of those paths is clear and straight, and this path is called the *Shariah*. *Shariah* law comes from a combination of sources, including the *Qur'an* (the Muslim holy book), the *Hadith* (the sayings and conduct of the Prophet Muhammad), and *fatwas* (the rulings of Islamic scholars).

Shariah deals with legal aspects of day-to-day life, including politics, economics, banking, business, contracts, family law, sexuality, and social issues. Doing business professionally, and holding fast to the values of truth, honesty, and trustworthiness, is the *Shariah* way. As all forms of social, economic, and political activities are governed by *Shariah* law, thus branding and marketing activities should also fall under *Shariah* law.

However, world trade, including trade with and between Islamic countries and companies, has largely been conducted under globally accepted laws and customs, and it is only in the last 30 years or so that a notable increase has been seen in trade and commerce of a truly Islamic nature, such as Islamic finance. Islamic law has often been perceived in a negative light by those Western observers who associate Islam with negative attributes, but legally it is now a system of law that is recognized throughout the world.

Islamic Economics

The underlying economic concepts behind Islamic business are fairly straightforward. Islamic economics aims to achieve the state of human *falah* by organizing the resources of the earth based on cooperation and participation. The word *"falah"* means to thrive, be happy, and be success-ful; and in the Islamic economic sense, it refers to being successful in this world as well as the hereafter, and so has macro- and micro-level implica-tions for spiritual, economic, cultural, and political issues.

In focusing on the economic conditions of *falah*, the following must be fulfilled in order to achieve it:

- *Infaq:* Spending on others and meeting the social needs of the com-munity from only part of one's total possessions.
  - Giving *zakat* (a financial levy on surplus wealth) to the poor and needy is compulsory, and is seen as an act of purifying one's wealth.
  - However, there is no compulsion to spend all of one's wealth.
- *Prohibition of riba:* Interest on capital is seen as perpetrating exploi-tation and inequity.
  - Islamic finance is a growing industry that is increasingly being seen as a viable alternative to the conventional financial system.
  - Some argue that the current Islamic finance system still has a strong profit motive and is a mere mirror-image of the conven-tional system.
- *Fulfillment of covenants and trusts:* Meeting all of one's social and reli-gious obligations, including to the environment.
  - When extended to corporations, this strongly correlates to corpo-rate social responsibility, where they are answerable to the society at large, and not just to their shareholders.
- *Justice:* Lawfully acquired wealth must be protected to avoid inequal-ity, impaired incentives, and social waste.
  - Personal property rights of all people are safeguarded, irrespective of their race or religion.
- *Enterprise:* Productive economic activity contributes to the *falah* of society and the individual.
  - The *Qur'an* exhorts man to "seek the bounty of God."

– The Prophet's statements urge people to work and earn their livelihood, and condemn idleness and beggary.
– Overall, mankind's spirit of endeavor is encouraged as long as it is for lawful and wholesome purposes.

Cultural conditions of *falah* should also be reviewed, as they have an impact on consumption by Muslims—in particular:

- *System of prayers:* Islamic prayers (five times a day, with Friday congregational prayers) teach discipline and organization to individuals and the community.
- *Knowledge:* The Qur'an emphasizes inquiry and the pursuit of knowledge, as well as prohibiting sorcery. This is so that society bases its actions on knowledge, rather than superstition.
- *Sexual chastity:* Legitimate sexual relations as a foundation for a stable family life, which when exceeded leads to various social and health problems.
- *Prohibition of drinking and gambling:* Seen as leading to numerous social problems, such as alcoholism, addiction, and so on.
- *Purification of the environment:* Being responsible for the environment ties in with the concept of stewardship. The current pollution of the environment due to material development is counter to Islamic economics.

The view of Islam in relation to consumerism can be explained as follows:

- Material possessions are a necessary part of human life and should not be forgone.
- However, they are secondary to one's moral and spiritual development, as the real destination is deemed to be the hereafter.
- Even then, material possessions are ultimately owned by God and must be consumed, saved, or invested within the limits of one's covenant with God.
  – Marketing and branding, if seen as not only satisfying consumer demand, but actually creating and perpetrating it, is at odds with

Islamic economics, which espouses moderation and a resource-based view of consumption.

- "Islamic consumption" must be governed by *Taqwa* (God-consciousness), based on conservation of resources and attaining satiable comforts, rather than pursuing insatiable wants.

Taking all of the above into account, any Islamic branding and marketing strategy must seek to create brand identities that address all these issues; otherwise, the result will be a mere market segmentation tool that might not be entirely acceptable.

Adhering to the principles of *Shariah* also means ensuring that certain ethical values are in place. The role of Islamic values in building and marketing brands will be discussed in detail in Chapter 5.

It's important to note at this point that Islam states quite clearly that profit optimization is acceptable, as long as it is in keeping with *Shariah* principles and the fulfillment of covenants and trusts meets all of one's social and religious obligations, including to the environment. The issues of social and environmental obligations are most interesting, representing great possibilities for Islamic businesses, and they will be discussed later in this book.

Islamic *Halal* Standards

The practice of Islam under *Shariah* law has for centuries been the basis of Islamic trade and business, and there are well-established rules and standards in place to ensure that the law is observed by practicing Muslims. Those rules have been described above. We shall now turn to the standards and guidelines for the consumption of products and services.

Any Muslim who wishes to buy and consume or use products and services must ensure, as far as he or she can, that those products or services are *halal*, an Arabic term meaning "permissible," which refers to anything that is rightful and permissible under Islam. The term is most frequently linked to food that is permissible according to Islamic law, but in fact it applies to *all* categories of products and services used in Muslim life. The opposite of this term is "*haram*," which means "not permissible." Conforming strictly to Islamic law means that everything a Muslim does must be *halal*. In reality, however, as will be seen in Chapter 3, there are different degrees of religiosity practiced, from orthodox to liberal. The concept of *halal* has been in existence from the birth of Islam, and Islam has always been involved in global trade.

The Interface between Islam and Trade

Several developments made Islam and the Muslim world the defining force in international trade for over 600 years (from around AD 640 to 1260), pushing Islamic civilization to the front of the world's economic stage. These were:

- the establishment of commercial law;
- the expansion of property rights for women;
- the prohibition of fraud;
- the call for the establishment of clear standards of weights and measures; and
- the uncompromising defense of property rights (even while calling for a greater responsibility for alleviating the plight of the poor and needy).

Some of the trading expeditions are quite legendary. For example, as described by Chinese Premier Wen Jiabao, "In the 15th century, the famous [Muslim] Chinese navigator Zheng He led seven maritime expeditions to the Western Seas and reached over 30 countries. He took with him Chinese tea, silk and porcelain and helped local people fight pirates as he sailed along. He was truly a messenger of love and friendship."[2]

Trading is still an innate skill and a natural activity in Islamic culture, and can be seen in many Muslim countries. The resource-rich countries of the Middle East continued to rely on commodity trading, as opposed to the building of diverse manufacturing and service economies, until recently.

The shift from trading to modern business is really a result of the depletion of oil in some areas—for example, Dubai in the United Arab Emirates (UAE). The poorer countries have had little choice but to rely on trading, but as economic development improves, the shift from trading to production and service-related industries tends to follow. And with this shift comes the demand for branded products and services. But if Islamic nations have survived through the centuries via trading, why do they need to produce their own brands? This question will be answered in depth in Chapter 2. Let's reflect first a little more on the situation to date.

How Are Islamic Brands Doing?

In short, the answer is: "Not very well." Given the clear benefits for any nation of developing and encouraging the growth of strong brands, it is perplexing to see that few, if any, truly global brands have come from Islamic countries. The reasons for this seem to be similar to those that accounted for the state of Asian branding 10 years ago, and are as follows:

- companies focusing on short-term profits and operational efficiency, and neglecting the longer-term nature of brand building;
- a tendency to rely on the Original Equipment Manufacturing (OEM) trap—that is, making products for other companies that would then put their own brand names on them;
- a prevalent mindset among chief executives that brand building is not strategic and is really only done tactically via advertising, promotion, and other communications activities;
- lack of acknowledgment that brands are assets with considerable value;
- over-reliance on the status quo, especially in those countries endowed with an abundance of natural resources; and
- lack of government support of brand building by companies in Islamic countries. This is reminiscent of Asian brands during the 20th century, when only Japanese and Korean brands succeeded due to their receiving government support.

Given the success of Islamic trade in past centuries, it is interesting to note that the focus is now switching from trading to branding and strategic marketing.

Why the Interest in Islamic Branding and Marketing?

There are many reasons for the increasing interest in Islamic branding and marketing. First, there is the compelling argument provided by the sheer size of the market, with its relatively young and growing population, and rising affluence. This, in itself, is providing a growth in demand for Islamic products. Second, there is a growing awareness of Islamic consumption as a result of the above, and a greater empowerment of Islamic consumers. A third reason is the fact that Islamic countries and companies have seen the power of branding in global markets, and witnessed Western brands moving into their markets. Coupled with this is the realization that Islamic brands have the potential to cross over to non-Muslim markets, due to:

- shared universal values in relation to purity, health, and wellness;
- increasing quality standard of Islamic products and services; and
- increasing availability of Islamic products and services in non-Muslim-majority markets.

Why Now and Not Before?

Stemming from the above trends, there is now a growing interest in establishing and growing Islamic brands. This interest is following a similar path to that of branding in Asia over the last two decades.

In Asia during the early 1990s there were few brands of importance, as local companies remained focused on profits and efficiency. A short-term, trader mentality was prevalent, and owners of businesses tended to seek short-term profits and operational efficiency, as opposed to investment in the intangibles of brand building—a long-term pursuit. It took several years for companies to change their business strategies to move out of the OEM trap and start to brand themselves. The same situation is now to be seen with companies from Islamic countries. But one more factor is speeding up the process of brand building for Muslim companies, and that is the acceleration of globalization.

Globalization has made an impact in three main ways. First, recent increases in exposure to global brands and lifestyles both abroad and at home have revealed to business owners and consumers what the power of branding can bring. Second, there has been an increase in Muslims studying and working abroad, who are bringing marketing and branding know-how back to their home countries. Third, and importantly, foreign brands have made vast incursions into the lives of Muslim people all over the world.

One extraneous factor that is also helping the brand movement is the need for some Islamic countries to diversify as their traditional resource base starts to reduce, such as Dubai and Brunei, which are now looking at finite oil horizons.

Finally, some countries—such as Kuwait, Qatar, and Abu Dhabi from the UAE—are investing their cash reserves in buying foreign brands in order to kick-start the brand-building process.

These and other possible reasons mean that the Islamic business world is waking up to the fact that brands are good news, and that we will soon be seeing a lot more of them.

Could There Be an Islamic Economic Union?

With this in mind, it has been suggested that such is the extent of the Islamic population and its spread across various countries that, just like the European Union, there could be an "Islamic Economic Union" stretching across the Middle East, Africa, and Asia, maybe as early as 2020. It could cover 77 countries where Muslims are the majority—or the largest minority—group, and would be a theologically based cultural and economic community, with a common economic platform and currency based on gold dinars and dirhams, according to the traditional weights and measures under the standards of the World Islamic Trade Organization. This Islamic bloc would control the majority of strategic and natural resources, including oil and gas; and the guiding principle of the "Islamic Union" would be the concept of "stewardship," or "*khalifah*," as prescribed in the *Qur'an*. This would differ from capitalism, socialism, and communism, as it would entail a resource management system involving sustainable development and accountability, as well as profits.

Whether this hypothesis is feasible or not is arguable, but the fact that it has even been thought of presents us with a view of the potential of the Islamic business world with its 1.57 billion people.

However, the huge number of people that constitutes the global Muslim market is by no means homogeneous from a consumer behavior perspective, and the distribution of Muslims across the globe means that the application and degree of adherence to the religion of Islam and *Shariah* ethics and law differs considerably, depending largely on the country and culture within which Muslims reside.

The scale and nature of the global Muslim market will be the subject of Chapter 3. However, let's first consider why branding is good both for nations, and for the companies and organizations that operate in them.

Notes

1. www.bbc.co.uk/religion/religions/islam/practices/fivepillars.shtml.
2. Excerpt from a speech by Chinese Premier Wen Jiabao at the University of Cambridge, February 2, 2009.

2 Why Muslim Nations Need to Develop Strong Brands

Introduction

In this chapter, we shall consider why Muslim countries should encourage brand building in both the public and private sectors as well as at the national level, in order to reap the benefits of branding and not get left behind in the titanic global struggle for national success.

It is no coincidence that countries such as Argentina, Australia, Iceland, Ireland, Kenya, Lithuania, Poland, Scotland, Slovenia, South Korea, Spain, the UK and others have been through some form of national branding exercise. They would not have done so without the expectation of considerable benefits accruing, and many have benefited tremendously. The benefits that can be achieved are discussed in this chapter.

Why Do Countries Need Branding?

Countries and sectors within countries, are just like large companies. And of course, like companies, they can be branded. *Anything* can be branded, as the principles are applicable no matter what the subject of the exercise. However, national branding is not an easy matter. Although the revenues of certain companies are larger than the gross domestic product (GDP) of some countries, branding a country is far more complex in nature than branding a company. But while the degree of difficulty is greater with nation branding, it is nevertheless worthwhile.

Some of the complexities of nation branding arise because there exists within countries a great deal of internal competition, as different institutions, government-related organizations, and ministries/departments compete for funding, public support, and talent. Other competitive influences exist via the private sector, from companies that clearly have their own agendas. Yet another difficulty is getting "inclusivity"—that is, buy-in from all the people who represent the country. This is difficult enough in a large company, let alone in a country.

However, there is no disputing the fact that nations and public sector organizations need branding, both as a means of differentiation and as a route to survival in commercial terms, because we now live in a world of parity and mediocrity.

The World of Parity

The trend that has caused most concern in every market in the world in recent years is that of parity. Faced with a situation where their products, services, systems, and technology are so easily replicable, the biggest problem for companies around the world is differentiation. How can they appear to be different and better than their competitors while marketing and selling the same things?

In the world of parity, the only true differentiator is brand image. This is why people pay 1,000 times the price of a Casio watch to own a Rolex, and why Nokia has for many years captured around 40 percent of the market share in mobile phones. It is why Armani makes greater profits during Asia's recessions than during normal times. And it is why the waiting list for Mercedes cars in some countries grows longer the more prices go up. It is because there are other associations in the minds of consumers: status, prestige, and the need for self-expression. These associations appear in people's minds because they have been deliberately positioned as such. The "commodity" label can be shrugged off with powerful branding.

But what has this to do with Islamic branding and marketing? Why should Islamic countries concern themselves with "brand image"?

Why Do Islamic Countries Need to Undertake and Encourage Branding? ━━━

There are several reasons why Islamic countries should be concerned with national, public sector, and private sector branding.

The first reason is because the problems they face are the same: parity and the need to differentiate in the face of increasing competition. Just like companies in Asia and the West, countries have to attract various customer groups and must market and sell their products, ideas, and services to people in other countries.

Just as companies have found that the best way to do this is not usually via the lowest price, but through building perceived value, so countries are beginning to do so as well. There is a dawning recognition that a nation's image is made up of "perceived value," and that value can consist of intangible as well as tangible elements. Countries have entered the world of branding.

Second, countries must change if they are to survive in a changing world, because relying on past reputation doesn't always ensure success in the future. What were good perceptions in the past may not be so good now. This is why New Zealand wants to portray itself as a country known for more than just sheep and rugby, by stressing its medical science expertise and transparency; why Canada wants to be seen as a hi-tech global player in addition to a good place to go for a holiday or an education; and why Britain wants to be seen as being more innovative, friendly, trendy, and "with it," rather than solid, conservative, reliable, and "past it." It is also why Malaysia, Oman, Brunei, and other Muslim countries are interested in developing national brands—a good image brings commercial power. For Qatar, a country rapidly establishing brand awareness around the world, winning the 2022 FIFA World Cup bid brings a massive opportunity to develop the country's brand image, and in turn attract investment, talent, jobs, tourism and trade. Sporting events are high level vectors for brand and national development.

Third, brands are strategic assets in their own right, and can bring both power and financial rewards. They can help countries by replacing the "push" factor with the "pull" factor. Strong brands differentiate and attract people to them, rather than having to chase after them. Islamic countries need talent and expertise in order to move forward, as well as retain the best and brightest people of their own nations.

Finally, countries need to manage perceptions and control their image in order to manage particular issues of national concern. This has specific relevance to Muslim countries, where differentiation is lacking, images are very unclear, and the country-of-origin factor can often be detrimental to exports and domestic sales.

Whereas many Western countries have already established their identity and strengths in certain areas, Muslim countries have yet to do so. Germany's reputation for precision engineering, Italy's association with fashion, and the romantic associations of France are examples. Indeed, countries such as Spain and Ireland have carried out deliberate branding programs to help them make a global impact. In Asia, Japan has closely linked itself to consumer electronics through its brands, but other countries in the region don't have such strong positive images or associations. Some countries haven't managed their brands well, resulting in negative associations that tend to stick in people's minds. For example, China is perceived as a producer of cheap, poor-quality products.

Muslim countries need to assess carefully what they stand for. While holding firm to their Islamic values, they also need to differentiate themselves from other countries. They also need to manage their brand image well by managing market perceptions, promoting their strengths, and eliminating their perceived weaknesses.

But throughout the world, even though geo-politics and national and foreign policy agendas still dominate government thinking in the race for power and influence and can constrain image-building activities, these are being eroded by the attention decision makers are giving to brand image and the benefits it can bring to the table. Doing so will bring them many benefits.

The Power and Rewards of Country Branding

If Muslim countries clarify what they really stand for and employ brand differentiation strategies, they will find that doors will open to the achievement of various national objectives, including:

- increase in currency stability;
- restoration of international credibility and investor confidence;
- reversal of international ratings downgrades;
- attraction of global capital;
- increase in international political influence;
- growth in export of branded products and services;

- increase in inbound tourism and investment;
- development of stronger international partnerships;
- enhancement of nation building (confidence, pride, harmony, ambition, national resolve);
- reversal of negative thoughts about environmental issues, human rights, and other matters of importance to global audiences;
- attraction and retention of talent (human resources and global knowledge);
- greater access to global markets; and
- improvement in their ability to surpass regional and global business competitors, and defend their own markets; and more . . .

Many of these issues revolve around how the various target audiences perceive the individual countries, in terms of positive mental associations and misconceptions, but some Islamic countries tend to have a perception gap between how they *want* to be seen (identity) and how they *are* seen (image). Perhaps Dubai would like to be seen as the link, the commercial hub, between East and West, but it has not quite achieved that status yet. Some say that Malaysia would like to be seen as the modern face of Islam, but it also has not yet achieved this position. Importantly, they are also competing against each other to gain a favorable "share of mind" with global tourists, investors, and importers of goods and services.

Great corporate brands are built on consistency of thought and deed, and countries are not used to doing this. What often happens is that there are many mixed messages sent, and mixed messages mean a mixed image. Also, in the world of perception, actions speak louder than words, and politics often can work against, as well as in favor of, a strong brand image.

Another complicating element is that different government departments have different agendas—to get more tourists, more investment, more talented professionals, and so on. They have their own communications plans, their own public relations strategies, and staff who focus on their own area and don't see "the big picture." In branding terms, they act independently almost as product brands do in the corporate world.

Are There Any Rules?

There is no magic to branding, but if the four rules outlined below are followed and Islamic countries work hard at managing their brand image, the rewards will come.

Rule No. 1: Action counts

Governments have to understand that there is more to branding than logos that mean nothing to the people whom they want to influence. It is action that counts. Government policies and public diplomacy influence a country's image much more than do advertising and promotion.

Rule No. 2: Have a clear strategy

Great brands are built on a clearly defined strategy. There is a very clear understanding of what the brand stands for (its values), the desired consumer perceptions of different target audiences, and why the brand is different and better than its competitors. These are brand promises, and they must be realistic, credible, and believable. Importantly, they have to be delivered.

Rule No. 3: Develop a consistent brand culture

There is a need for consistency across all "faces" of the brand. This means both consistency across all communications from government departments and agencies, as well as getting buy-in from the private sector. Successful corporate brands develop brand cultures, and countries need to do the same.

The ambassadors of a nation's brand are not just government agencies; they are every company that ventures into foreign markets, and every person a tourist meets. Many people think the hi-tech company Nortel is from the United States, when it is actually from Canada. Little surprise, then, that Canada isn't seen as a hi-tech country when its flagship brands don't publicize their country of origin.

Internal communication and involvement with the community is essential for brand building. Encouraging companies in a country, whether large or small, to carry out effective branding themselves will help build the country's image. Without their combined efforts, national branding is difficult. Singapore's Minister Mentor Lee Kuan Yew was absolutely correct when he said that Singapore must create more brands in order to survive. So must other countries. Where are the global brands from the Muslim world? There are none, and it is time now to do something about this situation.

Rule No. 4: Guard the brand

There needs to be "guardianship" of the brand. As brands are strategic assets in their own right, they have to be managed as such. This means putting in time and effort and involving everyone in the nation. In short, brand management is a strategic agenda item that requires meticulous care. Countries monitor currency flows and other important data carefully and regularly, but fail to do the same for their brand image.

Muslim countries (and those wishing to access Muslim markets) must move quickly to establish their brands in the face of the impending onslaught of legislated foreign competition, and branding must be made a top priority in national planning. At the very least, government ministers must be regarded as brand asset managers. But in truth, there is a strong case for a Ministry of Branding! I will discuss this in a little more detail later in the chapter, after we consider the need for national and corporate brands to be aligned.

The Connection between National and Corporate Branding

The above benefits of nation branding are substantial, but they will be less effective if the companies and sectors within the nation are not well branded. I call the link between the brand image of a nation and the brand images of companies and sectors within a nation the *Nation Brand Effect* (NBE).[1]

First, strong corporate brands are brand ambassadors for their countries and can have positive effects on their country's image. This is part of the NBE, described further below.

Second, strong corporate brands increase the value of the stock exchanges where they are listed, as the brand value contributes to the intangible asset value part of market capitalization. In Western countries, intangible assets can account for as much as 72 percent of a bourse's value, and much of the intangible base comes from the value of brands represented on those bourses. Now that it is becoming popular and mandatory in many countries for companies to disclose on an annual basis the value of their brands, this leads to higher market capitalizations. In many Islamic countries, this is not yet the case and thus they lag behind, and this provides little incentive for boards of directors to build their brands as they tend to do in the West.

Third, strong brands increase foreign direct investment, jobs, and wealth creation on their own, regardless of the national image, although they will do this less effectively if they are perceived to come from a country with a negative image. This is the country-of-origin effect and it is linked to the NBE.

The strength of the link between the national image and the corporate or sector image determines the NBE. For example, Germany has for centuries been a bastion of skill, craftsmanship, and hard work, perpetuated largely by the strong influence of craft guilds. Over time, these core values of hard work, quality, skill, efficiency, and innovation (especially in engineering) have become a large part of the literal national brand identity of Germany. This national brand identity—known the world over through German brands such as BMW, Mercedes-Benz, Porsche, MAN, and Audi—has had a big boost from the NBE (which, in turn, is sustained by the core values that give rise to the German brand identity).

In essence, a nation's people, beliefs, and history give rise to its brand identity (core values), which gives rise to its NBE, which in turn sustains and reinforces its core values—literally, one big reinforcement cycle. The same cycle can be observed in the case of Japan, whereby Japanese society and Japanese companies feed off of the identity and reinforce the successes of their national brand. Simply put, the Japanese core values of team cooperation, hard work, diligence, goal achievement, and learning give rise to its national brand identity, which leads to its NBE. The NBE then contributes to the success of its global brands, whose success in turn reinforces the ingredients (people, culture, history) and core values that started the process (see Figure 2.1).

Thus, a strong national brand image coupled with strong corporate brands gives rise to the virtuous circle of the NBE. As the world market continues to deregulate, brand-building skills diffuse across markets and societies, and levels of competition increase. Only nations with strong brands—both internally and externally—will be able to achieve and sustain leadership positions. This reality is where skillfully designed Second World nations (especially from Asia) will have an opportunity to "overtake" current First World nations, or at least dominate desired niches.

As more sophisticated models of brand management evolve, the NBE may become an essential part of the toolkit of companies the world over.

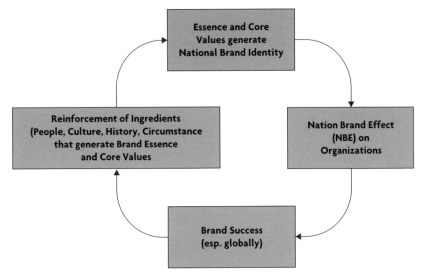

Figure 2.1   The Strong Nation Brand Effect (NBE) Cycle

It is possible that a direct calculation for NBE may one day be part of the asset section of the corporate balance sheet (differing for each country). A company's capability to capitalize on the NBE may, itself, even be part of its brand equity valuation. With up to 70 percent of a brand's value not being reflected in the company balance sheet at any one point in time, such a brand value factor as the NBE (when properly understood and quantified) could increase this figure to as much as 80 percent. The valuation of brands is now a rapidly growing business, and valuations can be used for many purposes.

This is the new reality for the next two decades: Nations that focus on developing both their brand strategy skills, and incorporating them into their national and corporate fabric, and NBE (both internal and external) will be the key success stories and leaders of the true new world order.

National Brand Structures

While we do not see many Ministries of Branding, as referred to in Rule 4 earlier, structures for the management of national brands are essential, as a common identity has to be presented to the world.

Creating and developing a national brand requires inclusiveness. Public and private sectors have to "buy-in" to the central message and core values of the brand. While industries, companies, ministries, and others need autonomy to market their own products and services, they have to be driven by the master (nation) brand. As with corporate branding, the more consistency of messaging there is to the marketplace, the better. Usually, there is some form of brand management structure to keep all communications and activities, such as promotions from sub-brands, aligned to the master brand. This can be a Brand Management Committee or Council or Unit—the name doesn't matter. What *does* matter is that this body is composed of representatives from the public and private sectors who are major influencers regarding the national brand image. Oman created an "Oman Branding Unit," for example, and Japan a "Japan Brand Working Group." The Swiss passed a federal act and ordinance aimed at promoting Switzerland's image and created "Presence Switzerland" under the Agency of the Federal Department for Foreign Affairs, a body that provides strict guidelines for the promotion of Swiss brands and monitors the Swiss national brand image. There are other examples.

This book is not the place to discuss national branding in any depth, but suffice it to say that more and more countries either have embarked, or are embarking, on such vital initiatives—creating an inclusive brand strategy and controlling and managing that strategy in the best possible way.

Few Muslim nations have undertaken significant branding programs, but the time is now right to do so if they are not to be left behind. Egypt is one of the rare examples of a Muslim national brand. While it has a thriving tourism industry accounting for around 20 percent of its GDP, it is not seen as a business destination. While it continues to maintain the strength of its tourism sector, recent branding initiatives have been focused on Egypt as a business destination, driven by the "Egypt Business Image Unit." Based on an in-depth SWOT analysis of Egypt's business image, it was clear that the country needed to accelerate the export of Egyptian products, attract more foreign direct investment, and generally get global businesses to see Egypt as a country that was on their radar and open for business. The Unit developed a strategy to brand Egypt as an attractive business destination, which included a variety of action plans such as visual identity, use of digital media for communication and promotion, an Internet strategy, public relations activities abroad, press tours of the country, and other branding initiatives. It remains to be seen how strong the brand resilience will be as Egypt now goes through a transition phase in political reform.

If branding the whole country appears to the government to be somewhat too large and difficult a task, a nation can have a significant positive impact on its overall image by branding a sector or industry, as with the example of Egypt, and thereby improving the image of a major part of its activities or interactions with the world.

Sector and Industry Branding

Countries, or states within countries, can create a positive overall national image by branding certain sectors or industries, such as tourism or trade. Tourism is the most popular sector to brand because it is both lucrative and perhaps the easiest to attempt. The problem with tourism is that most countries offer similar destinations and products, although it can be done well. Malaysia, for example, has had success with its long-running brand strategy and proposition encapsulated by the strap line, "Malaysia, Truly Asia." Singapore has branded its information communications and technology (ICT) industry in such a way as to wrap the strong and globally respected Singapore brand around its many small and medium-size enterprises (SMEs) that need image support when venturing overseas.

Notably, with the tremendous growth in *halal* markets, particularly food and lifestyle products, some countries and states are moving quickly to establish regional hubs in specific sectors. For instance, Malaysia has been very successful in branding itself as an Islamic financial services hub, and Brunei is currently attempting a similar initiative to brand itself as a *halal* food and lifestyle products hub. Both countries are attempting to trigger the Nation Brand Effect by developing a distinctive global position that will be a catalyst for the growth of local companies, infrastructure, exports, foreign direct investment, and other national objectives. The case of Brunei is an interesting one as it contains many challenges (see Case Study 1).

Another initiative currently under way at state level within a Muslim-majority country that will have a significant impact on the image of both the state and the country is Sarawak's Corridor of Renewable Energy (SCORE) (see Case Study 2).

CASE STUDY 1: BRUNEI HALAL BRAND

Brunei Darussalam is a Muslim country with a population of 381,000. The first Muslim arrived in 907, and in 1368 the first Muslim ruler, Sultan Muhammad, embraced Islam. Brunei Halal Brand is a government project initiated by the Ministry of Industry and Primary Resources along with the cooperation of the Brunei Islamic Religious Council, the Ministry of Religious Affairs, and the Ministry of Health. According to the official website (www.bruneimipr.gov .bn), through Brunei Halal Brand, Brunei Darussalam has set its sights on becoming a major player in the global *halal* industry, in terms of producing and certifying *halal* food, and catering to the worldwide market for premium-quality *halal* products.

The creation of Brunei Halal Brand is in line with Brunei Darussalam's aggressive efforts to develop a diversified, competitive, and sustainable economy. The oil-rich country, a Malay Islamic monarchy, has defined three sectors for development in a bid to move away from its dependence on oil and gas revenues. These are Islamic finance, eco-tourism, and *halal* products.

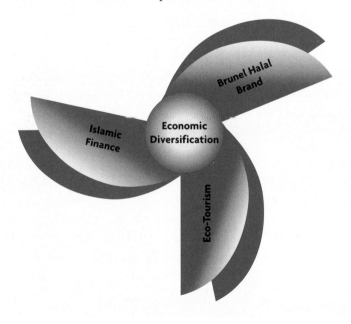

The development of Brunei Halal Brand is the key driver of these initiatives and has three main national objectives:

- economic diversification;
- SME capacity building; and
- fulfillment of a *fardhu kifayah*.

While the first two objectives might appear on many Muslim country agendas, it is the last one that perhaps sets Brunei apart. "*Fardhu kifayah*" means "collective responsibility," and it is this key element that ensures the achievement of the other objectives. Undertaking the obligation of *fardhu kifayah* means that the acclamation to provide pure *halal* food in accordance with the best Islamic standards is not just to the population of Brunei, but to the wider world—and it is a definite differentiator for Brunei, as no other nation has declared this as a priority. One of the challenges facing this plan is the many different *halal* certification and accreditation processes that exist globally.

ISSUES IN THE *HALAL* CERTIFICATION PROCESS

There are many *halal* labels globally, indicating which country or body has certified the products to be *halal*. For example, in Brunei the label is purple with a blue background. In countries such as Brunei and Malaysia, it is the government that certifies products' *halal* status, but in non-Muslim countries it may be a local mosque or other organization. As there are many interpretations of *Shariah* law, and *halal* accreditation around the world is very fragmented, there is often distrust among consumers, it is unlikely that universal achievement will occur in the foreseeable future. One of Brunei's main strengths is its high standards, which arguably are becoming benchmarks for others to follow. This is seen by Brunei as a huge marketing opportunity.

Brunei considered its position and decided to create a Brunei Halal Brand that would complement its own stringent certification processes. Having seen how powerful brands can be for nations—for

example, "New Zealand Lamb," "Swiss Chocolate," and "Aussie Beef"—
Brunei decided to create its own global brand.

THE LAUNCH OF BRUNEI HALAL BRAND

Brunei Halal Brand was launched in 2009 to address the certification
issues mentioned above and to gain a sustainable competitive advantage.
In the past, there was real consumer concern about only meat being
halal. However, consumers are now concerned about the *halal* status
of other products and ingredients. Checking every product for its *halal*
status against lists compiled by scholars can be a challenging process
for the average consumer. Products bearing the Brunei Halal Brand are
considered to be of high quality and come with a *halal* certification
label. This not only makes it easier for Muslim consumers to select
suitable products, but also reassures them that the products adhere to
the strict standards promised by the brand. The tight control exercised
over the audit and certification processes by the Ministry of Religious
Affairs Halal Food Control Division makes the Brunei Halal Brand
certificate more difficult to obtain than *halal* certification in many
other countries. Having obtained certification in Brunei, products can
generally be expected to pass audits undertaken by other countries.

The foundations for building a successful international *halal*
brand were considered carefully. The high standards required for
halal compliance had to be matched by high quality standards and
appropriateness of products for particular markets. If a *halal* product
is of good quality—and those are the values that Brunei Halal Brand is
built on—then it is suitable for Muslims as well as non-Muslims.
Product branding and packaging also needed to be exemplary. Above
all, Brunei Halal Brand had to embody the core values of the Sultanate,
as it had to become the flagship for positioning Brunei and its national
halal agenda for years to come.

One challenge that Brunei faced immediately was its lack of a
"home-grown" product along the lines of New Zealand's lamb. It
decided it would have to source products and encourage businesses

to join in the branding process. However, it could not do this without having access to appropriate expertise, and so it looked for a joint venture partner.

THE BRUNEI HALAL BRAND JOINT VENTURE

In what is widely regarded as a world first, Brunei Halal Brand was launched with the signing of a joint venture agreement with a partner from Hong Kong—Kerry FSDA Ltd.—to form a company called Ghanim International Food Corporation Sdn. Bhd. The combination of Brunei's highest standards of *halal* integrity and Kerry's product and marketing expertise enabled Brunei Halal Brand products to reach their markets.

The trading model is unique, according to Ghanim CEO Noel Shield. "It allows us the flexibility to source, manufacture and sell our products across a global market, as opposed to being a single country base, while maintaining the integrity of our systems—in particular, our strict *halal* accreditation procedures. This gives us the freedom to provide the global consumer with a wide range of quality *halal* food products. Currently, no country has a global *halal* brand and we believe our model will create an awareness of Brunei and its commitment to the *halal* food industry. The venture produces an income stream for the country, creates employment for Bruneians both here and overseas, and assists in showcasing Brunei as a destination for investment and tourism. It also benefits local and small and medium-size enterprises, as new technology from other countries can be introduced into Brunei to assist the development of this sector. As the company develops across the global market, it also assists the SMEs by marketing their products under the Brunei Halal Brand, and by allowing them to link into a strong supply chain. By having access to this supply chain, it will expand their export opportunities and create a more competitive environment."

All companies that want to manufacture products under the Brunei Halal Brand have to pass the *halal* compliance audit conducted by the

Ministry of Religious Affairs Halal Food Control Division. If successful, they then have to pass Ghanim's own audits for health and safety, plus environmental and social compliance, all of which are conducted by international third-party audit specialists STR, formerly known as Shuster Laboratories. Ghanim can thus ensure that suppliers meet all criteria, including *halal* compliance. Ghanim's aim is to position Brunei Halal Brand products at the top end of the market and gain global access for them.

A logo was developed to signify that a product had achieved Brunei Halal Brand status as well as the certification labeling. The logo consists of three main elements:

- a diamond shape with a stylized mosque dome, representing the core Islamic values;
- a green and yellow jewel in the center, signifying the values of the Malay Islamic monarchy, the customs and culture of the Sultanate, and a sense of responsibility to the rainforest; and
- stylish, modern, black and white typology, in tune with today's marketplace.

With this logo as the face of the brand, Brunei's values as well as products are brought to the market.

Bringing products to market

Another challenge for Ghanim and the Brunei Halal Brand was—and is—which products to produce. Noel Shield says that the choice of product has to be demand driven. "It is no good just pushing products out into the market; the failure rate is too high. Product choice has to be based on consumer demand. If you know you are producing something that consumers want, you stand a much better chance of succeeding." Taste, texture, and other attributes also have to be right for new products, he says, as these can vary greatly not just between countries, but even between regions within the same country.

The first 50 products were unveiled on June 3, 2010 for the local market only, and in particular for Ramadan. They are what Shield calls "comfort foods," such as snacks, confectionery, chocolates, biscuits, and drinks. This "Hari-Raya Hamper Programme" is the first of several campaigns to kick-start the Brunei Halal Brand and involves the internal Brunei market first in order to get the support of the whole country. As Shield points out, "The Brunei Halal Brand is owned by the people of Brunei."

BUSINESS OPPORTUNITIES

Looking forward, the target market for the brand includes the regional market, the Gulf Cooperation Council (GCC) states, and the European and American markets. Product category procurement and manufacturing opportunities will include food, pharmaceuticals, health and beauty, cosmetics, logistics, and tourism. There will also be retail partnerships, and investment opportunities in science, nutrition, ingredients, and manufacturing. Companies that have been certified can avail themselves of the international profile of Brunei Halal Brand, and Brunei is offering to absorb the costs of obtaining the *halal* certificate for companies coming under the Brunei Halal Brand. This is particularly valuable for smaller corporations that may not have the budget or leverage to gain access to international markets otherwise. Or, if they don't wish to use the Brunei Halal Brand, they can still benefit from the *halal* certification. The process of including the Brunei Halal Brand with the certification costs also provides an added incentive for global suppliers wishing to get involved in Brunei's national brand.

The intention is that anyone in any market who sees any Brunei's *halal* symbols on a product will automatically know that the *halal* compliance is of the highest standard. To bring about this global recognition is a tall order, and it will take some years and significant financial resources to accomplish.

Brunei is now constructing the Brunei Agro-Technology Park, where facilities for research and development (R&D) and production will be available to all companies, not just those from Brunei. The hope is that this will bring investment to Brunei and further add value to the Brunei Halal Brand.

CONCLUSION

No other country has attempted to introduce both *halal* certification and *halal* brand logos as Brunei has. Care will have to be taken to ensure that companies see the benefit of the Brunei Halal Brand in addition to the Brunei *halal* certification visual identity, and that consumers understand the benefits of having both. It is a unique brand positioning strategy that could give a small country a large footprint on the global *halal* map.

CASE STUDY 2: SARAWAK

Sarawak Corridor Of Renewable Energy and the Tanjung Manis Halal "Green" City

SARAWAK CORRIDOR OF RENEWABLE ENERGY

The Sarawak state government is very much aware that to stand out and attract global business in the 21st century, there has to be a strong image platform on which to build. By developing the Sarawak Corridor Of Renewable Energy (SCORE) and specific entities within that corridor, it is anticipated that Sarawak itself, one of the 13 Malaysian states, will become more high profile and be accepted globally with a strong brand image.

The concept of Regional Corridor Development, as encapsulated in the Ninth Malaysia Plan (2006–10) and the National Mission (2006–15), is one of the strategies formulated by the Malaysian government to achieve balanced development within the nation. SCORE is one of the five regional development corridors being created throughout the country. It is a major initiative undertaken to develop the Central Region and to transform Sarawak into a developed state by the year 2020 and beyond. It aims to achieve the goals of accelerating the state's economic growth and development, as well as improving the quality of life for the people of Sarawak.

The Central Region of Sarawak stretches for 200 miles along the coast from Tanjung Manis to Samalaju and extends into the surrounding areas and the hinterland. SCORE covers an area of approximately 27,000 square miles, with a population of 607,800 people. The major urban centers within the corridor are Sibu, Bintulu, Mukah, and Kapit. The distribution of investment is RM267 billion (80 percent) in industries and power, and RM67 billion (20 percent) in physical infrastructure, human capital, and institutional infrastructure.[2]

Major growth nodes of SCORE

Five new-growth nodes have been selected by Sarawak with the aim of focusing investment efforts within the corridor. These nodes are a key element of the corridor's strategic development plan. The Mukah node will be developed into a "smart" city, and will serve as the nerve center for the corridor. The Tanjung Manis node will be developed into an industrial port city and *halal* hub. The Samalaju node will become the new heavy industry center, while Baram and Tunoh will focus on tourism- and resource-based industries. The corridor's secondary growth centers—such as Semop, Balingian, Selangau, Samarakan, Bakun, and Ng. Merit—will also tend to benefit greatly from spatial development of the entire region and the development of these new-growth nodes.

In branding terms, the growth nodes are like sub-brands, with SCORE acting as a master brand. With this in mind, the Sarawak state government has realized that all brands are interdependent and that the image of any one of them is likely to impact the images of the others. Tanjung Manis is a sub-brand (a designated area) of SCORE, which in itself is a sub-brand of Sarawak, and using this as a case we can see how this ambitious development will play its part in enhancing the overall business capabilities and image of Sarawak.

Tanjung Manis could well be the flagship brand for SCORE and Sarawak, alongside many other development projects. By looking at the brand development holistically, with brands leading the way, Sarawak could be among the most prominent and ultimately successful players in the global *halal* market.

TANJUNG MANIS FOOD AND INDUSTRIAL PARK: MALAYSIA'S *HALAL* HUB AND "GREEN" CITY

Tanjung Manis is a large-scale development project in a delta area for three rivers, including the Batang Rajang, which is Sarawak's longest river. There is a land bank of 77,000 hectares, owned by the Sarawak state government, available for development of the Food and Industrial Park. Plans for the park are ambitious, including deep-sea fishing, palm oil, gas and petroleum, shipping, and *halal* foods. A range of international companies are investing in the park. The park will eventually become the "southern node" of the Sarawak Corridor Of Renewable Energy, and there is much emphasis on green principles.

The Tanjung Manis Halal Hub is a unique and industry-leading destination due to its unrivaled natural landscape and its position in the heart of one of the world's fastest-growing markets. The Tanjung Manis Halal Hub is referred to as an advanced hub because of the area's wide range of competitive advantages.

Tanjung Manis's large land bank available for agriculture and development differentiates it from other sites. The land is available for an assortment of *halal* industries, both upstream and downstream. As well as the unparalleled availability of land, Tanjung Manis has an extensive infrastructure system to enable the transport of products in and out of the area. There is a modern road system connecting the hub to Sarawak's major cities of Kuching and Sibu.

An airport and deep-water port can also be found in Tanjung Manis, thus providing easy connectivity to mainland Malaysia and the world. Both of these facilities are in the process of being upgraded, which will further increase the attractiveness of the site. There is a large, able workforce available in Tanjung Manis, with many human capital initiatives being implemented. Business-appropriate broadband is available throughout the area, with Telekom Malaysia (TM) being the principal provider. The *halal* hub will be a one-stop approval agency for streamlined project approvals, and there will be no barriers to foreign direct investment or repatriation of funds.

On a macro level, there are a number of other factors that make Tanjung Manis a priority for investors in the *halal* industry. First, the Malaysian government provides attractive tax incentives for green and *halal*-based industries and their related manufacturing activities, as well as biotechnology grants and other specialized incentives. Also, the project has the strong commitment and support of the Sarawak state government and the country has a stable political environment.

Agriculture and aquaculture can be carried out all year round due to the moderate, warm climate with minimal seasonal changes. This is helped by the fact that the delta region has adequate water resources which are suitable for a wide range of aquaculture and agriculture activities. Finally, the Tanjung Manis Halal Hub will practice green policy development, which will readily facilitate certification of the products of the *halal* hub as both organic and sustainable.

The following is a summary of a keynote address by Datuk Hajjah Norah Bte Tun Abd-Rahman Ya'kub, executive chairman of Tanjung Manis Food and Industrial Park Sdn Bhd, given at the Inaugural

Oxford Global Islamic Branding and Marketing Forum, held July 26–27, 2010 at the University of Oxford's Saïd Business School. (For a summary of the forum's proceedings, see Appendix 2.)

Tanjuk Manis is in Sarawak, and is approximately the size of Taiwan. Proposals for 16,000 hectares of the area to be turned into a Green Special Economy Zone are being submitted, and this is being combined with the idea of "halal."

Traceability and bio-security are two of the key factors underpinning the development of the area. One of the goals of the project is to ensure water quality is maintained, along with the quality of production. This is part of the overall ethos of having a local responsibility to community development, and this is born out of the concept of halal. As a result of the goals of bio-security and community development, Sarawak continues its policy of maintaining the rainforest, which has been in place in Sarawak since the 1950s.

This policy of sustainability will be extended throughout the Green Zone with methods such as organic farming, green feed, green road works, green buildings. For example, any road works that are undertaken must have a life span of 30 years. The airport will be relocated out of the Green Zone. That is to say that all activities must conform to the highest environmental standards. For example, water management must meet world-class levels. However, to deliver against all these policies can be expensive.

Companies are invited to set up in the Green Zone; however, if they are unable to meet the policies outlined above, they are turned down, and this has already happened. For example, shipbuilding was declined as an industry for the area.

One project which has shown great success in integrating these criteria and the ethos of the zone described earlier is the Tilapia fish project. . . . The area needs not only food security, but also cost-effective food production. This project was able to deliver those goals. This was done by partnering with a sea technology company from Taiwan, which as it happens is not Muslim. This is worth noting. The project had the support of the vice president of Taiwan. The company was selected because of their zero-waste policy—everything would be used. In establishing the project, the company spent a year with local villagers and got involved with the community in order to better understand the environment and their needs and to secure mutual support.

Tilapia is normally considered a low-end, low-value product. However, in this project, high-quality methods were used in order to reposition the fish from a low-end cheap commodity to something of sufficient quality to be used for high-end products like sushi. This new process was developed in conjunction with the company and the IP was shared with them. The process involved introducing corella algae, which was expensive but reduced white spot disease, cholesterol and improved the quality. It was expensive, but the whole process injected value into the product.

Part of the issue of food security is that food should be affordable, and this is a principle of "halal," and food security and affordability are also part of the development of the Green Zone. These are subjects at the heart of the "halal city," along with the green and organic initiatives outlined earlier. The halal city will focus on sports tourism, food production, and lifestyle companies. It will be marked at its entrance by a green gate after which point no fossil fuel cars will be permitted in the zone. Only transportation like solar, battery—or even horse and cart!—will be admitted.

Side by side with this, the halal city must have both corporate and aesthetic value because it is crucial in an area like Sarawak that young people feel a strong pull to remain in their communities and not leave them. By making the halal city attractive and investing these strong principles into it, there is the hope that they will feel strongly bound to their communities.[3]

Summary: Branding for Islamic Countries and Industries

Western and newly developed countries have been systematically working on leveraging the Nation Brand Effect for a long time. Countries such as South Korea have been successfully raising their national brand image by working on the NBE at the national and corporate level for 10 years or more, with very positive results.

China is now on its way to achieving the NBE, and is gradually overcoming the challenges of quality and trust in its brands. India, with its 161 million Muslims, is also encouraging its large branded companies to move further afield, as well as satisfying the needs of its burgeoning middle class.

For Islamic countries hoping to diversify into many different industries and encouraging their companies to go regional, or global, nation branding is a must. But little evidence is seen of activity on this front in the Muslim world. Muslim-minority country Singapore and Muslim-majority country Malaysia have both been involved in branding activities, providing branding and promotional grant assistance for all companies wishing to develop their brands overseas. Both have also carried out industry and sector branding, but neither has developed a composite, well-defined national brand strategy. Oman has worked on its national brand for a few years, but has not reached the end of the road, and destinations such as Dubai are presently recovering from what could be called a national brand image crisis. I would encourage these countries not to give up, and I would suggest that those countries that have not yet started to enhance and manage their national images encourage their companies to proceed with some urgency. Brunei and Sarawak are examples of this trend; both are moving toward their own brand objectives in connection with the *halal* industry. More Islamic countries could learn from the examples in this chapter and develop and diversify into powerful global economies.

The major lesson from this chapter is that any government has to work on its national image, and at the same time encourage both its large companies and its SME sector to build strong corporate brands. This is a strategic imperative, with significant benefits in terms of employment, tourism, trade, foreign direct investment, and economic growth.

I have introduced this issue of the Nation Brand Effect early in the book because of its importance to all brands that originate from any Muslim country. Entrepreneurs, SMEs, and large corporations all need help if they are to grow into international brands, and governments have a responsibility to assist them in this process.

Chapter 3 looks at another critical piece of branding and marketing knowledge, which is the latest research and information on the global Muslim market and possible segmentation strategies.

Notes

1. Paul Temporal, *Public Sector Branding in Asia* (Singapore: Marshall Cavendish International (Asia) Pte. Ltd., 2004).
2. www.recoda.my.
3. Datuk Hajjah Norah Bte Tun Abd-Rahman Ya'kub, executive chairman of Tanjung Manis Food and Industrial Park Sdn Bhd, "The Halal City of the Future: Building a City's Islamic Brand and the Marketing Challenges Faced," keynote address, Saïd Business School, Oxford University, July 26–27, 2010; www.sbs.oxford.edu/islamicmarketing.

3

An Overview of Muslim Markets

Introduction

This chapter looks at the size and distribution of Muslim markets using some of the latest research findings, discusses some of the market segmentation ideas that have emerged, and analyzes some of the implications for branding and marketing.

It is only in the last few years that any information about Muslim markets has been featured in the outputs of market research companies. Only as recently as 2009 were marketers able to get any firm and accurate figures on the size and distribution of the Islamic population, and these were provided by the Pew Forum on Religion & Public Life. Since 2007, we have also begun to see some data on the behavior of different Muslim populations, courtesy of the Gallup Coexist Index and JWT. Even so, there are many blanks yet to be filled in. For example, not all countries are covered by these pieces of research, and they do not deal in detail with specific markets, such as Islamic financial services, *halal* food, and so on. However, they do give us some valuable insights into how certain aspects of Muslim identity influence how Muslims behave, and their attitudes to brands and lifestyle, and this chapter looks at what brand managers and marketers can derive from these pieces of work.

We will start by looking at the latest information on the size and distribution of the Muslim market.

The Growing Global Muslim Market

The Pew Report[1] reveals that there are approximately 1.57 billion Muslims of all ages living in more than 200 countries in the world today, representing 23 percent of an estimated 2009 world population of around 6.8 billion.

Muslims live in all five inhabited continents, with 62 percent of the global Muslim population living in Asia-Pacific. In Asia-Pacific the total Muslim population stands at just over 972 million people. Indonesia has the world's largest Muslim population with 203 million (13 percent); and in South Asia, three out of seven countries (Pakistan, India, and Bangladesh) account for 31 percent of the world's Muslim population and 99 percent of South Asia's Muslim population.

About 20 percent of Muslims are in the Middle East and North Africa. The Middle East–North Africa region has the highest percentage of Muslim-majority countries. The study also highlighted that more than half of the 20 countries and territories in that region have populations that are approximately 95 percent Muslim or greater. The 10 countries with the highest concentrations of Muslims are Indonesia, Pakistan, India, Bangladesh, Egypt, Nigeria, Iran, Turkey, Algeria, and Morocco, and two-thirds of all Muslims live in these countries.

However, more than 300 million Muslims, or one-fifth of the world's Muslim population, live in countries where Islam is not the majority religion. India, for example, has the third-largest population of Muslims worldwide with approximately 161 million. China, at nearly 22 million, has more Muslims than Syria (20 million), while Russia is home to more Muslims (16 million) than Jordan and Libya combined (12 million).

There are about 38 million Muslims in Europe today, and over 4 million in North and South America. Approximately 315 million Muslims are in the MENA region (Middle East and North Africa).

Sub-Saharan Africa alone has 15 percent of the world's Muslim population, at 241 million people. Nigeria, Ethiopia, and Somalia have high concentrations of Muslims in this region.

Europe accounts for 2.4 percent of the total Muslim population. Russia has the highest number, at over 16 million, followed by Germany at over 4 million people. France has over 3 million Muslims.

Future growth of the global Muslim market

Of further and perhaps greater interest to marketers is the information contained in the latest Pew Research Center report,[2] where figures for the growth of the global Muslim market are given for 2101–2030. This information indicates very clearly that the global Muslim market will provide an increasing number of opportunities in this time span. According to Pew, "The world's Muslim population is expected to increase by about 35 percent in the next 20 years, rising from 1.6 billion in 2010 to 2.2 billion by 2030. Globally, the Muslim population is forecast to grow at about twice the rate of the non-Muslim population over the next two decades—an average annual growth rate of 1.5 percent for Muslims compared with 0.7 percent for non-Muslims. If current trends continue, Muslims will make up 26.4 percent of the world's total projected population of 8.3 billion in 2030, up from 23.4 percent of the 2010 world estimated population of 6.9 billion."

Importantly, within this growing market there are also expected to be some shifts in numbers among regions and countries, although Pew emphasizes that the report makes demographic projections and that projections are not the same as predictions. For instance, the Pew report says, "If current trends continue, however, 79 countries will have a million or more Muslim inhabitants in 2030, up from 72 countries today. A majority of the world's Muslims (about 60 percent) will continue to live in the Asia-Pacific region, while about 20 percent will live in the Middle East and North Africa, as is the case today. But Pakistan is expected to surpass Indonesia as the country with the single largest Muslim population. The portion of the world's Muslims living in sub-Saharan Africa is projected to rise; in 20 years, for example, more Muslims are likely to live in Nigeria than in Egypt. Muslims will remain relatively small minorities in Europe and the Americas, but they are expected to constitute a growing share of the total population in these regions.

In the United States, for example, the population projections show the number of Muslims more than doubling over the next two decades, rising from 2.6 million in 2010 to 6.2 million in 2030, in large part because of immigration and higher-than-average fertility among Muslims. The Muslim share of the US population (adults and children) is projected to grow from 0.8 percent in 2010 to 1.7 percent in 2030, making Muslims roughly as numerous as Jews or Episcopalians are in the United States today. Although several European countries will have substantially higher percentages of Muslims, the United States is projected to have a larger number of Muslims by 2030 than any European countries other than Russia and France.

In Europe as a whole, the Muslim share of the population is expected to grow by nearly one third over the next 20 years, rising from 6 percent of the region's inhabitants in 2010 to 8 percent in 2030. In absolute numbers, Europe's Muslim population is projected to grow from 44.1 million in 2010 to 58.2 million in 2030. The greatest increases—driven primarily by continued migration—are likely to occur in Western and Northern Europe, where Muslims will be approaching double-digit percentages of the population in several countries. In the United Kingdom, for example, Muslims are expected to comprise 8.2 percent of the population in 2030, up from an estimated 4.6 percent today. In Austria, Muslims are projected to reach 9.3 percent of the population in 2030, up from 5.7 percent today; in Sweden, 9.9 percent (up from 4.9 percent today); in Belgium, 10.2 percent (up from 6 percent today); and in France, 10.3 percent (up from 7.5 percent today).

Several factors account for the faster projected growth among Muslims than non-Muslims worldwide. Generally, Muslim populations tend to have higher fertility rates (more children per woman) than non-Muslim populations. In addition, a larger share of the Muslim population is in, or soon will enter, the prime reproductive years (ages 15–29). Also, improved health and economic conditions in Muslim-majority countries have led to greater-than-average declines in infant and child mortality rates, and life expectancy is rising even faster in Muslim majority countries than in other less-developed countries.

Other specific points of interest contained in the report include the following:

Asia-Pacific

• Nearly three-in-ten people living in the Asia-Pacific region in 2030 (27.3 percent) will be Muslim up from about a quarter in 2010 (24.8 percent) and roughly a fifth in 1990 (21.6 percent).
• Muslims make up only about 2 percent of the population in China, but because the country is so populous, its Muslim population is expected to be the 19th largest in the world in 2030.

Middle East-North Africa

• The Middle East-North Africa will continue to have the highest percentage of Muslim majority countries. Of the 20 countries and territories in this region, all but Israel are projected to be at least 50 percent Muslim in 2030, and 17 are expected to have a population that is more than 75 percent Muslim in 2030, with Israel, Lebanon and Sudan (as currently demarcated) being the only exceptions.

- Nearly a quarter (23.2 percent) of Israel's population is expected to be Muslim in 2030, up from 17.7 percent in 2010 and 14.1 percent in 1990. During the past 20 years, the Muslim population in Israel has more than doubled, growing from 0.6 million in 1990 to 1.3 million in 2010. The Muslim population in Israel (including Jerusalem but not the West Bank and Gaza) is expected to reach 2.1 million by 2030.
- Egypt, Algeria and Morocco currently have the largest Muslim populations (in absolute numbers) in the Middle East-North Africa. By 2030, however, Iraq is expected to have the second-largest Muslim population in the region—exceeded only by Egypt—largely because Iraq has a higher fertility rate than Algeria or Morocco.

Sub-Saharan Africa

- The Muslim population in sub-Saharan Africa is projected to grow by nearly 60 percent in the next 20 years, from 242.5 million in 2010 to 385.9 million in 2030. Because the region's non-Muslim population also is growing at a rapid pace, Muslims are expected to make up only a slightly larger share of the region's population in 2030 (31.0 percent) than they do in 2010 (29.6 percent).
- Various surveys give differing figures for the size of religious groups in Nigeria, which appears to have roughly equal numbers of Muslims and Christians in 2010. By 2030, Nigeria is expected to have a slight Muslim majority (51.5 percent).

Europe

- In 2030, Muslims are projected to make up more than 10 percent of the total population in 10 European countries: Kosovo (93.5 percent), Albania (83.2 percent), Bosnia-Herzegovina (42.7 percent), Republic of Macedonia (40.3 percent), Montenegro (21.5 percent), Bulgaria (15.7 percent), Russia (14.4 percent), Georgia (11.5 percent), France (10.3 percent) and Belgium (10.2 percent).
- Russia will continue to have the largest Muslim population (in absolute numbers) in Europe in 2030. Its Muslim population is expected to rise from 16.4 million in 2010 to 18.6 million in

- 2030. The growth rate for the Muslim population in Russia is projected to be 0.6 percent annually over the next two decades. By contrast, Russia's non-Muslim population is expected to shrink by an average of 0.6 percent annually over the same period.
- France had an expected net influx of 66,000 Muslim immigrants in 2010, primarily from North Africa. Muslims comprised an estimated two-thirds (68.5 percent) of all new immigrants to France in the past year. Spain was expected to see a net gain of 70,000 Muslim immigrants in 2010, but they account for a much smaller portion of all new immigrants to Spain (13.1 percent).
- The U.K.'s net inflow of Muslim immigrants in the past year (nearly 64,000) was forecast to be nearly as large as France's. More than a quarter (28.1 percent) of all new immigrants to the U.K. in 2010 are estimated to be Muslim.

The Americas

- The number of Muslims in Canada is expected to nearly triple in the next 20 years, from about 940,000 in 2010 to nearly 2.7 million in 2030. Muslims are expected to make up 6.6 percent of Canada's total population in 2030, up from 2.8 percent today. Argentina is expected to have the third-largest Muslim population in the Americas, after the US and Canada. Argentina, with about 1 million Muslims in 2010, is now in second place, behind the US.
- Children under age 15 make up a relatively small portion of the US Muslim population today.
- Only 13.1 percent of Muslims are in the 0-14 age group. This reflects the fact that a large proportion of Muslims in the US are newer immigrants who arrived as adults. But by 2030, many of these immigrants are expected to start families. If current trends continue, the number of US.
- Muslims under age 15 will more than triple, from fewer than 500,000 in 2010 to 1.8 million in 2030. The number of Muslim children ages 0–4 living in the US is expected to increase from fewer than 200,000 in 2010 to more than 650,000 in 2030.
- About two-thirds of the Muslims in the US today (64.5 percent) are first-generation immigrants (foreign-born), while slightly more

than a third (35.5 percent) were born in the US. By 2030, however, more than four-in-ten of the Muslims in the US (44.9 percent) are expected to be native-born.

- The top countries of origin for Muslim immigrants to the US in 2009 were Pakistan and Bangladesh. They are expected to remain the top countries of origin for Muslim immigrants to the US in 2030."[3]

Even given the possibility of such projections being slightly erratic, the trend is perfectly clear, and brands interested in pursuing Muslim markets will find these statistics extremely helpful in shaping their future marketing activities.

However one slices and dices the numbers, there is no escaping the fact that the Muslim population is not only huge, it is growing, and it represents some of the best global marketing opportunities for decades to come. Let's have a look at some of the implications of these large numbers and their distribution before we delve further into the details of segmentation.

What Does All this Mean?

Numbers on their own only give us a part of the marketing picture, and unless we understand what behavior lies behind numbers we are in danger of treating all audiences that make up the market as a homogeneous target. The spread of these numbers already suggests some differences, and we will now examine those. We will then consider some more detailed research that will provide us with more marketing ammunition.

Muslims number among the world's poor

Various studies, including *The Pew Report*, have indicated that the Muslim population is growing faster than any other segment, and it appears that the Islamic community has a tendency to be situated mostly in the poorer, developing economies where large families are the norm and, among all religions, there is the pattern of poverty.

These research findings lead us to believe that, unfortunately, the Muslim-majority nations are marked by inequality, poverty, and conflict. In wealthier, Muslim-minority countries, the Muslim population is (except in the US) dramatically poorer than the rest of the nation's citizens. These communities of immigrants and second- or third-generation children have been poorly assimilated into the host culture. Muslim neighborhoods are often marked by sectarian, ethnic, and tribal conflict, in addition to being alienated from the host culture.

Western and other developed economies tend to have smaller family sizes and dual-income families, resulting in more prosperity, and there seems globally to be an inverse relationship between family size and prosperity. The growth of the Muslim population, therefore, is not indicative of a more prosperous market.

Indeed, the spread of Muslims across the Asia-Pacific, Middle East, and North Africa regions suggests that most Muslims based in these regions are poor. Even in developed economies, or richer countries such as those in the Middle East, the majority of the Muslim populations tend to be poor. Saudi Arabia, for example, has an elite affluent segment and a majority of poor people, and in the UK, Germany, and France—Muslim-minority countries—Muslims are relatively less well off than other sections of the population. The exception to this is the US, where Muslim Americans tend to have similar social and economic profiles to other segments. Nevertheless, there are small groups of wealthy Muslims in European countries, and wealthy Muslims from other countries do tend to travel to European countries, but this has some limitations for some products, as will be seen later.

In Europe, the profile of Muslims differs in Muslim-majority countries. Muslims in minority European countries are predominantly first- to third-generation immigrants, with the third generation now semi-Europeanized in their upbringing and expectations compared to their parents and grandparents. Although they may be not as well off as the average populations in their countries, they do have more purchasing power than Muslims in developing countries, and they have access to a wide range of consumer brands. Additionally, these Muslims often have conflicts in terms of their identity—for example, being both a Muslim and British. These factors mean that their preferences may be quite different from those of Muslims in Muslim-majority countries in the Asia-Pacific, Middle East, and Sub-Saharan Africa regions.

In other parts of the world, notably China and India, very large populations encompass a substantial sub-segment of Muslims. But without data to establish where those populations are located in these nations, especially because of their huge land areas, as well as being unable to determine their income, education, and current lifestyles, it is extremely difficult to predict what the market for everyday products would be.

We will look at the implications of these discoveries for branding and marketing later in the book, but first it is also relevant to look at population growth and birth rates. Such statistics may prove to be essential in developing government-to-government programs to enhance the lives of poorer populations, and in giving direction as to which markets to focus on when developing other initiatives, such as small and medium-sized trade cooperation.

Growth and birth rates

According to the Population Research Institute, the Western world has birth rates well below the replacement rate of 2.1 children per woman, with only Muslims having high birth rates. Additionally, the United Nations Population Fund predicts that Muslims will make up over 1.6 billion of the world's population by 2015 and approximately 2.6 billion by 2050, which will be nearly 30 percent of the world's population. Interestingly, it is also estimated that by this time Muslims will account for two-thirds of the world's population under the age of 18.[4] It is a huge and growing market from a single religious perspective, and indeed Islam does govern to a large extent the way of life of all people who subscribe to that religion.

The overall figures shown above regarding the distribution of the Muslim population suggest a tremendous polarity between rich and poor Muslims. Sub-Saharan African Muslims and large Muslim populations in India, Indonesia, and others tend to be a part of lower-income communities. If we look even closer, we can see that even in the developed countries such as the UK, France, and Germany, the majority of Muslims there are not affluent. This contrasts with the US, which has approximately 2.3 million Muslims, many of whom are affluent. So, just from an affluence point of view, not all Muslim markets are the same.

On the issues of European and Muslim birth rates in Europe, the Pew Forum on Religion & Public Life comments:

. . . a rapidly growing Muslim population is making its presence felt in societies that until recently were largely homogeneous. Muslims are still very much minorities in Western and Central European countries, making up *roughly 5 percent of the European Union's total population. But a number of demographic trends point to dramatic change in the years ahead.*

Islam is already the fastest-growing religion in Europe. Driven by immigration and high birth rates, the number of Muslims on the continent has tripled in the last 30 years. Most demographers forecast a similar or even higher rate of growth in the coming decades. The social impact of this growing population is magnified by a low birth rate among native Europeans. After a post-World War II baby boom, birth rates in Europe have dropped to an average of 1.45 children per couple, far below the 2.1 needed to keep population growth at replacement levels. The US's Migration Institute says that Muslims will account for more than 20 per cent of the EU population by 2050.

Amid these demographic shifts lies a host of social challenges. While many European Muslims have become successful in their new homes, many others do not speak their host country's language well, if at all, and are often jobless and poor. Moreover, segregation, whether by choice or necessity, is common, with large numbers of Muslims living in ghettos or areas where the crime and poverty rates are high.

For Europeans, too, Muslim immigration poses special challenges. Unlike the United States—a land of immigrants with no dominant ethnic group—most nations in Europe are built around a population base with a common ethnicity. Moreover, these countries possess deep historical, cultural, religious and linguistic traditions. Injecting hundreds of thousands, and in some cases millions, of people who look, speak and act differently into these settings often makes for a difficult social fit.[5]

The inevitable conclusion arising from these important findings is that Muslims are largely poor, and growing in number due to high birth rates. In developed nations, early-immigration generations sometimes replicate that familial characteristic. However, in those countries, smaller family size is a necessary precondition for prosperity. Children are expensive to raise in the West, and having greater numbers of them exhausts resources rather than adding to wealth potential. Moreover, the road to upward mobility is strongly associated with dual-income households. As women go to work (and have access to contraceptives), family size tends to drop. Upscale economic status in the West, therefore, is consistently associated with a lower fertility rate. From a marketing perspective, the notion that the Muslim population is growing isn't necessarily the indication of a lucrative group of buyers. And, as mentioned earlier, it is certainly not reasonable to assume that the growth rate in Muslim-majority countries can be applied across the board to Muslim minorities in very different settings.

The above research can at first be confusing for brand and marketing managers, and indeed for Muslim nations that wish to explore the global market. But one possible approach is to distinguish between products that are intended for poorer Muslim markets and those that might be aimed at the more affluent market. Poorer countries are areas often afflicted by poverty and illness, and governments and companies could focus on enhancing levels of healthcare and standards of living in these countries. More developed Islamic countries might therefore concentrate on manufacturing basic *Shariah*-compliant drugs, pharmaceuticals, and household necessities for poorer countries, for example, and aim for the more developed countries with beauty products, cosmetics, and luxury items. A similar approach could be taken by companies.

Paradoxically, it is important not to assume that, because Muslims reside in developed Western countries, their level of affluence is comparable with the overall development in these countries. Muslims exist within the affluent, middle-class, and poor in these countries, and thus a hybrid design may be needed in marketing the *halal* industry to them. We also have to remember that Muslims in Muslim-minority countries have access to globally renowned brands and often have the purchasing power to obtain them.

So, rich and poor are two dimensions that influence brand and marketing strategies. But it is also important for anyone involved in branding and marketing to Muslim markets to understand the whole range of similarities and differences.

Brand and marketing managers must note that, despite the fact that Muslims in general subscribe to *Shariah* law and the practice of Islam, not all Muslim markets are the same. This disparity makes life interesting and challenging to brand and marketing professionals, and there is little in the way of research to help companies that are trying to understand Muslim markets identify meaningful, reachable segments, and how such different Muslim segments behave differently in market situations. We will look at market segmentation later in this chapter, as some very interesting developments have recently taken place. In the meantime, we will examine some of the similarities and differences that are most evident.

Similarities and Differences across Global Islamic Markets

Some of the similarities and differences across global Muslim markets are as follows:

Similarities

- Common faith, values, and identity as Muslims
- Similar dietary requirements (*halal*)
- Similar lifestyle requirements (finance, education, entertainment)
- Strong sense of community and welfare

Differences

- Diverse locations
- Multiple languages and dialects
- Various cultural and lifestyle differences
- Varying degrees of Islamic adherence
- Varying degrees of education, affluence, and marketing sophistication

These similarities and differences will be considered in more detail later in this book. For now, we need to delve into some of the other research studies that have taken place recently that add more data of interest to marketers, especially with respect to Muslim consumer attitudes and behaviors. The first of these studies is the Gallup Coexist Index.

The Gallup Coexist Index ━━━━━━━━━━━

In 2009, Gallup presented an interesting study on interfaith relations, with some in-depth data on Western Muslims as well as wider findings from a mix of countries across four continents.[6] This study helps us understand the economic and social standing of Muslims, particularly in the UK, France, and the US, as well as Muslim attitudes toward religious toleration, integration, values, and identity. The report also explores attitudes and perceptions among Muslims and the general public in France,

Germany, and the UK in regards to issues of coexistence, integration, values, identity, and radicalization.

While the study does not cover all Muslim-majority and minority countries, it confirms that religiosity (religion being identified as an important part of daily life) is negatively correlated with development. This means that developed countries are less religious than developing countries, and this in turn means that Muslim-majority countries are more religious than Muslim-minority countries. There is a dramatic shift from lack of religiosity/developed nation to religiosity/developing nation, and we can see this trend clearly in Figure 3.1. This difference, obviously, has a significant impact on the lives of Muslims in developed nations; not only are they struggling against a culture that may be prejudiced against Islam in particular, but they are also trying to follow religious lives in cultures where many don't generally value or respect religion. The footprint of the different countries' approaches to integrating

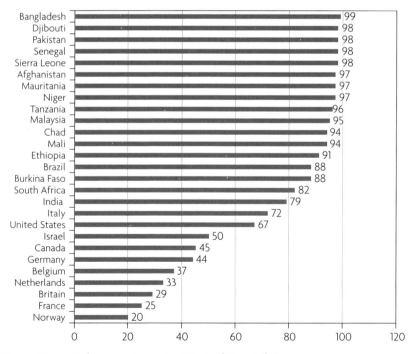

Figure 3.1 Is Religion an Important Part of Your Life?

Source: Gallup Coexist Index, 2009.

immigrants with different religions (meaning, specifically, Muslims) can be seen in the relative integration of these cultures.

In the study, Gallup goes a step further and assembles three levels of religious integration—Isolated, Tolerant, or Integrated—the definitions of which are as follows:

- **Isolated:** Isolated individuals tend not to be members of any particular faith group, but if they are, they tend to believe in the truth of their perspective above all others. They don't want to know about other religions. They also neither respect nor feel respected by those of other faiths.
- **Tolerant:** Tolerant individuals have a "live-and-let-live" attitude toward people of other faiths, and they generally feel that they treat others of different faiths with respect. However, they are not likely to learn from or about other religions.
- **Integrated:** Integrated individuals go beyond a "live-and-let-live" attitude and actively seek to know more about and learn from others of different religious traditions. They believe that most faiths make a positive contribution to society. Furthermore, integrated people not only feel they respect people from other faith traditions, but also feel respected by them.[7]

According to the Gallup report,

The United States and Canada top the European countries surveyed in the proportion of their general public classified as integrated. Within Europe, 35 percent of Britons and 38 percent of Germans are classified as isolated, compared with 15 percent of Americans and 20 percent of Canadians. Across African countries surveyed, Niger, Chad, and Djibouti have the highest proportions of respondents who can be classified as isolated. The highest proportions of integrated respondents are found in Senegal, Sierra Leone, and Mauritania. Among Asian countries polled, Afghanistan and Israel had the highest percentages of isolated residents.

In France, Germany, and the United Kingdom, Gallup Coexist Index data show some important trends. In each country, the general public is more likely than its respective Muslim population to be classified as isolated. Little variation is found in the percentage of tolerant individuals across the European general populations surveyed (45 percent among the

British public and 49 percent each among the French and German publics). But among European Muslims surveyed, the tolerant group spans a wider range, from 31 percent in France to 43 percent in Germany and 60 percent in the United Kingdom.[8]

Questions of tolerance and prosperity are also addressed in the Gallup Coexist Index. The survey asked people to answer how well they were doing economically now, and how they expected to be doing in the next five years. Three types of groups emerged among respondents—namely, those who saw themselves as either Thriving, Struggling, or Suffering. What this section basically shows is that even if countries have a high "tolerance" of other religions, unless they have a high rate of "integration," this may affect prosperity. So, in the case of France, which has a similar level of "tolerance" to Britain, British Muslims are likely to be "struggling" when compared to French Muslims, as France is more accommodating and has an integrative approach to immigration. In Britain, Muslims tend to group together in large numbers and self-isolate within the national culture. This trend is illustrated in Figures 3.2 to 3.4.

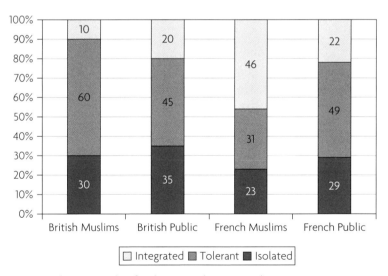

Figure 3.2   Relative Levels of Religious Tolerance and Integration: Britain versus France

Source: Gallup Coexist Index, 2009.

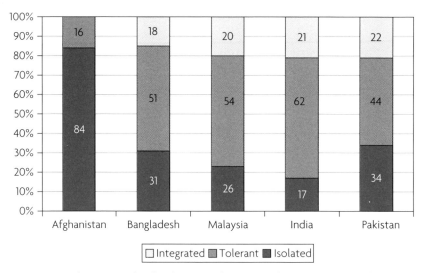

Figure 3.3 Relative Levels of Religious Tolerance and Integration in Selected Countries

Source: Gallup Coexist Index, 2009.

The US, UK, and France have taken, whether purposefully or unconsciously, very different approaches to their immigrant populations. The US, always a nation of immigrants, is often said to have a multicultural approach, though the net effect is virtually always a quick assimilation. The European countries have had less experience with immigration and so are, perhaps, a bit more exclusive and a bit more insistent on maintaining what they see as the markers of their national culture. France has an assimilative approach, though for contemporary Muslims, this emphasis has often meant prohibitions on expressions of ethnic and religious identity in the name of enforcing the interests of the secular society. The UK's Muslims have themselves pursued a segregationist approach, though the government has tended, at least in recent years, toward multiculturalism.

Some other results for these measures are also interesting. For instance, Pakistan has more people who feel integrated than Malaysia, but Malaysia has a much higher degree of tolerance and a much lower level of isolation. This helps account for Malaysia's image of a modern, multicultural Islamic country. Indeed, Malaysia's profile is much closer to that of the US than it is to

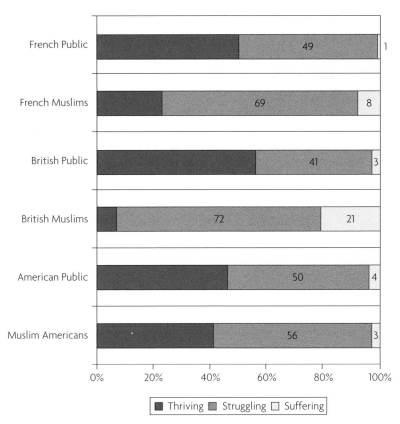

Figure 3.4   Thriving, Struggling, and Suffering Populations in France, Britain, and the United States

Source: Gallup Coexist Index, 2009.

Afghanistan or Bangladesh. Thus, in no way does Malaysia's greater religiosity compromise its willingness to support religious pluralism on the ground. By looking at the results of the study, many other deductions can be made.

Information like this emanating from the Gallup Coexist Index emphasizes the importance of tolerance and pluralism to national prosperity, and the fact that the bridging of the gap between the host culture and Islamic practices is a matter not just of social comfort but of survival for those living in Muslim-minority countries. Certainly, when positioning products in progressive ways to help consumers bridge the gap between their Islamic and modern identities, this reasoning should be kept in mind.

The implications for marketers of the Gallup study are many, but again we come back to the fact that clearly Muslims cannot be treated as one homogeneous segment across nations, whether in Muslim-majority or minority countries. This means that developing an understanding of the Muslim markets in each country is fundamental to marketing success.

We shall now turn to a body of research that has recently been carried out by J. Walter Thompson, the world's fourth-largest advertising agency. The research is interesting because of its strong mix of qualitative and quantitative methodology, and because it provides marketers with some very useful insights into how different Muslim markets are from each other (with some surprising results), but also how segmentation can be used to cut across those markets.

JWT Muslim Market Segmentation ▬▬▬▬

As with the research referred to earlier that reveals the true numbers and distribution of Muslims around the world, it is only relatively recently that information is emerging from Muslim markets on aspects of market segmentation, thanks to studies carried out by J. Walter Thompson (JWT).

The JWT Studies on Marketing to Muslims

JWT has carried out three major studies concerning Muslim populations in the UK, the US, and the Eastern Hemisphere (Asia, the Middle East, and North Africa). Using quantitative and qualitative market research techniques, JWT has unearthed some comprehensive and rich data that tells us a great deal about how Muslims might be segmented for branding and marketing purposes.

Below is a summary of this interesting study, which is extremely revealing about common and differential factors that make up reachable groups of people across the Islamic world. Also, at first sight, the findings might be applicable across many industries. The actual study is based on a combination of qualitative and quantitative surveys, plus in-depth interviews, together with narrative pieces given by chosen "influencers from various social and business backgrounds."

Like the other studies covered so far in this chapter, the JWT work notes several general elements that can be identified at a broad population level and outlines the fact that within and between countries there exist many differences. What makes it distinctive is that it goes further with its segmentation profiles, but it doesn't really possess enough clarity to show us how the segmentation, and possible differences or exceptions, might apply in different industry categories. Nevertheless, it is certainly worth discussing, as it is the first in-depth study into the psyche of Muslim consumers, and any information concerning collective consumer psychology is certain to be of use to brand and marketing managers.

Before we look at the actual segmentation of the Muslim market that resulted from the study, it is important to understand some of the key attitudes that were found among the populations studied. (The Eastern Hemisphere survey included the Muslim-majority countries of Egypt, Algeria, Saudi Arabia, UAE, Jordan, Turkey, Iran, Pakistan, Malaysia, and Indonesia.)

Key Findings from the JWT Research

One of the first things we see when we look at the findings is something that other researchers have found, which is that Muslims often find themselves in a state of tension regarding their identity as a Muslim and their identity as a citizen of a particular country. In answer to the statement shown in Figure 3.5, a much higher proportion of respondents from Iran and Turkey say that their nationality means more to them than their religion. This isn't surprising as regards Turkey, as it is a well-known secular Muslim country, but it is probably not the kind of perception that Western or other countries might hold of Iran.

Perhaps the most interesting information we get from the JWT study is the overall segmentation that is derived from the data. There are four basic attitudinal elements that form the segments, depending on how they are emphasized and combined. These are:

- *Self View and Mindset:* In this area of data collection, the survey looks for an individual's attitude toward the self, particularly to do with dreams, aspirations, and personal choices.
- *Practices:* By this the survey means the traditions and culture influencing respondents.
- *World View:* This is concerned with attitudes toward media and advertising.

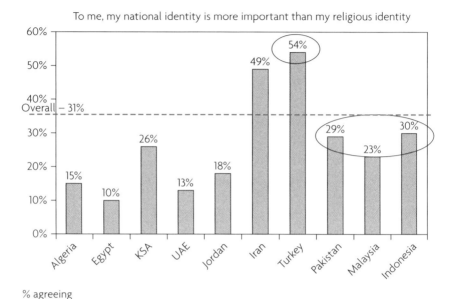

% agreeing

Figure 3.5 Differences in National versus Religious Identity

Source: Roy Haddad, Chairman and CEO, JWT MENA, from a presentation entitled "The Muslim World, Opportunities Unseen."

Note: KSA = Kingdom of Saudi Arabia

- *Relationships:* This area looks at attitudes toward men and women, family and friends, and generational differences.

Depending on the answers to the questions in the four areas, five attitudinal clusters or segments are revealed, as shown in Figure 3.6. The percentages given refer to the percentage of each segment across 10 markets in the Eastern Hemisphere, as seen in detail in Figures 3.7 and 3.8. I have chosen to look at the Eastern Hemisphere results, as these are the main Muslim-majority countries.

1. *Religious Conservatives (17 percent):* These are extremely religious individuals, and also extremely conservative. They don't approve of gender interaction, and they expect others to follow religious practices. They are anti-media and information averse. They are not

**Plus 5 Segments
Dimensions defining the segments**

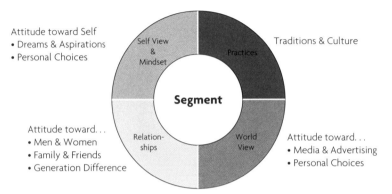

Figure 3.6   Five Attitudinal Clusters (Segments) and Their Dimensions

Source: Roy Haddad, Chairman and CEO, JWT MENA, from a presentation entitled "The Muslim World, Opportunities Unseen."

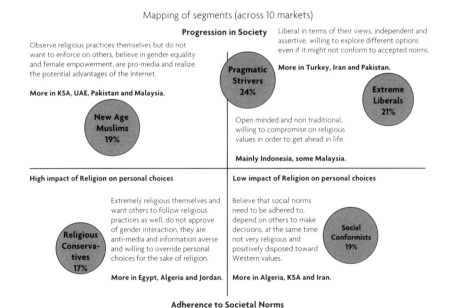

Figure 3.7   Mapping of the Five Segments across the 10 Markets

Source: Roy Haddad, Chairman and CEO, JWT MENA, from a presentation entitled "The Muslim World, Opportunities Unseen."

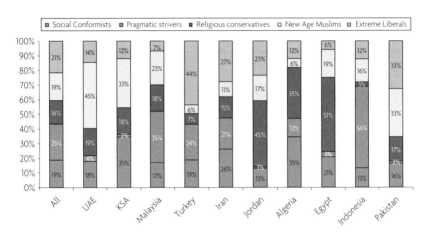

Figure 3.8 Clusters per Country

Source: Roy Haddad, Chairman and CEO, JWT MENA, from a presentation entitled "The Muslim World, Opportunities Unseen."

brand conscious as consumers and would override their personal choices for religious beliefs.

2. *Pragmatic Strivers (24 percent):* These individuals are non-traditional and ambitious. They are open-minded, and are willing to compromise on religious values in order to get ahead in life.

3. *Extreme Liberals (21 percent):* This set of people is very liberal, independent, and assertive. They are not very particular about traditional and religious practices. Instead, they are pragmatic individuals who like to explore different options even if it might not conform to accepted religious/societal norms.

4. *New Age Muslims (19 percent):* People in this segment are somewhat traditional and religious individuals, yet they don't expect others to follow religious practices. They are religious by nature, yet they believe in female empowerment and gender equality. They are pro-media and realize the potential advantages of the Internet.

5. *Social Conformists (19 percent):* These are individuals who believe that social norms should be adhered to, even if it means overriding

personal choice. They don't approve of the reason-based approach of "Generation Next." They lack self-confidence and depend on others to make decisions. At the same time, they are not particularly religious and are positively disposed toward Western values.

Mapping these segments across the 10 markets on the dimensions of how people feel about progression in society versus adhering to societal norms, and whether religion has a high or low impact on the personal choices studied, provides an interesting picture, as shown in Figure 3.7.

Figure 3.8 shows us how the five segments are clustered across the 10 Muslim-majority countries from the Eastern Hemisphere. We immediately see that every country is made up of a different percentage of these segments, and this gives rise to some unexpected differences in behavior and attitudes.

What these charts illustrate, as Roy Haddad, chairman of JWT Middle East and North Africa (MENA) Region, expressed it, is that: "Collective assumptions do not make a reality." A clear example of this is that in each of the 10 Islamic or predominantly Muslim countries, the need for respect of individual opinions is ranked considerably higher than the need to belong to a group and to share views collectively.

To illustrate this further, Haddad points out some interesting characteristics of different countries in the Eastern Hemisphere study that might provide some surprises to people who don't know these countries well. For example:

- Some 72 percent of Saudis believe that traditional practices need to adapt to changing times. The Kingdom of Saudi Arabia has one of the highest ratios of New Age Muslims, who:
  - drive societal change and progress;
  - have a very low resistance to change, as long as it is in accordance with their values;
  - are media friendly, and appreciate mostly its "edutainment" aspect; and
  - are conscious decision makers in all aspects of their lives.
- In Jordan, 65 percent of the population think that traditional practices don't need to adapt to changing times. This is twice the number in any other country.
- Some 47 percent of Turks would leave a restaurant if they were not served *halal* food.

- One in four Egyptian Internet users is a blogger.
- Among all Muslims, Malaysians feel the most secure about their marital life.
- Some 90 percent of Muslims in all countries agree with the statement: "It's good that today's generation voices opinions that they strongly believe in."
- Across all countries and segments, 79 percent of Muslims agree with the statement: "Media is responsible for making today's generation smarter."
- Yet, 63 percent think that "satellite channels have had a negative impact on their society."
- Iran has the second-lowest rate of religious role models. (Most of the survey respondents indicated they would like to become teachers.)
- The Kingdom of Saudi Arabia has the highest rate of role models that are businessmen (twice as high as in the UAE).
- Some 83 percent of Pakistanis want to be part of a social group where they can voice their opinion.
- Some 68 percent of all Muslims indicated that local products are now as good as imported ones.
- Saudis are the trendiest consumers across all markets.
- Some 87 percent of Indonesians would leave a restaurant if they were not served *halal* food, but one in two Indonesians prefer to deal with a more profitable non-Islamic bank.
- To Iranians, wearing Western clothes is less of a cultural denial than it is for Turks . . . and for all other Muslims.
- More women than men tend to believe that happiness is impossible without money.
- Half the Iranians considered their national identity was stronger than their religious identity.

Time spent reading all of the JWT research would provide additional insights into these Muslim countries and segments, and the work is packed with interesting facts and quotations from respondents. Overall, what it shows is that nothing can be taken for granted in the world's biggest untapped market, and this should remind marketers that they cannot assume anything about the collective Muslim world or the individual countries that are a part of it.

A recent survey by Ogilvy & Mather Worldwide has also produced some much-needed information for marketers wishing to gain an understanding of Muslim markets. However, that information is of a different kind to the JWT study, with different segmentations and insights into Muslim attitudes toward brands.

Ogilvy & Mather Worldwide and Ogilvy Noor

In trying to understand the market further and get to grips with the reasons Muslim consumers behave as they do, Ogilvy & Mather Worldwide has created a special practice—called *Ogilvy Noor*—to look at this global market. In June 2010, Ogilvy Noor published, in partnership with research agency TNS, a study called "Brands, Islam and the New Consumer." The study provides unique insights into the meaning of brands in Muslim life. Two years in the making, this is a groundbreaking piece of work, exploring completely new territory. One of the interesting results, with strategic implications for companies wishing to build Islamic-friendly and compliant brands, was the publishing of the Noor Brand Index.

Miles Young, CEO of Ogilvy & Mather Worldwide, recently gave a keynote address at the Inaugural Oxford Global Islamic Branding and Marketing Forum, held at the Saïd Business School on July 26–27, 2010, in which he revealed some of the interesting findings of the research. He has kindly permitted me to quote him here.

In his address, Young said:

Ogilvy Noor has just completed the first phase of a major qualitative and quantitative study. The primary findings I will quote from emerge from four majority Muslim markets—Saudi Arabia, Egypt, Pakistan and Malaysia; however, they have been qualified and sense checked in other both majority and minority markets. The research was conducted by our partner TNS, and is one part of a much larger study and report led by my colleague, Nazia Hussain, entitled "Brands, Islam and the New Muslim Consumer," which we are formally launching this week.

So, what did we learn?

While segmentations of Muslim consumers have been attempted before, they have often tended to merge into relatively simple scales of devoutness in terms of adherence to Islam on a scale of liberal to conservative. It seems more profound to look instead through the lens of the role that religion plays in their lives. On this level there are indeed six segments.

There are the "Connected," 27 percent of the sample, who see themselves as part of the web-like network of the Ummah (and who, therefore, tend to view technology as a positive enabler). Compassion ranks highly as a value with them. They would say, "religion connects me." Next are the "Grounded": Islam is their anchor; religion and culture are inseparable. They were 23 percent of the sample. They seek peace in all their thoughts by being close to Allah. They would say "religion centers me." Next are the "Immaculates." They seek disciplined perfection in religion, and many (not all) consistently reject the impure. At 11 percent of the sample, they tend to have a younger skew. They would say "religion purifies me." Then, we have the "Identifiers"—Islam is a uniform they wear with pride—"religion identifies me." They want to see it strengthened and defended. They are 27 percent of the sample. Next are the "Movers": successful change agents. For them, religion is what you do with it—"religion enables me." They're Internet-savvy, for instance. They are 6 percent of the sample. Finally, there is a segment we call the "Synthesizers," also at 6 percent. They are pragmatic, and adapt religious practice to their needs. As one said, "travelling by camel is Sunnah but we need to travel by plane." They would say "religion individuates me."

So we have six rather different and nuanced statements about the role of faith. But, they cohere within two rather different macro-groups. The first three—the Connected, the Grounded, and the Immaculate—represent a more traditionalist mindset. They have an overarching desire for harmony; they are collectivists, seeking a sense of belonging. They tend to be more strongly aligned with the Shariah values of tolerance and compassion. They are proud of their faith, in a quiet way.

By contrast, the second group, a younger group, which we call the Futurists, are more fiercely proud still. It is this group (statistically smaller at 40 percent), the sum of the Identifiers, the Movers, and the Synthesizers, who as practitioners of marketing and branding we should be fascinated in and focused upon. At the start, it is very important to avoid the Western journalistic temptation to see these as just another version of Gen Y or Millennials. The Futurists are differentiated by the degree to which they see themselves as steadfast followers of Islam in a modern world. They are driven by a purpose, a purpose very different from their peers. Herein lies the danger of glib segmentations along the lines of "impoverished religious conserva-tives" or "affluent modern liberals." The critical lesson is that global brands need to avoid seeing these consumers through Western eyes; rather they have an amazing opportunity to empathize with the cul-tural mores which mainstream journalism tends to at best misrepre-sent or at worst stigmatize.

In contrast to the Traditionalists, the Futurists are more individual-istic. Their religion is their own choice, not just imposed on them. Their pride is intense, regardless of the extent to which they would be catego-rized as "devout." In the broadest sense they believe in "struggle"—the struggle to remain true to their faith while carving out success in life. They believe in education, and with it, the right to ask questions—typically deeper and more probing about the intentions of businesses than the Traditionalists. They want to get ahead: as activists they see Islam as an enabler. They seek to integrate a more globalized lifestyle with their own culture, but do so without fundamental compromise. They value cre-ativity, and they're global. Muslim youth in Lahore exchange Ramadan tips with youth in Dhaka and in Jakarta at the click of a keyboard: it's a flatter, wider Ummah they are creating. But one in which they feel strong responsibility to an Islam to help change things for the better. In the words of a famous StyleIslam T-shirt, "Keep smiling, it's Sunnah."

One of the implications for us of Futurists is their attitude toward halal, especially in majority Muslim markets. The Futurists are increasingly prone to question the details behind what they buy. Where Shariah com-pliance is assumed to be a given, any maladroit behavior or slip-up will get headline status—and the Futurists will be particularly unforgiving.

Global marketers need to be acutely aware of this, and also that the ground rules are becoming more demanding. The scepticism of Futurists in particular means that a simple halal logo is no longer enough. In the words of one respondent, "we need to look at the halal logo, yes, but also at the ingredients." Or, again, "TGI today . . . they have the halal logos, but some of the food is quite doubtful. Let's say we order grilled chicken— the chicken will obviously be halal, but what about the utensils? They may be used for non-halal cooking as well."

In our research, Malaysian respondents tended to be the most discerning, being the most developed consumer market in relation to Shariah, and where Muslims live alongside non-Muslims. Increasingly, though, we believe Futurists everywhere will seek pure choices. In the frequent absence of facts, corporate reputation—and the apparent or not Shariah-friendliness of the corporate brand—assumes a critical importance.

In the research, we have derived a ranking of the relative importance of Shariah-compliance by product categories. At the top, food, dairy, beverages, and oral care scored highest. In the second tier, consumers ranked fashion, personal care, and "regular" finance. In the third tier were airlines, resorts, financial and insurance products. The essential continuum is from body-sensitive to less so. At the extreme end, Muslim consumers will tend to identify halal/haraam as irrelevant to some categories, for instance software, or even to imply a "halal usage effect" which makes it in effect compliant if the ultimate benefit of its usage is positive development for the community. So "justification of desires," by any psychological means necessary, becomes a marketing enabler. "If we use it for a good purpose then it is Islamic, and if we use it for an evil purpose, then it is not Islamic," said one of our Pakistani respondents.

From all of this we can deduce a very specific role for branding in the Islamic future. Brands must inform, educate, reassure the consumer about the highest levels of product quality through innovation; and also demonstrate a proactive anticipation of their informational needs—the surest way of garnering trust. In other words, techniques which may be regarded as marginal in the non-Muslim world need to be used or developed.

But that doesn't by itself make a brand. A brand is a relationship at an emotional level. And the Muslim Futurists are also an extremely emotional consumer group who want to be talked to on their own terms. "They see us only as a market," we heard of a certain global brand in Saudi Arabia. Rather they want the brand to be their friend. David Ogilvy indeed once said that people choose brands like they choose friends. A friend in need: when we asked our Saudi Arabian respondents to create a fictional bank brand, they said their first feeling was the need to "feel safe."

One finding which may seem surprising in terms of traditional media stereotyping is that we have seen no clear-cut preference in terms of global = bad, local = good, or the other way round. Global brands, for instance, are seen clearly as leaders in quality and innovation, and are appreciated for their values. They have heritage and longevity. On the other hand the lurking fear is that they are "ticking the boxes"—the clear opportunity is for global brands to communicate their genuine Shariah-friendliness.

On the other hand, local brands evoke national pride, are seen as less profit-oriented, and are often formed on deep local insights. But quality worries persist, innovation is questioned, the information can be woefully inadequate, they are sometimes seen to be opaque—and their advertising is clearly recognized as not being of a "global standard." For local brands, quality, innovation, and transparency are critical hills to climb.

So, perseverance is key. In the words of a respondent, "I think of Nokia as an Egyptian company. They did research and produced products that suit the Egyptian consumer. They have Islamic values and they know how to deal with Egyptians."

Young went on to talk about the Noor Brand Index, a significant output of the research.

One of the exciting outputs of our research is that we have been able to derive what we call the Noor Brand Index, a quantified ranking of brands' perceived Shariah-friendliness. All these brands are within the compliance zone, that is, none are haram. At the top of the index are Lipton, Nestlé, Nescafé, Nido, and Kraft—two corporate brands and three product brands. Hot drinks and juice brands do well, reflecting their role in communal consumption. In each local market, of course, local

brands such as Boh Tea, Maaza, Al Rabie, Juhayna, all fare well. The
two poorest-performing brands are HSBC and RBS. Global brands, in
particular, suffer from a belief that they cannot in principle be Shariah-
friendly, that in spite of heavy investment in arms such as Amanah, they
are contaminated by behaviors in non-Muslim markets. While Shariah-
compliance is much vaunted, it has not created friendliness. Brands like
Nescafé and Lipton, though, represent a gold standard which any aspiring global player in this area would do well to study carefully. At its roots
lie a holistic understanding of the consumers, and an active engagement
with Islamic values throughout every element of the marketing mix, and
beyond. "It is not just the products, but it's how the employees are treated
too," is just one message from our consumers to which we should pay
heed.

Ogilvy Noor, the agency's Islamic branding practice, describes the index
in more detail as follows.

What is the Noor Global Brand Index?

The Noor Global Brand Index is a preliminary exploration of the consumer perception of halal status and Shariah compliance, or relative
"Muslim-friendliness" of certain global brands across the world today.

How was the Index compiled?

The index averages the composite scores per each of our four markets,
and as a global average ranking can be taken as indicative of how
appealing these brands are to Muslim consumers relative to each other.
The numbers represent the percent agreement with the statement "this
brand is completely halal or Shariah-compliant" averaged across four
markets. The scores are on a 100-point index, where brands above 100
are perceived by consumers as being more Shariah-compliant and brands
below 100 are seen as less so.

The 35 global brands chosen to test quantitatively were the ones
regularly mentioned spontaneously in our qualitative research, as well
as other brands in the same category to provide a measure of comparison. The research was designed to be both pointedly specific and deeply

exploratory at the same time. Rather than try to achieve a representative demographic sample, Ogilvy decided that, for the purposes of the study, what was needed was a representative consumer sample. To this end, four culturally distinct majority-Muslim markets were chosen that Ogilvy believed represented four key stages in the level of consumer development when it comes to Islamic Branding—Saudi Arabia, Egypt, Pakistan and Malaysia—with Malaysia being, in Ogilvy's opinion, one of the most advanced consumer markets in the world when it comes to an understanding of halal and Shariah compliance. Additionally, one of the reasons the four culturally distinct markets were chosen was so that those markets could potentially reflect the habits of their wider regions. Thus the focus, in this initial report, was on majority-Muslim markets only.

The five main categories researched in the Noor Global Brand Index—Beverages, Food & Dairy, Personal Care, Financial Services, Aviation—are the categories that Ogilvy found were important to consumers when it came to *halal* status and *Shariah* compliance (discovered through developing the Noor Category Index, which is not covered in this chapter). The 2010 Noor Global Brand Index is shown in Table 3.1.

These results raised some interesting conclusions that have implications for Islamic business and brand strategy. As described by Ogilvy, these are:

- *Origin doesn't matter: Despite popular misconception, in the consumer's eyes an Islamic brand does not have to originate in a Muslim country, as the highest scoring brands like Nestlé and Lipton go to show. Emirates and Etihad, on the other hand, originating in Muslim countries, appear in the bottom ten.*
- *Food brands win: In the Noor Category Index we learned that* halal *compliance was most important for food brands, and by developing the Noor Brand Index we can see that food brands are also the most successful. The food category is the one where Shariah-compliant standards are the most developed, through the practice of* halal, *which clearly prescribes how a food product must be sourced and handled at all stages of manufacture.*

Table 3.1   Noor Global Brand Index, 2010

Brand	Noor Index Score	Brand	Noor Index Score
Lipton	131	Heinz	101
Nestlé	130	Nivea	98
Nescafé	122	Fair & Lovely	97
Nido	118	Pepsi	95
Kraft	117	Coca-Cola	94
Maggi	117	Air Arabia	91
Mirinda	110	L'Oréal	90
Pringles	110	Axe	88
Lays	110	Emirates	85
7 Up	109	Red Bull	78
Colgate	108	Etihad Airways	77
Lux	108	Singapore Airlines	63
Sunsilk	105	Cathay Pacific	62
Close Up	103	Citibank	59
Dove	103	Standard Chartered	54
Pantene	102	HSBC	51
Rexona	102	RBS	47
Head & Shoulders	101		

Source: Ogilvy Noor.

- *Islamic branding efforts must be holistic:* We have found that one of the reasons financial services brands do so poorly in the Noor Global Brand Index despite the large sums invested by global banking brands into their Islamic Banking arms, is consumer scepticism. Consumers seek reassurance that any Islamic Branding initiative from a global brand is not tokenistic or a marketing ploy. Instead, they want to feel that the brand genuinely understands and empathises with Islamic values in all aspects of their operations all over the world.[9]

All the studies I have described so far in this chapter are very informative, and yet they are only just scratching the surface of what we want to know about the global Islamic market, and how it behaves. There is a paucity of research data to help the marketer do his job well, and although some companies are doing their own studies in particular markets it will be some time before we have a really thorough understanding of Muslim consumer behavior. However, there is one more piece of evidence as to how the Muslim market can be segmented in terms of behavior that I would like to share before moving on to look at Islamic brand opportunities and challenges.

Retail Muslim Consumer Segmentation

One key variable that appears to influence the decision making of many Muslim consumers, whether consciously or subconsciously, and whether in Muslim-majority or minority markets, is the degree of religiosity they feel; in other words, how strongly they feel compelled to conform to the code of Islamic practice. This is, of course, not applicable in all markets and is influenced by the culture of the country within which consumers are making their decisions. But it does give us an important insight into consumer behavior. Figure 3.9 helps us to understand this behavior to some extent, and is based on the model that banks have discovered in their research on Islamic finance and kindly shared with me. However, having interviewed many companies outside of finance, I can see that this type of segmentation may apply beyond that specific category.

At the two ends of the spectrum are the extremes of observance in terms of allegiance to Islamic brands and products. On the far right are people who have a very high, strict observance of Islamic values and practices; they will

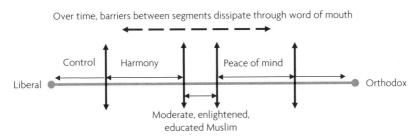

Figure 3.9   Retail Consumer Segmentation

always go for the Islamic option or alternative offered and might be described as very orthodox. On the far left are those who may not be concerned at all by the nature of the offer—possibly secular and global citizens who see themselves as being free to decide between Islamic and non-Islamic options. Between these two extremes are varying degrees of observance and behavior influenced by different factors, mainly religiosity, culture, and price.

Added into this complex equation are demographic elements, and in the case of Islamic finance the banks in Muslim-minority markets have tended to go for the middle part of the spectrum—namely, the moderate, enlightened, educated Muslim—those who have family ties to Muslim countries but have grown up in a Western culture. They tend to be second- or third-generation professionals who regard themselves as, say, British if they were born in Britain, but stay committed to their Islamic roots and values. They have a good Islamic knowledge, tend to understand what Islamic finance is and what the products are, and actively seek out Islamic financial solutions to their life-style problems. They are the most "available" segment, if you like. Those in the extreme right or very orthodox segment have been found to be difficult to penetrate, despite being the most religious and the obvious candidates for these kinds of products. The reason for this is that they are unlikely to buy unless their local *Imam* or scholar endorses it. The need to pursue and convince this segment is so great that it almost makes it not worth the resources required. If they can be convinced, they are, in essence, moving across to the next segment, which is the "peace of mind" group of consumers. This segment says, "Yes, I want to make sure that I practice my religion properly so that I can have peace of mind." So, they tend to take the attitude of "Prove it is *Shariah* compliant, and I will listen seriously to you and probably buy."

To the left of the enlightened, educated Muslim are the two segments of "harmony" and "control." They tend to be religious in terms of perhaps going to the mosque on a Friday and eating *halal* meat, and so on, and they try to live in accordance with Islamic practices, but they are quite price-conscious. Both groups will have the attitude that: "I don't understand your products, but if you can show me the real benefits, and if they are close to the cost of conventional products I will consider them, but they cost me more then I am not really going to buy."

The difference between the "harmony" and "control" groups is that the those in the "harmony" group are influenced heavily by their peers, and will probably buy what their friends and neighbors buy without the bank having to promote their products to them, while the "control" group is a little more price-conscious and harder to convince. They will say: "I don't understand the products. Explain them to me, but if they cost me more and there is a lot of paperwork, and so on, then I'm not interested and I'm happy to stay with conventional banking." The "control" group is very close to the extreme left of the spectrum, where we find the "liberal" segment. This segment takes the stance that they want to fit in with their society. "When in Rome, do as the Romans do," is their attitude. They will say, "Unless they give me the exact same benefits and don't cost me more, I'm not interested."

What will happen over time, according to the banks, is that due to word of mouth the bars that are between the segments will gradually start moving upwards and dissipate out, so that, for instance, more and more people from the "control" segment will come in to the "harmony" segment, and the "harmony" segment will come in to the "moderate, enlightened, educated" segment. According to the banks, that process is already occurring.

This kind of segmentation is now being used by marketers in banks and other organizations, although it certainly makes sense and is the product of proper validated research carried out by banks and research agencies, it doesn't necessarily show marketers where and how to reach the various segments. It would appear that the moderate, well-educated, and enlightened Muslim would be more likely to respond to media advertising and promotion, but it is also clear that marketers need to be extremely sensitive in the messages that they are delivering to Muslim consumers so as not to offend them in any way by assuming any degree of religiosity among them. In fact, most banks I have interviewed have said that it is very difficult to mass market their products, whatever market they are in—Muslim majority or minority. Moreover, if they are trying to attract customers who are more orthodox, especially in Muslim-minority countries, they have found it necessary to go out into the community and hold seminars or talks using the mosque as a conduit. From such outreach work they tend to get the interested consumers coming back to them to ask for more information.

Another reason not to rely on heavy advertising and media outreach is that customers tend not to understand the products. Conventional banking products, having been available in all markets (except Iran) for several decades, are understood by most customers who need financial products, but Islamic banking, despite its longevity, is an embryonic market and its products are complex to the ordinary consumer.

The main point of these findings, though, is that different people buy based on different points of view, and differing degrees of religiosity form a part of these points of view, but at all times an organization has to make it very clear that it is offering products that comply with *Shariah* law. They do this by working with independent boards of advisors who guide them on compliance and communicating factual information to customers who make their choices. Those customers who want a religious validation may still go to their local *Imam* or scholar, or indeed they can speak to the scholars who advise the banks if this is the situation.

It therefore becomes quite difficult to build a broad-value proposition that will work across all segments, and so the customer growth strategy is not easy and is very different to the conventional banking market. In Muslim-minority countries, it is a very niche market. In Muslim-majority countries, it is a little easier to communicate the value proposition, but these segments still seem to exist. This probably accounts for the success of the Western brands in offering Islamic products, as global brand names tend to have higher levels of trust, even in Muslim-majority countries.

What is very interesting in the banking sector is that Islamic banks in Muslim-majority and minority markets are beginning to bring in more non-Muslim customers than Muslims! Non-Muslim new customers can reach up to 60 percent of the total number for many Islamic and Western banks. This appears to be because Islamic financial products involve more transparency, the sharing of risk, and, since the last recession, are seen as less speculative and more ethical.

Summary: What Does All This Mean? ▬▬▬▬

There are some things we can take away from the data that is now beginning to be gathered by various organizations.

1. The Muslim market as a whole is extremely large, and certainly worth paying attention to, whatever your industry is.

2. Paradoxically, that market is not homogeneous in nature. There are many complexities that exist, which force companies to look carefully at different elements of the market and its Muslim population.

3. Branding and marketing activities in different countries need to be based on solid research. From what I have seen, there are some similarities and some differences in different country markets. The differences appear to be lodged in national cultures and the degrees of adherence to Islamic principles. The differences are distinct in Muslim-majority and Muslim-minority markets, and immigration patterns and government policy play a role in shaping the differences. Indeed, national identity seems to be as important, if not more important, in some countries. Sometimes, this is based on people's engagement with Western values.

4. In any Muslim market can be found very religious or "orthodox" Muslims and not-so-religious or "liberal" Muslims. This has a bearing on marketing initiatives, particularly communications and messaging, and is influenced by price as well as religious inclination—or "religiosity," as it is sometimes called.

5. It should not be forgotten that most Muslims in the world belong to the disadvantaged or not very affluent groups; indeed, hundreds of millions can be classified as "poor." This has a bearing on what products can and should be offered. It also provides opportunities for governments and SMEs, as well as for multinational companies.

6. For those firms wishing to build an Islamic brand (that is, Muslim companies), there are enormous opportunities in this vast market, but Western brands have seen these opportunities and are moving in. This point will be the subject of discussion in a later chapter.

7. The segmentation possibilities are quite revealing, and there is clearly scope for building and marketing niche and global brands. It appears there are various segmentation approaches being looked at now that might apply in understanding consumer behavior in all Muslim consumer markets, minority or majority—the financial services example being one of them.

8. There is a very clear message here that stands out above all others, and that is the lack of uniformity across all Muslim markets. Large, global, and growing though the total market may be, the different cultural influences and inconsistencies in lifestyles and behavior across Muslims residing in over 200 countries mean that brand managers and marketers will have to adopt multiple marketing strategies in order to build international Islamic brands.

Nevertheless, despite the challenges, there are a huge number of opportunities that marketers can pursue.

The Range of Opportunities in Islamic Branding and Marketing

Before we leave the broader aspects of Muslim markets, it is important to understand that Muslim markets, although differing in size and behavior across the world, provide opportunities across many categories, including:

- food and beverage;
- education;
- tourism and hospitality;
- medical and pharmaceutical products and services;
- entertainment;
- cosmetics and personal care;
- Internet and digital products and services;
- financial products and services;
- children's products; and
- lifestyle and fashion products.

It is interesting to note that many Western brands are already providing brands in most of these categories alongside brands that are indigenous to Muslim-majority countries. In the next chapter, I'll explain the sources of Islamic brands. In Chapter 5, we look at how brands are built, and in Chapter 6 we take a closer look at the above category opportunities.

Notes ━━━━━━━━━━━━━━━━━━━━━━━━━━━━

1. The Pew Forum on Religion & Public Life, *Mapping the Global Muslim Population: A Report on the Size and Distribution of the World's Muslim Population* (*"The Pew Report"*) (Pew Research Center, October 2009).
2. The Pew Forum on Religion and Public Life, "The Future of the Global Muslim Population: Projections for 2010–2030" (Pew Research Center, January 2011).
3. *Ibid.*
4. United Nations Population Fund.
5. The Pew Forum on Religion & Public Life, *An Uncertain Road: Muslims and the Future of Europe*, http://pewforum.org/docs/index .phpDocID=60, accessed December 29, 2009.
6. *The Gallup Coexist Index: A Global Study of Interfaith Relations: With an In-Depth Analysis of Muslim Integration in France, Germany, and the United Kingdom. Muslim West Facts Project; What the People Really Think* (The Coexist Foundation, Spring 2009).
7. *Ibid.*
8. *Ibid.*
9. Ogilvy Noor, www.ogilvynoor.com.

The Nature and Structure of Islamic Markets

Introduction

The previous chapter outlined the size and scope of Muslim markets, globally, regionally, and with respect to both majority and minority populations, and looked at market segmentation ideas originating from some of those studies. In this chapter, we shall look at the nature and structure of Islamic brands in much the same way as we would look at sources of, and relationships between, brands in the conventional corporate world— by way of *brand architecture*.

A Typology of Islamic Brands

In the conventional branding world, the phrase "brand architecture" is often used to describe where brands come from and how they might be linked to one another. Brand architecture is a bit like a family tree, in this respect, showing which brands are related and how. Brand architecture can also be concerned with how sub-brands (brand ranges or products) relate to master brands, and whether or not they should be related at all. The challenge in dealing with brand architecture issues is that there are no fixed rules and a variety of options, and these can be dynamic. In this respect, they are unlike human family trees, which—once formed—are usually fixed. Let's consider how brand architecture works, using a few examples from the world's top brands, before we examine Islamic brand sources and relationships. This will also be useful for organizations looking for other options to build their brand portfolios.

In the corporate world, there is usually one question that companies have to answer: "Does the corporation want to be a 'branded house' or a 'house of brands'?" "Branded house" means there is one master brand that becomes the sole focus of the branding effort; all sub-brands or product brands are subservient to and support that master brand. "House of brands," on the other hand, means that the sub-brands or product brands can stand on their own and don't have to relate to the master brand.

Using examples from the corporate world, BMW, Nokia, and Virgin Group are branded houses—their sub-branded businesses and products are always given little prominence in communications, while the master brand gets the spotlight. On the other hand, a corporation such as Procter & Gamble is really a "house of brands," because its products such as Pampers, Tide, and Head & Shoulders get the spotlight, while the brand owners have a lower profile. The choice of the "right" model will vary for every company. It is also common practice to see a mixed model, as in the case of Intel (master) and Centrino (sub-brand) or Microsoft (master) and Windows 7 (product brand).

The same brand architecture roles can be applied to nations. For example, underneath the master brand (the nation or country) can fall a number of sub-brands or product brands, such as tourism, trade and investment, foreign affairs, and others that relate to it. Alternatively, there may be "products" of a nation or country, such as particular destinations, that can stand on their own. In the national context, conflicts can sometimes arise. For instance, a national tourism authority (sub-brand) is usually set up to promote the nation, despite the fact that within the country there are several destinations (product brands) wanting to promote themselves in their own right. The tourism authority will want a branded house, where—whatever the destination—the country comes first, while the destinations want to spend their budgets on promoting themselves in order to maximize tourism revenue and return on investment.

As an example, the Malaysian Tourist Promotion Board (MTPB) wants to promote Malaysia as a country destination, but the 13 Malaysian states want their own international advertising, as attracting people directly to the individual states guarantees more visitors—and thus more prosperity—than does a general national campaign. Similarly, the Tourism Authority of Thailand is the national brand champion, but Phuket, Chiang Mai, Ko Chang, and other destinations within the country want a louder voice. The sub-brand destinations would thus prefer a house of brands, where the individual brands are promoted more heavily. By contrast, in the UAE, Abu Dhabi is now implementing a tourism strategy that could either work with, or compete against, that of its next-door emirate Dubai; the difference here is that the UAE doesn't operate an overall tourism strategy. But there may come a time when, as the other emirates also start to provide tourism facilities, the UAE creates an "umbrella strategy."

Which is the best option to choose? A combined model usually works best if all parties can agree, so that the master brand supports the sub-brands and the sub-brands reinforce the master brand. In the corporate world, this works with firms such as Intel (Centrino) and Microsoft (Windows 7).

It is not easy to apply this architectural framework with Islamic brands, and I find it a somewhat confused marketplace. Nevertheless, in trying to understand Islamic branding and marketing we have to get to grips with what levels and categories there are, and this has to be done at a macro level before we get down to the more "corporate" level. So, before we analyze the opportunities available for Islamic brand and marketing managers, it is useful to look at how Islamic companies are evolving in terms of structure. Figure 4.1 summarizes the "architecture"—or "typology"—of different Islamic brands in terms of their origin or source.

As mentioned in Chapter 1, Islam is a way of life. As a religion, it is based on a set of shared values and principles that influence every Muslim person's life on an everyday basis to a certain extent, depending on how

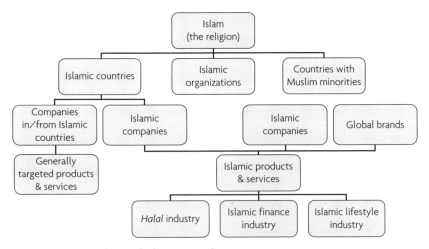

Figure 4.1   A Typology of Islamic Brands

strictly they adhere to the faith. If we start from the point of view of Islam as a brand in itself, as it clearly is, then we can link everything that is considered to be "Islamic" in business nature to three main groupings. It is from these three main groups or sources that most brands, products, and services are derived. The three sources are: Islamic countries (with Muslim-majority populations), Islamic organizations, and countries with Islamic-minority populations. Let's now look at these sources in more detail.

Islamic Countries

Islamic countries are those countries considered to be Islamic due to the fact that they have a Muslim-majority population—for example, Malaysia, Saudi Arabia, Pakistan, Bangladesh, and Oman. Some non-Islamic countries have Islamic-minority populations, such as India, China, Russia, and France.

It is important to emphasize that any country, whether an Islamic country or not, will have a wide brand image, intentionally projected or otherwise. Because it exists in the marketplace, it will possess an image formed by perceptions held by the rest of the world. Whether or not a country likes that image is a different matter. In the context of branding and marketing, these images are extremely important as they are often associated with the companies, products, and services that emanate from the country, and the country-of-origin effect is well known to be capable of helping or hindering a brand's success.

For example, a product endorsed with the phrase "Made in Japan" may have a much easier time gaining acceptance as possessing the quality attribute, as opposed to one that bears the label "Made in China." This country-of-origin or nation brand effect can be so strong that many countries have now embarked on branding exercises to polish up their national images. Others have yet to do so. This subject was discussed in some detail in Chapter 2, but some points are worth emphasizing again here.

The global perception of "Islam" also influences the images of Islamic countries. Some of the most talked-about brand images on the Islamic religious dimension are those of Saudi Arabia, Iran, and Afghanistan, which appear to be—or are perceived as being—extremely conservative, and which may have negative connotations for some audiences. At the other end of the religious scale are secular Islamic countries such as Turkey, which consistently reject traditional Islamist ideologies and have fewer negative associations. In between these two ends of the spectrum there is an increasing prominence of "moderate Muslim" countries such as Malaysia which try to project a more modern image of Islam that embraces economic development. No detailed survey has as yet been carried out across Islamic countries to determine how much their national image has affected the branding and marketing of companies and products, and this remains a research and development opportunity.

As the discipline of country branding itself becomes more widely accepted, there is an opportunity for Islamic countries to leverage on branding concepts to promote both an image of Islam, as well as an image of their country, in ways that are both relevant to them and more universally acceptable to global consumers. One model of a national brand image that might have such appeal is that of a "modern Islamic country," which not only promotes associations of modernity but also positive connections with respect to moderation. This could be a highly favorable position to hold in a global context with regard to tourism and trade, but no one country has yet reached the position of being perceived as the "Modern Face of Islam," although Malaysia desires to acquire that position and the UAE to some extent has been moving in this direction.

Malaysia also has an internal branding agenda, which is interesting if we consider that in the world of corporate branding the external corporate brand image is never likely to be better than the internal brand image. Thus, the "1 Malaysia" sustained branding campaign that is currently running, and which is designed to unite all people and races within Malaysia, while being political in nature with the intention of clearing up some internal challenges, will have an impact on the world's view of Malaysia. Unless Malaysia continues to be seen as politically stable with multiracial harmony, then negative effects may impact on externally driven economic elements such as tourism and foreign direct investment.

From this example, it can be seen that Islamic countries wishing to enhance economic growth and the quality of life of their people should become focused on their internal, as well as their external, image. This doesn't just mean the pursuit of advertising and promotion, which largely is unsuccessful in changing perceptions; rather, it means the pursuit of policies and public diplomacy that deliver on the promises that advertising makes.

Another component of the building blocks of any national brand is its companies, whether government-related or not, which are brand ambassadors and have an impact on their country of origin through their own brand images. If they are successful, then the national brand is likely to be more successful; and if they are tainted with poor reputations, then their national brands will suffer similarly. This Nation Brand Effect is discussed in Chapter 2. But before we look at corporate brands as a source of positive image ambassadors, we should first examine the types of Islamic organizations that can be found nationally and internationally that are one level above companies.

Islamic Organizations

Islamic organizations are those institutions that are Islamic and may be based in one Islamic country, but which belong to many Islamic countries. These brands serve the Islamic world and are usually based in one country, providing products—but usually services—to many Islamic countries. Islamic organizations are those such as the Organization of the Islamic Conference (OIC), a group of 57 member states, headquartered in Jeddah, Saudi Arabia. Another example is the Islamic Financial Services Board (IFSB), "an international standard-setting organization that promotes and enhances the soundness and stability of the Islamic financial services industry by issuing global prudential standards and guiding principles for the industry, broadly defined to include banking, capital markets and insurance sectors. The IFSB also conducts research and coordinates initiatives on industry-related issues, as well as organises roundtables, seminars and conferences for regulators and industry stakeholders."[1]

A further example is the World Islamic Economic Forum Foundation (WIEF), based in Malaysia, "a global conference that acts as an international business platform where the business sectors of the Muslim world meet for business opportunities and together with the government leaders, act as a hub where policy proposals on economic development can be formulated."[2]

An additional source of Islamic brands within this second level is companies domiciled in Muslim-minority countries who offer brands that address Muslim markets at home or abroad. This leads us to the third level in the typology, which is Islamic companies. It is to this level that most attention will be given in this book, in the form of case studies.

Islamic Companies

This next level down in Islamic brand architecture doesn't include international Islamic organizations, but rather companies and brands that originate from Muslim-majority and Muslim-minority countries.

In Islamic countries—that is, countries with Muslim-majority populations such as Indonesia, Malaysia, and the Middle Eastern countries—we find two types of companies: non-Islamic and Islamic. By "non-Islamic companies," I mean those not necessarily owned by Muslim shareholders, but which operate in Muslim countries and markets and offer their products and services to Muslim markets. For example, in Malaysia, they may be foreign companies with branches or subsidiaries operating in the country, such as Rolls-Royce (British) or Bombardier (Canadian), or local companies owned by Malaysian Chinese or other non-Muslim shareholders, such as Resorts World or YTL Group. Also in these Muslim countries we find Islamic companies that are owned by indigenous Muslims, or in some cases by governments. They may offer Islamic products (such as CIMB Bank in Malaysia) or general products—as is the case with Petronas, the Malaysian national oil company. Similarly, Zain from Kuwait offers general telecommunications services to the Middle East and North Africa, and Zam Zam Cola is an example of an Islamic-branded product from Iran.

In Muslim-minority countries—such as India, France, and Singapore—there may also be two types of companies that offer Islamic products and services even though they are not Islamic themselves. Examples are global brands such as UK-based HSBC and Standard Chartered Bank, which both offer Islamic financial products and services, as well as conventional banking products; and smaller brands such as Overseas Chinese Banking Corporation from Singapore. Nestlé, Unilever, and McDonald's would also feature in the global brand area, being foreign companies involved in offering Islamic products.

If we place these and other examples on a brand architecture chart, we will see something like Figure 4.2.

The figure shows us that there can be a variety of sources for Islamic brands, both those specifically aimed at Muslims and those that are not,

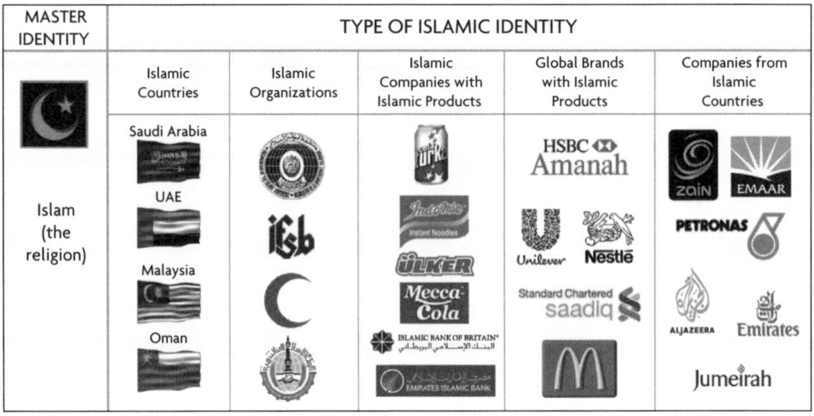

MASTER IDENTITY	TYPE OF ISLAMIC IDENTITY				
	Islamic Countries	Islamic Organizations	Islamic Companies with Islamic Products	Global Brands with Islamic Products	Companies from Islamic Countries
Islam (the religion)	Saudi Arabia UAE Malaysia Oman			HSBC ⟨X⟩ Amanah	ZAIN EMAAR PETRONAS

Figure 4.2   Islamic Brand Architecture Continuum

and generated by Islamic countries and companies, or not. This wide variety of brand sources creates several opportunities for Islamic branding and marketing.

Implications for Marketers

In the architecture described above, we can see two distinct ways of branding and marketing Islamic products and services.

First, companies can provide specifically designed and developed Islamic brands that are not intended for non-Islamic audiences, although they could purchase them. Mecca Cola and the Burquini (Islamic swimsuit for women) would be examples in this dimension. Second, they can develop and market branded offerings that are conventional in nature, but modified to suit Islamic audiences. The modifications may be merely in terms of brand communications and connected via these to Islamic values, as is the case with Zain's telecommunications services; or they may be in the way the product is made, ensuring a different and acceptable formula for consumption. Nestlé's *halal* products would be an example of the latter. A more fundamental third option is for a foreign company to create an Islamic subsidiary to cater strictly for Muslim audiences, as Standard Chartered Bank has done with its Standard Chartered Saadiq Bank.

We can see that there are various ways of dealing with the marketing issues, and there are many opportunities for many companies to reach both Islamic and non-Islamic audiences. In Chapters 6 and 7, we will take an in-depth look at the range of categories that is currently being expanded by companies looking to brand and market Islamic products and services. How companies might overcome the challenges they may face in taking advantage of these opportunities, and which strategies they can use to greatest effect, will be the subject of the remaining chapters.

Before we move on to consider these practical branding and marketing issues, it is appropriate to look at how brands are actually built.

Notes

1. www.ifsb.org.
2. www.wief.org.my.

5 Building a Brand Strategy

Introduction

In this chapter, I will focus on what it takes to build a strong brand. The principles are the same for any kind of brand-building exercise, whether for a person, a product, a company, a public sector organization, or a nation. Whether you are involved in building an Islamic brand for a Muslim company, organization, or nation, or a brand that addresses any market, there are certain steps that must be taken. The chapter makes reference to some well-known Western brands to illustrate how the world's top brands have achieved their positions. The chapter also examines in detail two cases of brands from Islamic countries that have adopted these globally recognized brand-building principles.

Building a great brand is a strategic activity. Branding isn't just advertising, promotion, or a nice-looking logo; these are tactical activities and devices that help with brand communications. What distinguishes a *great* brand is a well-conceived strategy, as this chapter will explain.

Brand Strategy

In 1999, the incoming chief operating officer of Nissan, Carlos Ghosn, said: "One of the biggest surprises is that Nissan didn't care about its brand. There is nobody really responsible for the strategy of the brand."[1] Although this comment was made over a decade ago, to my mind it is perhaps the best articulation by a global business leader of the most common mistake made by companies that would like to have a strong brand but just don't make the grade—*they don't have a brand strategy*. Without a brand strategy, brand management and the creation of great customer experiences become very difficult, if not impossible, to achieve. Strategy gives focus and direction to brand management, and provides the platform that enables brand managers to gain consistency in all their brand-related activities.

Whether the audience your brand is intended to attract is Muslim or non-Muslim, developing a robust strategy for that brand is a must.

But we all know that strategy starts with the business. And for too long, companies have been refining the art of inside-out thinking; researching and developing products *they think the market will want*. In fact, the most brilliant strategies come from deep consumer insight—really getting inside the minds of the consumers that you hope will build your brand (that is, outside-in thinking). It is this continual search for outside-in thinking that can lead to unusual but real insights into how people perceive things, and what "hot buttons" will switch them on to your brand.

If we use consumer insight, the business of the brand might be different from the business of the business; so, before we look at the key elements of brands, let's think about the *business* of brands. It's quite easy—all you have to do is ask yourself one important question: "What business is my brand in?" Consider the following examples.

What Business is Your Brand in?

I was once engaged in discussions with a CEO whose company made products that "make things shine," such as car polish, shoe-care products, and so on. We talked about what business he was *really* in. When he moved away from the obvious answers relating to cleaning products, and so on, he decided that his brand was in the "feelings" business, because when consumers use his brands the end-result is that they feel good about themselves and their self-image improves. This paradigm shift in thinking has since impacted the CEO's company greatly and has taken it into product areas he had previously not considered, resulting in more new products and brand extensions and a larger, more profitable business. The key to the development of his business and his brand image was having insights into the feelings of his customers, and then tapping into their emotions. As we shall see throughout this book, the engagement with human emotions is at the heart of any successful brand strategy.

Many of the world's top brands use the inner emotions of consumers as key drivers for their brand strategies. This is because it is now a well-known fact that emotions are the basis for nearly all brand purchase decisions, and any brand worth its salt has to appeal to the innermost emotions of every prospective customer. If we look at the emotional strategies of some of the world's top brands, we can see this in action. For example, Nike isn't in the business of marketing sports shoes and accessories; the brand aims to help athletes and ordinary people get the best out of themselves. Nike stands for *winning*, an attribute strongly supported by endeavor and doing one's best. And Nokia isn't just "Connecting People," as its strap line suggests; it has a brand strategy based upon the emotional driver of *empowerment*. Thus, by choosing emotional areas of universal appeal that are relevant both to the business and their consumers, brands get closer to customers by demonstrating that they understand them better than the alternatives offered by other brands.

Perhaps one of the best examples of a business that focuses on human emotions in building its brand image is Hallmark Inc., profiled in the following case study.

CASE STUDY 3: HALLMARK INC.

The Business of the Hallmark Brand—a Paradigm Shift in Thinking

Most people, if asked what business they thought Hallmark is in, would say that the company is in the business of manufacturing and selling greetings cards—and indeed, Hallmark is famous for that type of product. But this isn't what the Hallmark brand business is all about. The Hallmark brand is focused clearly on the business of enriching people's lives. The brand wants *"to be the very best at helping people express themselves, celebrate, strengthen relationships, and enrich their lives."* This is a powerful brand vision statement, and taking this view of the business has led Hallmark Inc. into a tremendous array of business opportunities that have proved to be highly successful and profitable.

The company, which has existed for 100 years, had consolidated revenues of US$4 billion in 2009, with products in 30 languages distributed in 100 countries around the world. Hallmark Entertainment is now the leading producer/distributor of mini-series, TV movies, and home videos, and the *Hallmark Hall of Fame* has won more Emmy awards than any other series. The company is also involved in cable TV, real estate, and the retailing of other relationship-building products such as Crayola Crayons, Silly Putty, party plates, gifts, wrappings, and more.

The whole of the Hallmark brand and business is built around emotion, and it genuinely cares for its customers. The company always has emotion as the base of the business and the brand, as this statement explains:

> *For 100 years, Hallmark Cards, Inc. has helped people connect with one another and give voice to their feelings. Our employees are personally passionate about caring, creativity, quality and innovation—values that have guided us from the start and remain at our core.... We're with you at holidays and any-days, at your most important milestones and unexpected occasions, when you want to share a laugh and when you seek to offer comfort.* Creativity, innovation, quality and caring *have guided our decisions and earned us the trust of the people who work with us, buy our products and live in the communities we call home. It's a trust we intend to keep.*

The Hallmark beliefs and values statement says, "Our products and services must *enrich people's lives*" (www.hallmark.com). Such statements, made to employees and the public at large, are not just the foundation for good brands; they are a powerful driver of human emotion and behavior. Hallmark manages to build emotion into every touchpoint with the consumer, and it generates brand loyalty in return. Another example can be found in Hallmark's strong corporate social responsibility program, which emphasizes its commitment to building relationships and enriching people's lives. The program involves, among other initiatives, employee volunteerism to assist community projects, philanthropic contributions to various programs that will improve the lives of the underprivileged, and helping people to connect with their loved ones who are far away.

By expressing its business in a brand-related way based on enriching lives, Hallmark found the key to becoming one of the top privately owned brands in the non-Muslim and Muslim worlds alike.

The Role of Consumer Insight ━━━━━━━━━

Hallmark and the other examples referred to above indicate that brands are now driving business strategy, but *only* when they reach deeply into the psychological world of consumer insight. The really "hot buttons" that consumer insights unveil are emotional, not rational, and lead to excellent brand performance.

It is the brand manager's responsibility to work with brand strategy consultancies and other agencies to discover these insights, which are sometimes far from obvious. However, as it is consumers that create brand power, brand managers must discover the underlying motives that exist in their minds that will trigger favorable attitudes and compulsive desires toward their brands.

Living with the Consumer

In the never-ending search for consumer insights that may provide a paradigm shift in thinking for brands and businesses, some companies hire research crews who live for a few days with "prototype" consumers, in order to learn how they think and behave in their everyday lives. Traditional research—both quantitative and qualitative—has the drawback of relying on what consumers *say*, which is sometimes different from what they actually *do* in real life. What brand management has to do is find out how to press the "hot buttons" that motivate consumers, and this means gaining a full understanding of what drives them in real-life situations.

Companies trying to create consumer brands are waking up to the fact that the place to start understanding consumer behavior is in the home— where people's real lives are lived in the context of wide-ranging emotions, the sometimes-conflicting demands of different relationships, and relaxed, rather than ideal, personal standards—as opposed to the office or a research room. For example, when Procter & Gamble filmed housewives going about their daily routines, the company noticed mothers multi-tasking. One mother was seen feeding her baby while preparing a meal and snatching glances at the television. In natural scenarios such as this, companies can see what programs and advertisements attract homemakers, and what products they use or could use. Banks often carry out similar research to discover the process by which families at various stages of their life cycle discuss and make major financial decisions.

Another good example of gaining consumer insight comes from Unilever. The company has sent staff out into rural villages in underdeveloped areas of Malaysia to live with the villagers and learn more about their way of life, in order to help with brand relationships and product development, as described in the following case study.

CASE STUDY 4: UNILEVER MALAYSIA

Romancing the Consumer

Unilever's emotional brand and business driver has always been "helping people get more out of life," and the company is always looking for new ways by which it can deliver on this promise. In the 21st century, one of Unilever's "Path to Growth" strategic agendas has been "reconnecting with the consumer" with the aim of:

- focusing everyone in the company on the consumer;
- turning knowledge gained about the consumer into creative insight; and
- anticipating and responding to consumer change.

According to Unilever, the only way to achieve this is by:

- deepening its knowledge of consumers' habits and attitudes;
- having a culture of "getting close" to the consumer; and
- having the skills to tap insights into the consumer and to turn them into business opportunities.

Unilever has this strategic thrust as a global initiative, and this case shows how it has been implemented in its operating company in the Muslim-majority country of Malaysia, through a program called "Romancing the Consumer."

Preparations for the "Romancing the Consumer" program involved the following:

- Managers of Unilever Malaysia visited 50 homes and held face-to-face interviews bi-monthly to gain consumer insights.

- Twenty staff brought 120 consumers to the factory quarterly for face-to-face-understanding dialogue.
- All staff were given cross-category training so that not only could inter-brand communications be enhanced, but also staff could answer questions about any brands asked of them by consumers.
- A specific project—Project Rambo—was devised. The whole company was closed for one day, and every employee—old and young, from the tea lady to the chairman—went out to do merchandising of products in shops to ensure that the visibility of Unilever products at retail customers' premises was first class, and to get retail feedback.

Project Rambo saw high energy and a high commitment by Unilever Malaysia's entire workforce to work with trade partners to enhance product displays to better attract shoppers' attention. The experience even inspired Unilever's employees to tidy up merchandising in stores where they usually shop!

The Rural Marketing Program was another initiative aligned with reconnecting with the consumer, but primarily with those in the rural market. The idea of this program when it was conceived was to raise the awareness of Unilever products in the rural areas of the country by having rural-relevant activities, and at the same time putting products on sale. The program was also aimed at providing Unilever Malaysia with the opportunity to engage rural consumers with Unilever brands and people. The first event—held in October 2000—was a tremendous success, and similar events followed over subsequent years in different parts of the country.

Additional activities included marketing staff staying in villagers' homes for two days to gain a detailed insight into the usage and buying patterns of household, personal care, and food products. All such events were planned well in advance and started with a meeting with the head of the village and his committee. The team was briefed on the objectives of the event and the type of activities to be organized. These often included traditional games to enable participation by all age groups. The local villagers took charge of these activities, and Unilever staff organized prizes and appearances by special guests. Each of the events attracted between 3,000 and 6,500 people.

With its "Romancing the Consumer" program, the company has been successful in developing a culture of getting consumer insights and using them to drive its business.

Intel is another company that constantly seeks consumer insights. It employs anthropologists and ethnographers—people who study human behavior and culture—to gain insights into what people really want, and why they like to buy. The insights gained from studying "the minutiae of daily life" help in making technology much more friendly and fun for consumers. Again, this involves making visits to people's homes, and accompanying them on shopping trips and other excursions away from the home. Intel, like many other companies, has come to see that creating products, and then trying to persuade consumers to buy them, isn't enough. If companies *really* want to understand what makes consumers tick, they must look closely at their behaviors and gain insights into what they want, and why they like to buy. In Asia, in both Muslim-majority and minority countries, Intel has found that people are less individualistic and tend to share a lot more than do people in the West; as a consequence, it is developing devices that will facilitate the sharing of technology. As Intel moves deeper into healthcare, education and other markets with its products, it is now employing greater numbers of scientists, doctors, and healthcare workers in order to understand what consumers really need and want.

Consumer insight is the gateway to understanding people's rational and emotional behaviors, and there is no doubt that brand strategies that are built on emotion and the realism of everyday life have a better chance of success than those that are not.

In the following section, we will see how powerful the world of emotion can be in building and managing strong brands.

Creating a Brand Strategy

The following are the main things that need to be considered when creating a brand strategy.

The Rational and Emotional Sides of a Brand

We must never forget that brand promises are often made in the world of commercial reality—in terms of exceptional quality, service, and, nowadays, innovation. However, this isn't where the source of success for brands lies. These elements are merely the price a company has to pay to get into the branding game, and the branding game is a mind game. As parity becomes the norm, and brands match each other feature-by-feature and attribute-by-attribute, it is becoming harder to create a brand strategy through rational means. So, while consumers screen the rational elements of quality and other compelling product attributes as part of the buying process, the real decision to buy is taken at an emotional level.

A brief excursion into modern science tells us why this is so. The notion that the rational, conscious part of the brain dominates the non-rational parts has now been disproved. MRI scanning has revealed that people's decision making is mostly quick and emotional, is often done subconsciously, and is much more intuitive than was previously thought. It is now an undisputed fact that emotion drives reason, and not the other way round. Our feelings happen with great rapidity and precede conscious thought. The emotional part of the brain is considerably larger than the rational part and outpaces it in terms of intensity, sending 10 times as many signals to the rational brain as opposed to the reverse. What's more, recall and memory have been proven to be a result of emotional experiences.

The following questions and statements provide a simple example of how this takes place. The *rational* thoughts tend to be analytical, but it is the emotional statements that drive the purchase decision.

Rational	Emotional
Do I need it?	I want it!
What does it do?	It looks cool!
What does it cost?	I'm going to get it!
How does it compare to . . . ?	I only want this one!

Studies in neuro-science make it clear that brand managers need to employ emotional brand strategies, as the end-game for any brand strategy is to achieve the dual aims of trust and loyalty, and both of these are based on emotional, not rational, thoughts.

Given the increasing scientific evidence of the power of emotion in people's decisions and actions, we can categorically state that without emotional brand strategies it is impossible to build great brands! If we look at the powerful brands around the world, we see that they elicit thoughts like those listed above on the right. Great brands build tremendous emotional capital with their strategies.

Characteristics of Power Brands—Emotional Capital

Brand managers are increasingly turning to the emotional side of strategy in order to win and keep customers. Power brands develop emotional capital, because:

- *They are very personal*—people choose brands for very personal reasons, whether they be self-expression, a sense of belonging, or other reasons.
- *They evoke emotion*—brands sometimes unleash unstoppable emotion, arousing passion and unquestionable excitement.
- *They live and evolve*—they are like people in that they live, grow, evolve, and mature. But luckily, if they are well managed, they have no life cycle and can live forever.
- *They communicate*—strong brands listen, receive feedback, change their behavior as they learn, and speak differently to different people, depending on the situation, just as people do. They believe in dialogue, not monologue.
- *They develop immense trust*—people trust the brands they choose, and often resist all substitutes.
- *They engender loyalty and friendship*—trust paves the way for long-lasting relationships, and brands can be friends for life.
- *They give great experiences*—like great people, great brands are nice to be with, good to have around, and are consistent in what they give to their friends.

Given these facts about the emotional capital that brands develop, we need to understand that brands are relationships. The head of Starbucks,

Howard Schultz, once said in a note to his employees: "I want to emphasize that the key to our success lies in our values, our culture and the relationships we have with our partners and customers. When we're at our best, we create emotional experiences for people that really enhance their lives." If this is true for all top brands—and I have no doubt about that—what is the process of establishing an emotional relationship with consumers? How do the top brands build such relationships?

The Emotional Brand Relationship Process

In order to build an emotional brand strategy there are certain steps brand managers have to take, like the steps of a ladder, as shown in Figure 5.1. Let's think of it as a relationship between two people, as opposed to a brand and consumers. One person sees another across a room at a particular function and wants to meet them. Following this awareness, an opportunity to meet may arise, and although the conversation is short, it leads to the decision as to whether or not the interest is sufficient to carry the relationship further. Further meetings reinforce this mutual respect, and the two people become friends. If the friendship blossoms, it generates trust and loyalty between them and it is highly likely that they will become friends for life or have a lasting relationship.

The brand–consumer relationship grows in a very similar way. Awareness comes first, followed by involvement and purchase—a few meetings— which can lead on to the friendship and trust levels, which in turn lead to

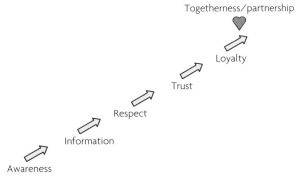

Figure 5.1   The Emotional Brand Relationship Process

brand loyalty and lifetime customer relationships. The power brands get to and past the friendship and trust levels. If they *didn't* become friends with customers, and develop that sense of comfort, familiarity, and dependability, then they would never have reached power brand status. Companies that don't get to the critical friendship level often get stuck at the awareness stage.

Big spending on awareness follows many brand launches, but the subsequent management of the brand may not take it up the ladder. Lots of awareness may build a level of familiarity and interest, but as we all know, true friendship and love go much further than the initial excitement. Building friendship takes a long time and has to be earned through consistency and dependability; without these qualities, there is no trust. Great brands develop such emotional relationships, but some brands sometimes forget what it takes, and consequently fail. For example, one Internet-based brand received 84 percent brand awareness ratings but only a 17 percent trust rating. Some brand managers spend millions on awareness—which is an essential step to achieve—but then neglect the emotional side of the brand–consumer relationship, which is necessary for real long-term success.

The Importance of the Emotional Ladder for Muslim Brands

The best brands in the world climb this emotional ladder of brand success, but I believe the nature of it gives much hope to brand builders in the Muslim world, for several reasons.

First, the issues of awareness and respect can be dealt with without too much trouble, as they really depend on marketing communications and product or service quality. Also, respect is more likely to be given if, say, the product is deemed to be *halal*, or recognizably Islamic in nature. However, I must qualify this statement: respect won't be given if the product doesn't reach adequate quality levels. For instance, *halal* food products from some Muslim countries cannot be exported to the EU, as they don't meet the stringent quality controls imposed.

Assuming that a product does reach top-quality levels, and receives due respect, then we come to the three critical elements that are required of a top brand—friendship, trust, and loyalty. Here Muslim brands may have an easier time as they can appeal through a range of widely accepted beliefs and values to Muslim audiences that can recognize them easily and really appreciate them—in other words, Islamic values. These values are discussed later in this chapter.

Second, trust or *amanah*, in itself, is one of the strongest words in the Muslim language (so strong, in fact, that a Western brand—HSBC—has used it as a product brand name, with great success). In this human value, we see the inculcation of centuries of faith, and it is a much sought-after value that, although not exclusive to Islam, is a great attractor for Muslim audiences, who are likely to trust brands that originate from an Islamic source or a source that transmits this value, or is perceived to have it in its belief system.

Third, the issue of loyalty is unquestionable in Islam, and so holds much import for branding. Indeed, although there is no confirmatory data, it is highly likely that, given all things being equal, Muslims are likely to remain loyal to brands that reinforce their beliefs and values, although these brands may not be from Islamic sources, as we can see from the examples of HSBC, Nestlé, and others. This, no doubt, will be a subject for future research.

Thus, the development of powerful emotional brand strategies should be well within the grasp of Islamic companies by linking them with Islamic values and beliefs, which will influence consumers in a significant way. Let's now look in a little more detail at how this can be accomplished.

The emotional part of any brand strategy is derived from what the brand stands for, as explained earlier in this chapter. If we examine how the world's best brands implement an emotionally based strategy, it is usually through the development of a strong personality for the brand that is used to build attraction, trust, and loyalty.

Brand Personality, Attitude, and Trust ━━━━

One of the most important components of a brand strategy is the personality of the brand, and how that influences a brand's attitude and the trust it gains.

Building Brand Charisma

Probably one of the most successful ways to build an emotional brand strategy is to create a personality for your brand. The people in the real world who stand out from the crowd always seem to have some kind of "charisma." They have a personality and attitude that others respect and are sometimes in awe of. They have a presence that almost commands people to follow without asking, and others always want to be around them. They aren't necessarily extroverted or introverted, but people feel good when they are around. Great brands are like great people in this respect, and the role of the brand manager is to manage the brand–consumer relationship by building a powerful and irresistible brand personality.

Like human relationships, whether they turn out right or wrong isn't usually a function of logic and rationality; rather, it is a result of emotional hits and misses. Given this reality, it seems strange that in many cases brand management continues to focus on the non-emotional side of the relationship, promoting features, attributes, price discounts, and so on, which have little impact on the growth of the brand–customer relationship. Such activities might bring in short-term sales increases, but they are open to imitation and won't attract and retain customers by developing an emotional relationship with them. In fact, they may well discourage this and "cheapen" the brand in the eyes of consumers.

Relationships thrive on emotions; they survive or perish, depending on the emotional fit between people. Brands have therefore to reflect personalities that people like, and this means having an emotional basis or edge to them. Indeed, the best brands have personalities carefully crafted to suit them and their target audiences. People have a universal longing to be liked, given attention, and to be loved. But brand management often ignores this. Research clearly shows that companies lose 68 percent of their customers because they feel neglected or aren't given attention. (For details of this research and similar findings, see my book, with Martin Trott, *Romancing the Customer*.[2]) This makes the emotional dimension of the brand–consumer relationship very important, and it is the personality and attitude of the brand that attracts and keeps people loyal to it.

Nike is a brand that has risen to fame through its "Just Do It" attitude, symbolizing the urge to get the best out of oneself, to push beyond one's limits, to win—a truly heroic brand. Brands such as these manage not just to develop a personality that the target audience likes; they also have an "attitude" toward life that attracts people.

Brands are Relationships Built on Strong Values

The best definition of a brand I know of is: *A brand is a relationship.* When you build a brand, you are building a relationship with your customers, and relationships, especially strong ones, are normally built on the basis of shared values.

The emotional connections that brands use at the heart of the brand-building process, such as the ones referred to above, are normally supplemented by a strong brand personality made up of rational and emotional values or characteristics. We have seen that successful Western brands are often driven by emotional values of universal appeal, but can Islamic brands be developed in a similar way? The answer, as can be seen by my remarks on Islamic values and the ladder of emotional success, is a strong "yes!"

Islamic Values for Brand Building

For good reason, I believe that Islamic brands can harness the values of the religion in order to build brands of universal appeal to both Muslim and non-Muslim audiences. A study of Islamic values shows us that they can be drawn from various sources, including:

- the *Qur'an*
- the practices of the Prophet Muhammad;
- the practices of other prophets, such as Yusuf, Ibrahim, Ismail, and Idris, for example; and
- the 99 names of Allah.

They can be seen in Arabic words and their meanings, such as:

- *shiddiq*—true and honest;
- *amanah*—trusted, responsible, and credible;
- *fathanah*—intelligent and wise; and
- *tabligh*—communicative.

There are other generic Islamic values with universal and emotional appeal that are not exclusive to Muslims, and so can be used to appeal across all markets. They include:

- purity and wholesomeness;
- honesty and consistency; and
- fairness and kindness.

A list that contains the above and more would give aspiring Islamic brands a variety of powerful values to use that not only are derived from Islam itself, but would also be attractive to all global audiences. Here is a summary of some of the most notable Islamic values:

Pure	Trusted
Wholesome	Responsible
Honest	Credible
Consistent	Intelligent
Fair	Wise
Kind	Communicative
True	Respectful
Modest	Peaceful
Considerate	Authentic

The list consists of words that all people can subscribe to; that all people agree with; that all people would like to be associated with. The opportunity to use such strong values in building brand personality is open to Islamic brands. What is more, when building a brand personality with emotional appeal and a brand culture that will inspire employees, including these sorts of brand values and personality characteristics ensures a very good chance of success.

It is not surprising, then, that some Islamic brands are doing just that, and are becoming well known for having strong "values" propositions. For example, Al Rajhi Bank, from Saudi Arabia, has built a strong brand on the three values of *truth, honor, and respect*. The Al Rajhi brand case is discussed in more detail in Chapter 9.

Brand Attitude

Brand attitude is a complexity of things, but for the consumer it is based largely on what the brand stands for, and in particular, on how the brand personality is communicated. Brand attitude is a product of brand communications—how the brand talks to the consumer. It is contained in the visuals and the copy of advertisements, for example. If a brand has a personality constructed around the words "warm," "friendly," and "approachable," and communicates this well, it will be perceived as having a "caring" attitude. The words "knowledgeable," "trustworthy," and "professional," when brought to life through communications, suggest a more businesslike attitude.

The key to the way in which the brand should be communicated is often found in matching the attitude and personality of the brand to that of the consumer, so the importance of understanding what makes a target audience tick shouldn't be underestimated. If that understanding isn't there, then the attitude of the brand may turn off the emotional relationship process. It may either "invite" or "alienate" consumers. So, for example, if a brand's character exudes confidence, it may make some consumers feel inferior and others smart. An ambitious or sophisticated brand attitude can invite those with ambition, but turn off those who think they will never be able to climb to those heights. A fun brand might make some people feel shy and others feel really good about themselves. A reliable brand could make someone feel either secure or bored, and a tough brand might attract the active but turn off the less active, and so on. Attitude is a two-way street, and brand managers have to manage these inner thoughts and self-directed feelings of consumers.

Flexing the Brand Values

Some brands cleverly mix the rational and emotional characteristics of their brand's personality, so that they can flex the brand character to suit the audience they are addressing. By having several brand personality characteristics, they can emphasize different aspects of their character to different target audiences. So where, for example, a telecommunications company brand has a set of characteristics such as

- friendly,
- innovative,

- trustworthy,
- understanding, and
- contemporary,

it can put across all these characteristics to each of the two main target audiences, but emphasize "friendly," "contemporary," and "trustworthy" a little more than the others for the residential consumer, and emphasize "innovative" and "understanding" more to the business community. In brand communications, the attitude of the brand personality would thus appear more emotional to the residential audience—because they are more attracted by an emotional attitude, and more rational to the business audience—because this is their attitude toward decision making. The brand–consumer relationship will still be based on emotional strategy, but the degree of emotion exhibited is controlled according to the needs of the consumer group that the brand is trying to build a relationship with, and is represented by the attitude of the brand when communicated.

So, brands often mirror consumers' thoughts, feelings, attitudes, behaviors, lifestyles, and personality. Several successful brands have achieved global status because of brand management's ability to relate to and keep in touch with consumer emotions, mirroring their minds. Brand managers must be specialists in "coaching," bringing out the best of the relationship between all the players—the brand and consumers. And there is no better way to do this than by managing attitudes, feelings, and emotions. Brand management is in the reflections business—anticipating what consumers want to see reflected back at them through the brand mirror.

An example of a brand from Kuwait that has an optimistic attitude to life is the telecommunications company Zain. The name "Zain" means "beautiful, good, or wonderful" in Arabic, and the company's tagline is: "A Wonderful World." In Chapter 9 you will read more about Zain's values, and how it communicates them to a multinational audience.

Brand Trust

An essential part of any brand management strategy must be the establishment of trust in the brand. This is really the key to reaching the long-term emotional relationship with consumers that makes brands famous. Many writers say that trust is derived from the quality of the brand experience that the branded product or service provides. Trust in the corporate brand also derives from this. While it is true that meticulous attention must be paid to quality, reliability, and, these days, innovation, there is much more to it than that. Trust is a very emotional issue, and not particularly a rational one. If consumers own and build brands, as I have stated, then there is more that can be done to catalyze this process, in addition to the development of personality and attitude as described above.

Adding Brand Attraction

If we look at some of the brands that really have captured people's emotions and spirit, we see that they also build in a degree of romance and sensuality. Some do this on the service side, but others manage to do it on the design side. Apple's iPod and iPad are good examples of the creation of an emotional connection with consumers via design. People want to hold them, touch them, and choose from among the attractive colors. Good design enhances the "wanting to own" process, by touching the mind of the consumer in a highly emotional way.

Montblanc was the first company in its category to achieve this emotional sensuality with its writing instruments. Such design features built into brands trigger passionate responses in the subconscious mind. And this is where emotions outweigh rational thoughts, making brand decisions easier. A lot of people don't know everything that an iPad can do, yet many still want one, and they may not realize that other brands have the same attributes of a good writing instrument as a Montblanc pen. Emotions trigger the mind 3,000 times faster than rational thoughts, so brand managers must give thought to owning the dimensions of passion, sensuality, "coolness," nostalgia, mystery, and spirit.

While good design is a must-have for consumer brands, it cannot be sporadic. Indeed, design has now become a part of the innovation process, and innovation now takes place at an increased pace in a continuous way.

Speed, Agility, and Innovation

If a company wants to develop a great brand in today's world, then it will need to develop the attributes of speed, agility, and innovation. These attributes used to be a "nice-to-have" set of characteristics, and companies could utilize them as they preferred. However, the situation today is different. Consumers are demanding new products, and they want them with increasing frequency; this is forcing companies to use these characteristics constantly. Speed, agility, and innovation are now a part of everyday corporate life. However, if firms can respond to these demands, they can generate huge success. The examples of the conventional brands Zara and Samsung below illustrate how two brands have made innovation and speed a part of their business process, and how this has provided them with a competitive advantage. Islamic brands will need to build speed, flexibility, and innovation into their businesses if they are to go global.

The fashion brand Zara is a prime example of speed, agility, and innovation in retailing and it has become a global brand by demonstrating its prowess in these three areas.

Zara produces around 11,000 products each year reaching across Muslim and non-Muslim countries, far more than most fashion retailers, and to accomplish this it has developed the ability to drastically shorten the product life cycle. Indeed, from the design stage to in-store can take as little as four to five weeks. If the design is just a modification, it may take only three weeks. No one design stays in the stores for more than four weeks, and if the first week's sales are not up to scratch, the item is withdrawn and production stopped.

This has an interesting and positive impact on the consumer. First, it means that Zara shoppers have a constant source of new, fresh products to choose from. Second, customers know that any item they buy will be more "exclusive" than those from other stores, as their items will only be on sale for a month. The benefit for the company is that Zara customers tend to visit stores around 17 times a year, as opposed to the fashion retailing average of three to four times. The frequent turnover encourages them to buy, as they know the products will only be available for a short time.

The time limitation for fashion clothes is the speed of design, with traditional fashion houses tending to have few designers who take up to six months to produce new designs and thus only have two or three collections per year. Zara has a large team of designers, which enables the company to react quickly to new trends and consumer demands. Zara's founder, Amancio Ortega, calls this business model "instant fashions."

The speed required is augmented by a computerized inventory system that links the factories producing Zara's large number of products to the retail outlets. This system significantly reduces the need to hold large inventories. All in all, it's a win-win situation for Zara and its customers.

Samsung is another famous global brand that has gained ground because of its speed, innovation, and agility, focusing on getting innovative technologies to market quickly and providing consumers with more choice.

The strategy of speed, which Samsung has developed to a fine art, allows the company to take advantage of decreasing product life cycles. In some product categories, they have been reduced to a number of weeks. This tremendous life-cycle compression is likely to be a permanent feature of the consumer electronics marketplace, where, paradoxically, the sheer ubiquity of mass-customized products has led to commoditization. They are now regarded by Samsung (and consumers) as perishable goods!

With this in mind, Samsung has moved away from the lower-volume, higher-priced products to much higher volumes of products and more line extensions offered to consumers at lower cost. Another piece of smart thinking is that Samsung now plays in both business-to-business and business-to-consumer markets, producing not just the end-user products but also their components. This has given the company the diversity, massive scale, and cost leadership that generates acceptable margins in commodity markets. One of the clear benefits to consumers, apart from lower pricing, is more choice.

Additionally, in order to enhance innovation, speed, and agility, Samsung has reduced its involvement in research and development work, which is both costly and slow, and instead uses technologies invented by others quickly, focusing on getting its products to market at least as fast as, if not more rapidly than, its competitors.

In commodity markets, Samsung has also realized that more is better. Consumers want choice. They want customized products to reflect their lifestyles and personalities. While some competitors haven't got to grips with such market trends, Samsung has used its cost and diversity advantages to produce more products in the categories in which it operates. For example, while Nokia launches around 20 new models a year, Samsung produces around 100. This allows its brand to cater for the very fragmented market that now exists in consumer electronics, where individuality is demanded at low prices and where the number of segments is rapidly increasing.

Mass customization is the name of the game, and Samsung has been the best at reinventing itself as a way to deal with this through the route of huge design improvements.

Islamic brands must take on board these lessons. Speed, agility, and innovation are no longer "nice-to-have" characteristics; they are essentials. Islamic brands need to demonstrate that they can think and act in an innovative way, and later in this book we will consider some examples of companies that are doing just this and setting the pace. All of the above factors in building the brand contribute to the way in which it is positioned in the marketplace, as we shall now see.

Brand Positioning

Positioning is vital to brand management, because it takes the basic tangible aspects of the product and actually builds the intangibles in the form of an image in people's minds. It focuses on the chosen target audience(s) and influences their thoughts about the brand in relation to other brands. Through the strategies described in this chapter, positioning seeks the best way of convincing people that a particular brand is both different from and better than any other brand.

Avoiding the Perception Gap

All brand managers aspire to build a great image for their brands. Brand image, however, may not turn out to be the same as the identity and personality we want the brand to be perceived as having, because image is subject to perception—the way in which people think about something, or even imagine it to be. So, if we project the identity wrongly, or not strongly enough, the people whom we want to acknowledge our identity might view it as something entirely different. They might not see us as honest, or might think our packaging looks cheap. Image can be based on fact or fiction, depending on how people perceive things. The difference between identity and image is what is often called the *perception gap*, which must be avoided at all costs.

To avoid the perception gap between identity and image, we must ensure that what is offered is what is acknowledged—that the target audience sees and relates to our brand personality or identity, and this will depend on their perceptions.

Positioning is also about creating a perception of difference, and brand managers use a variety of strategies to convince and persuade people that they are both different from and better than the brands of the opposition. The main goal of positioning is to create a perceptual space in people's minds that your brand owns, and that differentiates it from others.

Positioning is more than just differentiating a brand on personality. In positioning a brand, the brand's actual performance can be introduced, as well as its personality. This brings into play competitive business dynamics, as well as brand attributes and values. The idea is to portray a brand's strategic competitive advantage, and positively influence the perceptions of the target audience(s) so that the brand stands out from the crowd.

Whatever strategy or combination of strategies are chosen, there are certain points to be remembered:

- The position must be salient or important to the target audience you are trying to reach and influence. It is no good communicating messages to them that are of no interest, as they will either ignore them or forget them quickly.
- The position must be based on real strengths. Making claims that cannot be substantiated can cause enormous loss of credibility.
- The position has to reflect some form of competitive advantage. The whole point of positioning is to inform and persuade people that you are different from and better than the competition, so whatever that point of difference is, it must be clearly expressed.
- Finally, the position must be capable of being communicated simply, so that everyone gets the real message, and of motivating the audience. The aim of positioning is to provide a call to action to the target audience, and so communications must be created carefully.

The Need for Positioning Statements ━━━

Unless you are in total control of all aspects of creating your image through communications, which is most unlikely, there needs to be a communications brief for people to follow. This is one of the main reasons for having written positioning statements. If positioning statements aren't in writing, there is a real danger that the ideas might be misinterpreted, the strategy warped, and the key messages not expressed clearly. The result could well be confusion in the minds of the audience. Positioning statements are essential if you are to keep messages clear and develop a consistent image and position.

What are Positioning Statements?

Positioning statements are internal documents, not meant for public consumption. They summarize strategy, and act as a guide for strategic marketing and brand management. They state specifically and briefly what you want people to think about you, your product or company, or your country. They not only spell out the desired image you wish to have, but are also a good test for strategy, as they quickly tell you whether the perceptions you wish people to hold are believable, credible, and achievable. Positioning statements aren't easy to write, and often need several attempts. It is best to write them with inputs and agreement from other people. In companies, for instance, a corporate positioning statement would need to be considered by as many senior managers as possible to gain consensus agreement and buy-in, and to ensure execution. Product managers would also need to seek other opinions and endorsements.

Before writing a positioning statement, it is vital that there is a complete understanding of the following areas:

> *Your brand:* This seems obvious, but you have to be very clear about what you can really offer that will attract the people you are trying to influence. With products, this will mean looking closely at all the features and attributes, and the benefits that people will derive from them. All the time you should be looking for factors that will help differentiate what *you* have to offer from what the competition are offering. The same goes for services. What service standards can you present that will give you the opportunity to suggest a competitive advantage? Companies often have distinguishing characteristics, such as global stature, track record, personality, and other unique features that can be highlighted and used as differentiators.

- *The target audience(s) you want to influence:* Knowing what people need and want is critical, and there is a difference between the two. I might *need* some food to eat, but what I *want* is couscous. It becomes important, therefore, to understand people's intangible requirements as well as their more tangible ones. Unless there is precision in customer understanding, the messages we send may be irrelevant and lose us credibility.
- *The competitors you are up against (competitive set):* No strategy is complete without a thorough understanding of the competition, whether you are a football manager, marketing manager, entertainer, managing director, or government minister. Some of the questions to ask might include:
  - Which competitors do customers consider?
  - What positioning strategies are the competitors using, and why?
  - What key messages are they sending?
  - What appears to be their competitive advantage and the key points of difference?
  - Why do customers buy from them?
  - What image do they currently have?
  - What differences do customers see between them and us?
  - What competitor would they switch to if they moved from us?
  One of the major problems that can arise here is deciding just who the competition is. This issue is particularly relevant for fast-moving consumer goods, where the definition of categories becomes extremely important, but it does need to be considered in any positioning situation. For instance, is an iPhone a mobile phone or a handheld computer device? Definition of the product category is therefore a critical first stage in competitor analysis, and is vital to the positioning effort.
- *Why you are different from and better than the competition:* Analysis of the above areas will allow you to make some accurate judgments as to what position to choose and which positioning strategy you need to employ in order to influence the perceptions of the target audience(s).
- *The desired perception you would like people to have of you:* Always set a goal in terms of how you want to be seen by people. When you are writing down this goal, try to do it using the language of the customer or the persons you are trying to influence. If you put yourself in their

shoes, there is a greater likelihood that you will understand how they think and be successful in managing their perceptions, and you will find it easier to track whether you have achieved the intended image. When you write your positioning statement, certain things contained in it may be aspirational in nature and some factual. This doesn't matter, as these statements are for internal purposes only. However, the aspirational or desired consumer perceptions must be worked on hard in order to deliver on the promise. Communicating parts of the positioning may have to be delayed, therefore, until the brand can actually do what it says it can.

Some of the above analysis might entail commissioned research if you don't have the internal resources to carry it out, and it may take some time, but the quality of your communicated position will end up much more focused and accurate. Once you are ready to write the positioning statement, it has to be done in a concise way.

How to Write and Use a Positioning Statement

There are many ways of writing positioning statements, but they should all contain certain elements. From past experience I have found the template shown in Figure 5.2 to be the most practical.

Note on the Brand Personality or Values (Character)

The personality or values your brand has, as discussed earlier, can be stated separately at the end of this statement to guide those people responsible for brand communications; or, more usefully, the words can be used in the text of the positioning statement itself.

If you work methodically through this statement, you will achieve answers to the main questions of:

- Why are you better?
- Why are you different?

BRAND X (your brand)

is better than

COMPETITIVE SET
(The main competitors for your brand in its category, industry, etc.)

for

TARGET MARKET
(The customer group or groups you are aiming for, stated, if possible, in terms of their needs and wants. For a master brand this would be broad, but for each customer segment it would be more clearly defined.)

because it

STRATEGIC COMPETITIVE ADVANTAGE (SCA)
(The SPECIFIC advantage(s) your brand has, compared to others, in meeting those needs.)

with the result that

KEY PROPOSITION
(The real emotional and rational benefits to be experienced by your target audience, derived mainly from the SCA.)

Figure 5.2   A Positioning Statement Template

These two questions are of utmost importance to consumers, who want to know why they should buy your brand in preference to others on offer. Only if these questions are answered truthfully and adequately will you be able to persuade customers that you should be their preferred choice. Great care must therefore be taken to ensure that the content of positioning statements is credible, believable, deliverable, and relevant to the wants and needs of the audience whose perceptions you are trying to influence.

When you have carefully positioned your brand in this way, these statements must then be applied rigorously to product, service, staff, communications, and so on, and this is the role of brand management.

So, while brand strategy development and constant speed, agility, and innovation are extremely important, there is one more element of strong brand building that must be present, and that is brand management.

Brand Management

The chapter so far has dealt with how to build a brand; in other words, how to develop a brand strategy. However, it is one thing to have a strategy in place and another to make sure that strategy is implemented correctly. The task of ensuring that a brand strategy is correctly applied is called *brand management*. If a brand is not managed well, there is a greater chance of failure, so brand management is an important role in any organization. Brand management is a complex, everyday task. It seeks to ensure not only that the strategy gets implemented as it is meant to be, but also that customers get the best possible experience. One can think of it simplistically as managing "moments of truth."

Moments of Truth

Moments of truth determine success or failure, weakness or strength, loyalty or desertion, resolve or retreat. Moments of truth are not defined by companies or brands, but by ordinary people who experience things that make an impact on their everyday lives.

The really smart companies in the world of branding accept the fact that powerful brands are the only route to survival and differentiation. They occasionally have massive worldwide defining moments of truth in the form of a major crisis, but they also recognize that they face moments of truth every day in terms of the brand–consumer relationship. As brands exist only in consumers' minds, then *every contact with consumers* can potentially be a moment of truth. This philosophy is similar to that described by former CEO of Scandinavian Airline System (SAS) Jan Carlsson, who famously told his workforce that with 12 million customers a year and an average contact rate per customer of five SAS people on a single journey, this translated into 60 million moments of truth—60 million opportunities to get the brand experience right or wrong. His message was that *all* touchpoints with *all* consumers count, and companies have to look meticulously at how they can manage these. That's brand management thinking.

Many people with responsibility for company and brand image might say, "If only it were that easy!" However, Carlsson didn't rely just on rhetoric; he changed his company's structure, systems, technology, and many other things, and—importantly—he empowered staff at the frontline to make decisions that have immediate impact on the consumer's brand experience. He succeeded in bringing the SAS brand to life by motivating and empowering employees so that they saw how their actions contributed to the value of the brand and the business. In short, he created a massive organizational change project based around the brand–customer relationship and involving every function in the company—no easy task.

The big challenge for CEOs like Carlsson, and for brand managers in charge of Islamic corporate and/or product brands, is to bring brands to life through strategy and change, and to motivate people to deliver on the brand promise. This is particularly important for those involved in any business that uses a corporate- or house-endorsed branding approach. This can be achieved through careful management of the "brand management wheel," shown in Figure 5.3.

The brand management wheel shows how every aspect of the consumer experience, every touchpoint, must be carefully managed. Few companies do this well. For most, the reason for lax brand management here is the absence of a brand strategy to drive out from the center to the spokes of the wheel. If a company has a clear brand strategy, then it is much easier to manage the outer areas. The innermost part of the wheel represents the brand strategy in the figure, and this gives everyone in the organization a guide as to how the execution of the brand should be carried out in each area of responsibility. The spokes of the wheel are those activities that can influence whether the strategy is deployed well or not, as they are all activities that interface with consumers and provide those "moments of truth."

Without a clear brand personality and positioning, there is little hope of brand consistency. As there is no guide for practitioners who manage these different areas, the different spokes of the wheel are executed on an

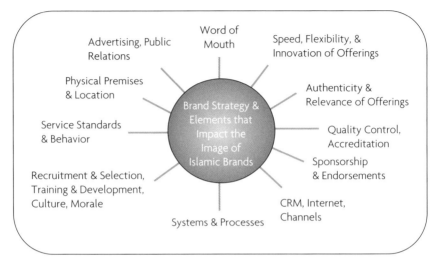

Figure 5.3   The Brand Management Wheel

ad hoc basis. The result of this is usually a confused, mixed, and relatively poor brand image, and those responsible for brand image come under fire because they are receiving ratings that are perceived as detrimental.

The absence of a clearly defined brand strategy means that agencies commissioned by the company have little idea of what the brand stands for, what the brand platform is, and what the key messages should be to address the different target audiences. In the case of one of my clients (an Islamic brand from a Muslim-majority country), I was called in to find out why the advertising agency wasn't portraying the brand messages in a way that met the client's expectations. When I asked the client if the agency had been given a proper brand brief, the answer was "yes." But when I asked to see the brief, the client said it had been done verbally, and not in writing. The client hadn't clearly defined its vision, brand positioning, or personality for the agency, and so interpretations of the "brief" by the advertising agency's creative team were far removed from the client's expectations. This accounted for the history of continuous misunderstanding with respect to what was required of the agency and what the client actually got.

Great brands are built on consistency, and this necessitates consistent and appropriate behavior in all areas of operation. But consistency depends on a clearly defined brand strategy. This is where the skills and influence of brand managers need to be at their peak. My suggestion is that you take a really hard, analytical look at the spokes of the wheel, and ask yourself and your colleagues:

- Is our brand vision and platform clearly articulated in written statements?
- What is currently happening in each area to manage the brand consistently?
- What needs to be done to improve on management of the brand in each area?

Every spoke of the wheel is important, although some of them might be more relevant to your brand than others. An action plan should be developed incorporating the improvements, and this should be reviewed frequently at meetings by those people who are responsible for managing and guarding the brand.

Managing the wheel well results in positive, consistent experiences for customers, and they become brand advocates, spreading the good news by word of mouth, physically or through the Internet. One bad experience can immediately reach thousands of other people by a comment on a social networking site, for example. Do all things right, and word of mouth will become your biggest brand-building weapon.

Who is Responsible for Brand Management?

Finally, many people ask me, "Who is responsible for brand management?" The answer is "everyone," because *everyone* can make an impact on it. Every department and every employee can, and should, help to manage and guard the brand. Nevertheless, the CEO must drive the efforts, and there should be a structure in place to make this happen. The structure often takes the form of two groups of people. The first group is a brand management committee or council that is responsible for signing off on major brand initiatives and has the power to veto anything that doesn't reflect or implement the strategy properly. The second group is the brand working committee, whose job it is to collect ideas and create action plans from all divisions and departments as to how the values of the brand can be projected, in various ways, around all the spokes of the wheel.

Can Islamic Brands Use Western Techniques to Go Global?

Most of the examples of successful brands in this chapter have so far been non-Islamic, although some, like Unilever, have interacted with Muslim consumers to show they are serious about wanting to have them as customers. While many Islamic brands want to be more clearly associated with their faith and values, there are also many companies with the same considerations but use the techniques learned from Western branding to help them achieve international success.

In order to illustrate this, there follows a case study of a successful brand that has been built using the above principles. (In Chapter 9, we shall consider DUBAL, another brand that has achieved significant success by applying these principles.)

CASE STUDY 5: OPUS INTERNATIONAL GROUP Plc

Branding Means Commitment and Total Change

INTRODUCTION

The introduction to this case refers to the company by its old name, Kinta Kellas plc. The company's change of name to Opus International Group plc was just one important part of a huge re-branding and repositioning exercise to create a powerful international brand.

Kinta Kellas plc, well known as an industry leader in project management of large-scale transportation infrastructure and infrastructure development projects, was originally a tin mining company when it began in 1926. The company has a rich corporate history. Today, it extends beyond project management into facilities management services for expressways, infrastructure and built environment, and healthcare services.

Kinta Kellas is an asset management and development company, "assets" meaning property and construction, not financial assets. It is a professional and specialized consultancy, and is a part of the huge UEM Group Berhad. As a Malaysian company, it has been the proud manager of most of the huge infrastructure projects that have put its country on the world map, such as the North-South Highway, the 1998 Commonwealth Games stadium, and many others.

But the heady days of huge projects required by government have gradually diminished in Malaysia, and Kinta Kellas, in its endeavor to move forward in a continually changing and sometimes turbulent operating environment, had to make urgent decisions about its future strategic direction in the face of the more challenging economic environment ahead, coupled with international liberalization and competition.

The group managing director, Suhaimi Halim, realized that the route to success in an ever-changing world, where parity rules, is branding. He understood that only a strong brand can provide the means of differentiation necessary for long-term survival and profitability, and that a strong brand name can actually be worth multiples more—in dollar terms—than the other tangible assets of the company.

Suhaimi commented:

Like many companies, we are faced with challenges that arise from shifting trends in the domestic market, the need to expand internationally, and a need to change our business accordingly. Whilst considering our response to these challenges, the opportunity arose to re-name our main company in Malaysia and link it with our fully owned subsidiary in New Zealand.

We decided to take full advantage of this situation to change our whole business, but there had to be a focus for this, and we decided that the catalyst for change should be the brand. By this I mean we needed to develop a brand strategy that would drive all the changes necessary for us to be successful in the future.

We knew that a brand-driven business means holistic change and that it would be no easy task. We have been working hard at this now for over a year, and are in the midst of changing mindsets, systems, processes, procedures, services, and communications. Nothing is to be excluded.

It is a challenging and exciting time, but the brand implementation is already bringing benefits to us. We are determined that Opus International Group plc will become a global brand name.

Kinta Kellas thus decided to seek out new strategies to retain its position as a leading provider of project management services domestically, and as a leading supplier of road asset management services in New Zealand, where it has a 100 percent fully owned subsidiary called Opus International Consultants Ltd., formerly a part of the government public works department. This meant that the company needed to be more efficient in its services and to accelerate its growth and performance, including introducing new and improved quality and added value services.

However, several challenges lay ahead that needed urgent attention, identified as follows.

THE BRAND IMAGE AND ARCHITECTURE CHALLENGES

Kinta Kellas had an image challenge to overcome if it was to forge greater growth and brand preference. In 2004, the company name was still perceived by some to be that of a mining company (historically, this was true), although it had achieved some degree of new brand awareness as a project and asset management company. There was a perception gap—internally and externally—as to what Kinta Kellas was and was trying to become. There was also another heritage factor—that of shareholder UEM Group. Kinta Kellas had very specific targets and not the mass market, but the need still existed to develop trust in the company and an image driven more by emotional associations and less by rational factors.

There was also an issue of brand architecture. The parental image had some negative imagery, which had to be handled carefully. Additionally, a subsidiary company had achieved more awareness than the parent company. Consequently, there were brand architecture challenges to overcome. For instance, should Kinta Kellas grow via stand-alone brands, or should it try to lift its image through association with them? Would a Kinta Kellas endorsement add to or dilute other brand images, and what would be the financial consequences of the strategic alternatives?

The architectural strategy for managing such a combination of brands within the company, at that moment, was still unclear, and so these and other questions needed to be resolved urgently within the context of the international business strategy.

THE NAME ISSUE

Kinta Kellas had to make a very important decision in 2004—whether to change its name to support the intended corporate and brand strategies. It not only had to face a domestic market that was moving away from large infrastructure projects, and thus the need to shift its business focus to managing assets as well as developing them, but it also had to move more into international markets. Its wholly owned New Zealand subsidiary, Opus International Consultants Ltd., already had a better business balance and a solid brand name both in and beyond New Zealand.

It was decided that the Kinta Kellas brand name would not travel very well across markets and cultures, but that "Opus" would, and so a new organizational name was adopted: "Kinta Kellas" was replaced with "Opus International Group plc." This decision was to have many implications for all aspects of the business, not the least of which was brand communications. However, first, the new entity needed a brand platform and strategy to move forward—one that tied in the master brand to the New Zealand brand.

THE BRAND PLATFORM ISSUE

The Kinta Kellas brand had no clear brand vision, but management realized that a powerful brand vision that connects the future of the brand emotionally with consumers across all markets and segments is vital; that true value lies in the emotional power of the brand itself, which leads consumers to pay price premiums and gives companies higher margins.

But the brand platform wasn't clear, and needed to be reviewed. A brand personality (set of brand values) would be needed to support the new brand vision, and these brand elements would be used to develop a strong brand culture. In a service organization, these elements are essential for differentiation and for building strong relationships with clients, suppliers, investors, and others.

Brand positioning statements would also be required to help create a communications strategy that would pull all messages together consistently across all international markets, and develop brand awareness for the new brand name.

THE NEED FOR A COMPREHENSIVE BRANDING STRATEGY

In sum, Kinta Kellas needed a comprehensive brand strategy to defend and improve its business, market share, and profitability, and to expand internationally. It was agreed that this strategy should be driven by a powerful vision, supported by relevant brand values and a clear differentiation path via positioning statements.

The top management of the company also saw the need to undertake a clear review of the systems, processes, and culture that would enable the new brand promises to be delivered. The company's philosophy was that power brands drive everything in successful businesses, and that this approach should be adopted by Kinta Kellas, under its new name of Opus International Group plc.

If a company doesn't know where it stands with respect to its brand image, then it is difficult to move forward. Opus therefore began its brand journey with a brand audit to assess its strengths and weaknesses.

The brand audit

As a part of the brand audit, a selection of people from inside the organization were interviewed, as well as a substantial number of external third parties, such as a government officer, contractors, suppliers, and clients. The results were in some ways expected and in some ways a shock. Positives and negatives were clearly identified in terms of the brand's current image as perceived by various audiences. Interestingly, the company also received valuable feedback as to where everyone's future expectations lay, and how the image could be improved.

The brand vision, personality, and positioning process

All powerful brands have a brand vision that drives their business strategy. After analysis of interview research findings and a senior management workshop, the vision for the brand was agreed, followed by a well-articulated and defined brand personality and values.

Many successful companies use closely defined brand values to attract and retain customers. The aim of defining brand values in terms of a personality and its characteristic traits is to take the focus away from ordinary attributes and features, and move toward the kind of relationship companies want to establish with the consumer, and consumers wish to have with them.

The brand personality characteristics for Opus were agreed as follows, with the meaning of the words defined in the brackets. The brand personality contained both rational and emotional elements. It is interesting to see the mixture of attributes that are needed by many companies today, such as "Innovative" and "Versatile," with more emotional Islamic-type values such as "Helpful."

Rational
- *Innovative* (Creative, Resourceful, Entrepreneurial)
- *Reliable* (Trustworthy, Dependable)
- *Professional* (Competent, Knowledgeable, Expert)

Emotional
- *Friendly* (Warm, Approachable, Passionate)
- *Versatile* (Adaptable, Flexible, Responsive)
- *Helpful* (Understanding, Proactive, Sincere)

The more rational personality traits tended to be brand strengths of the company, but it was seen to be weaker on the emotional side, which isn't surprising for a professional consulting business. The strategy, therefore, was to maintain the strengths and eliminate the weaknesses. However, the characteristic of "Innovative" was regarded as essential to transform the business and the brand image, so this was one of the personality traits that attracted more focus when the brand implementation started.

BRAND MANAGEMENT STRUCTURE

The development of the brand, as described above, had to be inclusive, and needed to have commitment from both the Malaysian and New Zealand sides. To this end, the vision, values, and positioning statements were subject to a process of iteration with involvement from both sides via management workshops. But, importantly, a structure was put into place that would ensure that everything to do with brand implementation was agreed, synchronized, and implemented in all geographical areas of the business.

Early on in the strategic thinking process, a brand management committee (BMC) was set up to facilitate this process and in anticipation of the tasks to be determined under the implementation program to follow. This is essentially a top management team, chaired by the CEO, that makes all important decisions regarding brand implementation, and gains support from the board of directors where necessary.

As soon as the brand strategy elements were agreed across the companies, a brand working committee (BWC) was created to look at all the detail of the brand transformation and implementation over the next two years, to 2006. BWC reported to, and received direction from, the BMC regarding focus, priorities, and high-level decisions for brand execution.

BRAND IMPLEMENTATION

The task of implementing the new Opus brand is an ongoing process, as it is with all top brands, but many initiatives have already taken place. The critical issue to enable the repositioning of the brand is described well by the former general manager of group human resources and administration, Tunku Siti Raudzoh Tunku Ibrahim:

> Human capital is the key to any professional services brand, and at Opus we are focusing very hard on training, development, and performance management systems that are linked directly to the brand.

> We have trained a pool of trainers so that everyone can understand not just what the brand means, but also how they can impact it in their everyday work. After all, everyone is a brand ambassador for the company, and they will be recognized and rewarded for performing well in this role. To help them, every employee—from the top management to the receptionists—has undergone training to represent the brand in a way that is relevant to their work, but consistent with our desired image.

> Talking of receptionists, we have also renovated our reception area and staff working spaces to reflect the new brand personality. A new corporate visual identity is in place and the website has been revamped. We have a detailed public relations program in place, and each department has submitted plans for how they will bring the brand to life. We believe that a strong brand is the only route to sustainable success, and it is our people that will make it happen.

Below are a few of the activities referred to.

Brand action planning

The first phase of brand implementation was to get senior management groups to work out plans for action in executing the brand strategically across all business units. This involved a series of workshops with prioritized short- and long-term goals as the outputs.

These workshops were then taken down to departmental level, with a similar process and outputs at a more functional and specific level. While these were going on, a Training-of-Trainers program was being designed and developed so that the brand could be rolled out to all staff, to explain to them what it was, and to help them think through how they could contribute in their jobs, both individually and in their teams.

Brand training handbooks

For the brand training programs, a brand handbook was produced for all staff, and was used as a vehicle for training as well as information purposes. A trainer's guide was written for the trainers. Both of these booklets were used by the trainers in their practice sessions.

The trainers' programs were completed for both Malaysia and New Zealand, and the roll-out occurred in May 2005, to coincide with the launch of the new brand name.

Induction and orientation

The brand has now been incorporated into the orientation and induction programs, so that all new employees are told about the importance of the brand and why they should reinforce it within their job scope.

Human capital

The Opus human capital policy is that people must be recognized and rewarded for performing well on the brand values, just as they are with other important aspects of their work. Doing so would reinforce the training initiatives, and make employees realize that the company is taking its brand image seriously. This motivation was important in building the brand culture with speed.

- *Recognition:* The recognition of people who help make any brand come to life is important and can be achieved in many ways. Opus embarked on a scheme to recognize employees who have performed well on one or more of the brand values, which includes possibilities such as:
  - role model recognition;
  - nominations for awards;
  - values performance certificates;
  - an OPUS annual award for outstanding all-round brand performance; and
  - team awards for certain important areas, such as innovation.
- *Rewards:* Rewarding people in monetary terms by incorporating values performance into annual performance appraisal schemes has proved to be very effective, and it shows the seriousness with which the company is taking its brand-building task.

  Linking pay, increments, and promotions to the brand values via the annual appraisal scheme rewards people for good performance on the brand values. It entails the analysis of jobs at various levels, and possibly role model analysis, to determine what constitutes good and not-so-good performance on each value. While it is not easy to do, it certainly motivates employees and lets them know that the issue of branding is of high importance to the company's future.

With this in mind, Opus devised ways in which it could incorporate the brand into its performance management scheme, in conjunction with other aspects of individual performance scorecards.

With the introduction of a new brand name, inevitably there has to be a carefully designed and managed corporate communications strategy, and the brand management structure managed this and other aspects of the brand strategy implementation. Thus, any activities such as corporate communications became the responsibility of the BWC, with the final green light given by the BMC to which it reported. Activities consisted mainly of corporate identity changes and a public relations plan.

A corporate identity manual

Opus decided not to change its logo and to base its corporate identity on that of the New Zealand subsidiary, but there were still many changes to make. A new corporate identity manual emerged that produced consistency across the companies, and guidelines for all aspects of communications.

A public relations plan

An agency was selected and briefed to work with the BWC to produce an appropriate 12-month plan to take the company up to and beyond the brand name change. This included looking at all the target audiences that needed to be informed about the new brand and what it stood for, and why the re-branding had been done. As Opus is an international group, the public relations plan had to take into account careful timing of announcements across global markets, as well as events and media placement. The soft launch of the new brand was carried out in May 2005.

The Opus brand is now well known, and has achieved its transformation, while the brand action plans continue to play a major role in the company's success.

The Opus Group of companies has been extremely successful and has over 80 offices in Australia, Canada, India, New Zealand, Malaysia, and the United Kingdom.

The next case is about one of the Islamic world's most successful brands—Petronas from Malaysia. While many oil and gas companies from Muslim countries have done very well in terms of revenue and profit, Petronas stands out as the only example from a Muslim country I know of in this category that is, despite its wealth, committed to brand building and management as an ongoing process.

CASE STUDY 6: PETRONAS

Malaysia's Global Brand Ambassador

BACKGROUND

PETRONAS, an acronym for Petroliam Nasional Berhad, was incorporated on 17 August 1974 and is wholly owned by the Malaysian government. The *Petroleum Development Act 1974* vested in Petronas the entire ownership and control of Malaysia's petroleum resources. Ranked among the Fortune Global 500 companies as the 107th largest and the 25th most profitable in 2010, based on 2009 revenues and profits, Petronas is an integrated international oil and gas company with four listed subsidiaries (six by the end of 2010) and business interests in more than 32 countries.

The group is engaged in a wide range of activities, including upstream exploration and production of oil and gas, and downstream oil refining; marketing and distribution of petroleum products; trading; LNG, gas processing and transmission pipeline network operations; petrochemical manufacturing and marketing; shipping and property investment.

Petronas recognizes the significance of balancing economic, environmental, and social objectives in all its business undertakings without compromising the needs of present and future generations. The group is therefore committed to sustainable development, giving utmost priority to protecting the safety and health of its employees and local communities, as well as preserving the environment and its biodiversity. Various community projects in the fields of education and health, among others, have been and will continue to be undertaken, some of which are referred to later in this case study.

During its growing years, Petronas developed a mission statement to provide clarity of purpose, a strong set of shared values which have remained at the core of its corporate culture, and a vision statement which defined its future direction. All of these elements were the foundation upon which Petronas's unique identity began to take shape in the minds of its domestic and global stakeholders.

The corporate vision

The vision statement is fairly general, much like that of many other corporations: "To be a leading oil and gas multinational of choice."

The corporate mission

The mission of the company articulates four statements, which are:

- We are a business entity.
- Petroleum is our core business.
- Our primary responsibility is to develop and add value to the natural resources.
- Our objective is to contribute to the well-being of the people and the nation.

Corporate shared values

Petronas has four shared values, which are defined as:

- *Loyalty:* Loyalty to nation and corporation.
- *Professionalism:* Committed, innovative, and proactive, and always striving for excellence.
- *Integrity:* Honest and upright.
- *Cohesiveness:* United in purpose and fellowship.

THE DEVELOPMENT OF THE BRAND

In the late 1990s, in line with its vision and aspirations, Petronas moved increasingly into the highly competitive and volatile global arena. It began to compete with major multinationals with long histories that were already household names with established corporate identities, such as BP, Shell, and Exxon-Mobil.

By this time, too, Petronas was fully involved in the broad spectrum of the industry, as well as in areas outside of its core business. Its growing and diverse portfolio of companies included some that didn't even bear the Petronas name. Its workforce had swelled by several thousands, embracing people of diverse nationalities from around the globe.

Against this background, it became increasingly critical to create a clear and consistent understanding of what Petronas stood for as an organization among all of its global stakeholders, not least of all its employees. In order to compete effectively in the global arena, it would need to proactively manage the development of a strong, consistent identity for the Petronas group as a whole. Petronas thus embarked on a brand-building exercise aimed at articulating and ensuring the successful delivery of its business promise consistently throughout all significant touchpoints within the group.

The brand journey began in 1999 with an analysis of stakeholder perceptions, giving a clear picture of the brand strengths and weaknesses. This effort culminated in the crafting of a brand essence statement, which encapsulated the founding philosophy and values of the organization and linked the mission, vision, and shared values into a single statement.

The Petronas brand essence is as follows:

Drawing On Our Unique Heritage
Born out of a need to serve Malaysia and its people, PETRONAS has been genuine in fulfilling national aspirations. The people it deals with on a daily basis acknowledge and commend its strong sense of duty to the nation and its employees, loyalty to the organization.

> PETRONAS' passionate spirit is one of its most enduring traits and has been largely responsible for its business success. As a group, it is committed towards excellence and progress. It continually pushes its own limits to discover new strengths and capabilities.
>
> As it grew and expanded into other corners of the globe, it retained these valuable traits, exporting its own unique economic model that espouses a philosophy of "Growing With The Nation" wherever it operates.

This was further elaborated as follows:

Encapsulating Our Essence
> PETRONAS receives energy in the form of natural resources, human talent and commitment.
>
> This energy is returned to the nation and the world as both physical and emotional energy, supporting people everywhere in their aspirations for the future.

Petronas felt it reaffirmed what the organization stood for and was capable of connecting emotionally with the outside world. Internally, it would create a new impetus for the development of a strong and brand-led business culture. To reinforce and provide clarity for its day-to-day stakeholder interactions, a set of corporate brand values was created, enabling Petronas to forge enduring stakeholder relationships and build distinctive value for the brand. The brand values are:

- trusted;
- passionate;
- progressive; and
- enriching.

From the time of its inception, Petronas has aspired to advance humanity through business by returning the value that it creates to its stakeholders in a meaningful and sustainable manner through the sharing of benefits, experience, knowledge, and wealth. At the very heart of this philosophy is the company's aspiration to excel in its business performance, thus enabling it to share its success with the nations and communities wherever it operates. For example, it never forgets its obligations to Malaysian society, with programs such as "Schools Outreach," which provides education-based outreach activities such as drug abuse prevention, road safety, environmental awareness, and a mobile library to inspire and enrich the community, the words "inspire" and "enrich" reflecting the brand and its values.

Petronas has always been very particular about doing things right; professionally, ethically, and morally correctly. As a result, it has an impeccable reputation and image.

DRIVING PETRONAS TO GLOBAL BRAND STATUS

Petronas uses a variety of means to promote and manage its brand globally. This case study provides a brief overview of a number of key methods the company employs in this respect. However, we will first take a look at its early entry into the global brand world through the platform of Formula One.

Formula One as a global branding platform

Petronas first entered the highly competitive and prestigious world of Formula One motor racing in 1995 with the deliberate aim to position itself as a global brand. Since then, Formula One has not only catapulted Petronas's image onto the international stage, but also fast-tracked its experience in hi-tech fields, advancing both the company and the nation to the brink of a new technological frontier. The Petronas partnership with Team Sauber provided IT with an ideal test-bed for its products and has since made significant advancements in various aspects of automotive engineering. Most significant are breakthroughs in fuel and lubricant development proudly achieved by Malaysian engineers who developed the advanced fully synthetic Petronas Syntium engine lubricant and the Primax Formula One fuel, both powering the Sauber Petronas Formula One cars.

The glamor and high profile of motor racing aside, there is a deeper underlying and more socially conscientious motivation at the heart of Petronas's pursuance of automotive and racing technology. The technological expertise and insight acquired by Petronas through the various transfer of technology projects is ultimately reinjected into the very pulse of the nation, thus providing impetus to the company's ambition of helping Malaysia reach the status of being a fully industrialized nation.

Using the concept of partnership for growth, Petronas, through the Sauber Petronas Engineering (SPE) team, first showed its determination in developing its human capital. Perceived as national heroes for their significant contribution to the local engineering industry, the Malaysian SPE engineers have achieved numerous successes over the years.

Petronas's serious involvement in an array of motor sports activities, inclusive of Formula One, is driven by its desire to harness a deep reservoir of technological expertise. It is envisaged that this powerhouse will have the potential of advancing national growth and instilling the seeds of interest in high-end technology among future generations.

However, things move quickly in the world of Formula One and Petronas has been involved with other teams. On December 21, 2009, a press release issued by the Corporate Communications Department, Group Corporate Affairs stated:

> PETRONAS today announced a five-year agreement with major auto-manufacturer Mercedes, making a new partnership for the company in Formula One. Under the terms of the agreement, PETRONAS will become the title partner to the Mercedes GP team, the reigning Formula One world champions. The team will from 2010 be officially known as the Mercedes GP PETRONAS Formula One Team.
>
> The exclusive rights of a title partner and association with the premium, internationally renowned Mercedes brand will further enhance PETRONAS and Malaysia's ongoing global brand positioning efforts. PETRONAS will also be able to continue to leverage on the extensive international exposure offered by the sport to grow its existing business activities.

The partnership also presents PETRONAS with the opportunity to utilise and leverage on Mercedes' long motor sport heritage to further supplement its talent development initiatives as part of its contribution towards the development of Malaysia's motorsports industry.

In addition to enhancing its brand, PETRONAS' association and involvement in international motorsport over the past two decades has been a significant contributor to the growth of its business—in particular its lubricants business in the global arena. The association has also paved the way for technological and knowledge acquisition relevant to the oil and gas industry.

PETRONAS will also continue to be the title sponsor of the PETRONAS Malaysian F1 Grand Prix, which is proven to be an effective platform to promote Malaysia on the global stage.[3]

And there was a further bonus for Petronas, as arguably the world's best-ever Formula One driver, Michael Schumacher, and rising star Nico Rosberg were driving for this team in 2010–11. That's not a bad brand-building combination! Petronas also sponsors MOTOGP. (See www.petmos.com.my for a total view of the company's commitment to motorsports.)

Managing the consistent development of the corporate brand globally

We saw in the previous section how Petronas has successfully leveraged its strategic involvement in Formula One to build its global profile. Today, its association with powerful brand icons such as Formula One and the Petronas Twin Towers in Kuala Lumpur greatly facilitates its entry into new markets while reaffirming its standing among existing stakeholders.

Since it launched its corporate branding efforts at the turn of this millennium, the company has introduced a number of branding initiatives aimed at further building and enhancing the Petronas corporate brand across the span of its global operations. This section provides some insights into how the company manages its employee brand communication programs, as well as the methods it engages to ensure the consistent development of the corporate brand group-wide.

Employee brand engagement

Petronas understands that key to the success of any branding initiative are the company's employees, who ultimately represent the brand. At the outset of its branding efforts, therefore, a conscious decision was taken to focus on engendering internal buy-in of the staff, so that any subsequent efforts to communicate the brand externally would be clearly supported by their actions and behaviors.

With this in mind, the company held an internal launch of its brand essence and values to senior executives from across the group. An internal brand communication program was carefully planned and executed to create meaningful engagement with the brand that would, ultimately, inspire the desired behaviors. An employee brand communication package was designed to articulate the brand messages in a manner that would win the hearts and minds of employees, and also, just as importantly, guide them through what it means in their day-to-day interactions with stakeholders.

Subsequently, a comprehensive series of road shows was undertaken throughout the group's operations worldwide to promote global consistency. Today, every new employee is initiated into the brand at entry point so that nothing is left to chance.

Brand integration programs

To promote a more brand-led business culture within the group, brand workshops were held with several key units in the corporate center that play a key role in shaping and defining the organizational culture. It was recognized that Petronas's systems and processes needed to be aligned with the brand in order to support brand delivery.

Subsequently, a pilot was undertaken to institutionalize branding into a key business unit interfacing with domestic stakeholders—

Petronas Dagangan, which operates its retail business. An important part of organizational learning to be built upon, this pilot forms a springboard for other subsidiaries operating within the Petronas group to leverage the corporate brand strengths while growing their respective global businesses.

Strategic brand direction

Building a great brand, as we know, takes many years and a lot of hard work, commitment, and discipline. It also requires rigorous planning, execution, and monitoring. Underpinning its seriousness in this respect, Petronas's management established a Corporate Brand Unit to spearhead, direct, and manage its corporate branding exercise. Today, the unit provides strategic brand direction and guidance to units within the Petronas group of companies on matters impacting the corporate brand. Among other things, it works in close collaboration with key business units within the group, as well as with Petronas's regional and global representative offices worldwide, to formulate brand positioning strategies for Petronas's entry into new markets and to ensure that any brand promotion or development programs are aligned with the aspirations of the corporate brand.

Corporate brand website

To further promote consistent understanding of the Petronas brand among employees, a corporate brand intranet website was created. Aside from information about the brand essence and values, it contains guidelines for the development of any printed communications such as reports, brochures, and newsletters undertaken by members of the group and a user-friendly guide to execution of the company's corporate identity/logo.

The website also contains an interactive section on the principles that drive the planning and design of the company's corporate environments to ensure experiential consistency throughout its global offices.

Corporate brand architecture

It is easy to become overwhelmed by the sheer magnitude of this challenge, but the trick lies in maintaining simplicity in the core brand platform across the broad spectrum of the business. Anchored in very universal human values, Petronas's brand essence and values have broad appeal across all cultures and peoples and are therefore capable of creating meaning in many different contexts.

At the same time, the corporate brand essence and values are capable of being interpreted at many different levels throughout the business. The corporate brand architecture, by determining that the many sub-brands of the group reflect off the mother brand, helps maintain clarity and consistency in approach across the group. At a corporate brand level, the brand essence and values provide an overarching meaning to all of Petronas's diverse investments, while at the business level they can be translated into differentiated product or service offerings that are meaningful in the context of those businesses.

Brand audits

One of the key challenges for Petronas in working toward global brand consistency is to maintain a constant watch on how its brand is surfacing and performing in the various aspects of its diverse portfolio across the breadth of its global operations. An important part of this exercise is brand audit. Commencing with an overview of the visual identity of the company, the exercise aims to promote greater consistency in the visual manifestation of the brand, through its corporate identity, stationery, livery, uniforms, and corporate gifts or merchandise. Subsequently, this effort will necessarily encompass all other activities undertaken by the group which impact upon the corporate brand, including its stakeholder engagement programs.

PETRONAS AS A GLOBAL BRAND AMBASSADOR

All aspiring nation brands need good corporate ambassadors. The ambassadors of a nation's brand are not just government agencies; they are every company that ventures into foreign markets, and everyone a tourist meets. As mentioned in Chapter 2, national and corporate brands have a symbiotic relationship that can work very favorably for all, and brands that move around the world help improve a nation's image, not to mention its "bottom line." They are national brand ambassadors.

Petronas falls into the brand ambassador category. Its country, Malaysia, realizes the need to strengthen its brand image. Although it has accomplished a great deal over the last three decades, few people in the world are aware of its successes and talents. Petronas is undoubtedly helping Malaysia globally with its image.

Not only is the company highly respected by the global business fraternity, but also it is helping to put Malaysia on the radar screen of ordinary people around the world. When international research was carried out on Malaysia as a tourist destination in the late 1990s, Malaysia was an unknown to many travelers. The global reach and brand communications of Petronas has increased awareness of the national brand and enhanced the country's image. The only challenge the country has now is to find more companies like Petronas.

THE FUTURE DEPENDS ON STRONG BRAND MANAGEMENT

Petronas has realized that having a brand strategy is one thing, and implementing it is another. The world's best brands are able to keep their eyes on the big picture, the vision, and strategic brand issues, while also meticulously managing the everyday detail and building a strong brand culture.

Petronas is clearly totally committed to managing its brand properly; no easy task for a giant corporation. No doubt, mistakes will be made and lessons learned, but this relatively young and fast-growing company has made a great start.

Source: Petronas Brand Management Unit and corporate website.

Summary

For Muslim brand managers in the 21st century, there are many complex tasks to undertake. However, their main challenge is to achieve brand loyalty and lifetime relationships with consumers, because only when these are achieved will the brand last and grow in value. Brands are at their most powerful when they determine business direction and bind themselves to consumers through emotional associations.

The power of emotion has been present since life began—it is the great motivator and the prime driver of the human spirit. Make sure your brand develops more emotional attributes, because, although rational attributes may attract, emotional attributes sell. Use personality characteristics that define what your brand stands for and have universal emotional appeal. Islamic values, among others, are ideal for this purpose.

In building powerful brands, emotional associations are greatly enhanced through good design, and design coupled with innovation can add a competitive edge to a company's business and brand strategy.

Building a brand strategy for any organization is critical to sustainable high performance, but it is not enough to ensure this. Strong brand management is required to build consistency into the brand–customer relationship.

The next two chapters describe in detail the many opportunities available in all categories for branding and marketing in Muslim markets.

Notes

1. *BusinessWeek*, October 1999.
2. Paul Temporal and Martin Trott, *Romancing the Customer* (Singapore: John Wiley & Sons, 2001).
3. www.petronas.com.my.

6 Opportunities in Islamic Brand Categories

Introduction

Having examined the scope and sources of the global market for Islamic brands and discussed how powerful brands are built, in this and the following chapter we will examine the tremendous possibilities that now exist across a wide range of industries. As Islam represents a lifestyle as well as a religion, the appeal of tapping into the total market for Islamic-branded products and services has spawned a great deal of recent activity across many categories, including:

- Islamic foods and beverages;
- Islamic finance—wholesale/retail;
- Islamic education;
- Islamic entertainment and "edutainment";
- Islamic travel, tourism, and leisure;
- Islamic medical, pharmaceutical, and beauty products and services;
- Islamic products for women; and
- Islamic Internet, media, and digital products and services.

This chapter describes what these categories contain and the opportunities they provide, along with some case material. The opportunities for media and the digital world are discussed in Chapter 7.

Islamic Foods and Beverages

This is a huge category that deals mainly in *halal* foods and drinks. The discussion will be restricted to the size of this market and brand opportunities, and will not delve into the meaning of *halal* or the thorny issue of *halal* accreditation.

According to *The Halal Journal*,[1] the global *halal* food market was estimated to be worth US$580 billion in 2004 and US$632 billion in 2009.

Although this figure is growing, it represents only around 16 percent of the world's total food expenditure, as Muslims have a relatively low purchasing power in terms of food products. Asian countries represent the largest market, with 62 percent of Muslims living in this region.

Most Asian countries consume basic primary and non-tradable products. The six Gulf Cooperation Council (GCC) countries, by contrast, where the *halal* food market is estimated to be worth US$43.8 billion, import more than 90 percent of their food products. In Europe, the value of the market is estimated at US$66.5 billion, reflecting Europeans' greater purchasing power and better education. These figures may not be totally accurate, as a proper survey has not yet been carried out, but they are likely to be reasonable estimates.

The *halal* food and beverage market thus provides a huge opportunity for Islamic companies to go global. Some companies are attempting to develop their own *halal* brands, and some countries are assisting places and destinations to do the same, as we saw in Chapter 2. However, many of the branding opportunities are being taken up by global Western brands such as Nestlé, as we shall see in a later chapter.

Some brands are content to continue to serve their own market, despite having the capability to go global. Yildiz Holding from Turkey, owner of the famous Ülker brand (among many others), started in this way, and then moved into other markets as it gained expertise and capacity. This is a good strategy for building brands—become number one in your own market before moving out into international markets.

CASE STUDY 7: YILDIZ HOLDING

Yildiz Holding was formed in 1944 around the idea that "Everybody has the right to a happy childhood, no matter where in the world." At the center of Yildiz Holding's values is an abiding respect for "people and society." In all its relations with society and individuals, Yildiz Holding operates legally and ethically. It is managed according to these values, which were instigated by its founder, Sabri Ülker. These values have turned Yildiz Holding from being a small biscuit production facility into an integrated food company.

Yildiz Holding, founded on a single type of biscuit, now carries its leadership into the global area through the production capacity, distribution power, product variety, and vision of the businesses under its umbrella.

One of the oldest food production companies in Turkey, Yildiz Holding is today a market leader. It operates 68 companies over eight divisions, with the company's traditional area of expertise—biscuit and chocolate manufacture—remaining as the core business. Yildiz Holding is a pioneer in many segments.

Yildiz Holding's 29,500 employees and 53 factories in Turkey and abroad manufacture food items demanded in every area of life. It has annual revenues of US$10.9 billion, and 13 of Yildiz Holding's companies were listed among Turkey's largest 500 companies in 2008. Companies in the group export to 110 countries, bringing a large amount of foreign exchange to Turkey.

Long known around the world as a "Turkish brand," Yildiz Holding has always been an important option for international food conglomerates seeking strategic partnerships. Such partnerships have brought Yildiz Holding closer to the global arena.

In addition to their contributions to the industry, Yildiz Holding's companies also play an important role in the utilization of national agricultural production. As one of the largest primary product buyers in Turkey, it is also an important supporter of Turkish farmers.

Yildiz Holding consists of eight main groups, namely:

- *Ülker (Biscuits, Chocolate) Group:* This group is responsible for production, marketing, sales, and distribution of traditional goods, including biscuits and chocolate, as well as products such as cakes, flour, and baby food.
- *Food, Beverage, Confectionery, and Chewing Gum Group:* This group operates the production and sales of vegetable and olive oil, margarine, milk and dairy products, soft drinks, starch-based sugars, ready-to-cook soups and other culinary supplements, breakfast cereals, functional food, confectionery, and chewing gum.
- *Packaging, Information Technologies and Real Estate Group:* This group produces basic packaging materials used for its well-known subsidiary company, Ülker, as well as a variety

of packaging materials for customers both in and outside of Turkey. Yildiz Holding united its businesses operating in the IT sector under this group in 2007. The resulting synergy has helped it create successful IT products and strengthened its strategic position in this field. The Real Estate Group is involved with projects such as shopping centers, and residential and commercial buildings.

- *Food, Frozen Food, and Personal Care Group:* This group is responsible for the management of subsidiaries operating in the fields of tea, frozen foods, and personal care.
- *International Operations Group:* This group is responsible for identifying the feasibility of international projects and manages the investments of Yildiz Holding in seven countries.
- *Financial Services Group:* This group is responsible for Yildiz Holding's purchasing, legal, and IT functions, as well as for management of its financial and treasury operations and coordination of its financial subsidiaries.
- *Marketing, Strategy, and Retail Group:* This group is responsible for managing all the brands, including Ülker, and preparing strategic plans. The Group also manages Yildiz Holding's investments in the retail field.
- *HR, Legal Affairs, Trade and Media Purchasing Group:* This group is responsible for managing the human resource activities and legal affairs of all the groups and companies, as well as purchasing activities related to both trade and media.

In late 2007, Yildiz Holding ventured into a totally new category when it acquired the leading global luxury chocolate brand, Godiva. This case is discussed in Chapter 9, It will be interesting to see in years to come if this excellent acquisition is used by Yildiz as an opportunity to learn from an established international brand, and to transfer this learning to some of its other products, and enter new markets.

Source: www.ulker.com.tr.

Islamic Financial Services ▬▬▬▬▬▬▬▬

Islamic financial services is an area of extreme importance and opportunity for both Islamic and Western brands. (I will not examine the structures of the various Islamic finance products on offer, as that information is available elsewhere.)

It could be argued that the Islamic financial services industry is both old and new. It is relatively old in that it was frequently used in medieval times for trading purposes—for example, between the Arabs of the Ottoman Empire and the Spanish—with financial arrangements made on a profit- and loss-sharing basis, as opposed to an interest-based mechanism. Indeed, until the Middle Ages, Christianity also prohibited the charging of interest. Gradually, as trade expanded across the globe, European and Western companies became more involved in business and established their own banks that financed business activities using the notion of interest. They went on to dominate world trade, and although there had been some local Islamic banking in Egypt in the 1960s, it was not until the 1970s that Islamic finance really began to establish itself again, this time as an alternative to "conventional" banking. When people refer to Islamic finance as a relatively new industry, they are referring to this post-1970 era. The first sustainable and recognized Islamic bank was Dubai Islamic Bank, which was founded in 1974, followed by the Islamic Development Bank in 1975. Now, hundreds of banks offer Islamic finance.

Countries are also racing to capitalize on this trend, with a few countries aspiring to become Islamic finance hubs—such as Malaysia, Singapore, Hong Kong, London, and others. Recent issues regarding lack of trust in the conventional banking system have added impetus to the growth of Islamic finance. While the breakdown of conventional global finance between 2007 and 2009 caused havoc in most countries, Islamic finance was largely unaffected, although there were a limited number of *sukuk* (corporate bond) defaults in places such as Dubai. The resilience of Islamic finance under such trying circumstances has led many players and observers in the industry to call it "*Shariah*-compliant," "*Shariah*-based," or even "ethical" banking. The implication of this is that the success of Islamic finance is based on principles that are accepted widely within non-Muslim as well as Muslim markets.

Under Islamic principles, *Shariah* law (as prescribed in the *Qur'an*) defines the framework within which Muslims should conduct their lives.

The overarching principle of Islamic finance and banking products is that all forms of interest are forbidden. The Islamic financial model works on the basis of risk sharing. Put simply, the main difference between Islamic and conventional finance is that money from an Islamic finance source is viewed as a trade facilitator, as opposed to the conventional view of money as a store of value. So, the notion of "interest"—or "*riba*" in Islam—is prohibited. This is to ensure that the value of money is only recognized when it is employed as capital, and it is the performance of that capital that determines the reward, or profit.

Islamic banks were founded on the principle of sharing profits and losses. The ratio by which profits and losses are shared between the bank and the customer is determined by a pre-agreed contract between the two parties, who are "partners" to the agreement. Profit is negotiated, and risk is determined, by the ratio of ownership. This is the case whether the financial product is a retail product (such as mortgages, personal loans, and deposits) or a wholesale product (such as company bonds, or "*sukuk*").

There is occasional discussion among observers and writers as to whether or not Islamic banking is really conventional banking that has been "tweaked" for Islamic audiences. However, the general view is that the stability, transparency, and non-speculative nature of Islamic finance does indeed appear to make for a different system to that of conventional banking, and is more ethical in nature.

Market deviations

It is important to note that although Islamic finance is based on *Shariah* compliance, the interpretation of Islamic law found in the *Qur'an* and the *Sunnah* can differ. In other words, there are different schools of thought, and although this is a technical aspect, marketers should be aware that differences in contractual and operational practices do exist between markets. For example, Middle East markets tend to be more strict in interpretation and South East Asia somewhat more open. The shortage of *Shariah* scholars that has culminated in some sharing of these experts across banks has helped toward more consistency, especially in some country markets as has institutional agreements generated by institutions such as the Accounting and Auditing Organization for Islamic Financial Institutions (AAOIFI), which has produced standards for Islamic accounting, and the Islamic Financial Services Board (IFSB), which issues standards for regulation and effective supervision. In addition to these variations, there are also variations banks can choose in terms of structure.

There are three main ways in which Islamic finance can be implemented with respect to the structure of a bank. These are:

- *A fully-fledged Islamic bank:* It is a proper Islamic bank that doesn't carry out conventional banking activities and are thus standalone entities offering only Islamic products. They tend to have a full range of such products. Examples include Sharjah Islamic Bank of the UAE and Al Rajhi Bank of Saudi Arabia.
- *A conventional bank with an Islamic banking subsidiary:* Here a conventional bank operates a separate subsidiary, so that the distribution and operational infrastructure is completely separate from the parent bank and more in line with total *Shariah* compliance. A well-known example in this category is Standard Chartered bank's Saadiq subsidiary.
- *A conventional bank with an Islamic "window":* This is where a conventional bank elects not to have an independent Islamic subsidiary company, but instead has a divisional business that deals entirely with Islamic products and services, and may even have dedicated branches. Islamic products may be offered through their main distribution network, for instance, where branches provide both conventional and Islamic banking products. Nevertheless, *Shariah* restrictions around mixing of funds apply, so funds, accounts and reporting are kept separately. This means that the Islamic window operates as a separate entity but leverages on the conventional bank infrastructure. The most well known of these is probably HSBC.

Making things more complex from a marketing perspective is the fact that the structure chosen may also depend on local country requirements, as well as the preference of the bank itself. For example, in February 2011 Qatar ordered conventional banks to stop offering Islamic financial services by the year end. Conversely, where standalone Islamic banking is not practical in some Islamic majority or minority markets due to challenges in satisfying legal and regulatory requirements, some banks use Islamic windows. In general, the use of Islamic windows has been more common in Europe and Asia, and the standalone Islamic banking model in the Middle East.

There are many more examples, and the banks concerned always have a point of view as to why they have chosen that particular model, and why it has worked well for them. The successful banks in the global arena for Islamic finance tend to be on the retail side, with HSBC and Standard Chartered Saadiq Bank being prominent. It is interesting to note that, from a branding and marketing point of view, the most successful retail banks are mainly non-Islamic. Although this is a generalization, it does appear that the strength of these brands as global entities helps not just brand awareness but trust and customer acquisition as well. There are exceptions, of course, such as Al Rajhi Bank, mentioned above, which is one of the most profitable pure Islamic banks.

Finally, marketers also have to understand that the choice of structure may determine the nature of customer acquisition depending on degrees of religiosity, but this is not straightforward. Logically, Muslims who strictly adhere to their faith are more inclined to seek standalone Islamic banks, and those who are more liberal might be more open to the use of Islamic and conventional products. In practice, however, it seems that customers do not behave in this way. More research is required on customer behavior in Islamic finance, but some findings on customer segmentation have been mentioned in Chapter 3 page 58. Suffice to say that entering markets without adequate market research would not be a good idea.

The rapid rise of Islamic financial services over the last 30 years has been quite noticeable, with the rate of growth outstripping that of conventional banking. However, it is a very young industry, and even growth rates of 20–30 percent don't yet make Islamic finance a major segment. While the growth figures vary, one fairly reliable statistic is that, between 2007 and 2008, there was a 27.8 percent growth in *Shariah*-compliant bank assets among the Top 500 (from US$500.4 billion to US$639 billion).[2] This increase was against the backdrop of a collapse in the value of conventional banking and a worldwide loss of confidence in conventional banking institutions. By 2009, the value had increased to US$822 billion, an extremely healthy increase of 28.6 percent.[3] At a time when asset growth in the Top 1000 World Banks slumped to 6.8 percent from 21.6 percent the previous year, Islamic institutions were able to maintain the 28 percent annual compound growth achieved in the previous three years.

The industry also continued to expand, with 20 new entrants bring-ing the number of *Shariah*-compliant institutions to 435, with a further 191 conventional banks having *Shariah* "windows." The Islamic banking geographies are stretching beyond the existing strongholds of Iran, Saudi Arabia, Bahrain, Malaysia, and the UAE to Europe, South Africa, Kenya, and Indonesia. Despite its dramatic growth, the *Shariah*-compliant aggregate asset total is still less than 1 percent of the Top 1000 World Banks' aggre-gate asset total. While its innate conservatism, risk-sharing philosophy, and asset-linked strategy provide many attractions to both Muslims and non-Muslims alike, according to *The Banker*, the benefits of Islamic finance's risk-reduced approach (no speculation) mean that there are "deficiencies in the standardization of products, the secondary market in financial instru-ments, transparent pricing and effective liquidity management."[4]

Most banks I have talked to say that Islamic finance provides good alter-natives to conventional banking that have been welcomed by customers. Islamic financial products are now offered not just by Islamic financial institutions, but also by conventional-branded banks such as HSBC and Standard Chartered. The products range from deposits and mortgages on the retail side to Islamic bonds on the wholesale side.

On the wholesale banking side, products such as *sukuk*, thought to be very resilient in the recent recession, are "yet to be fully tested in tough legal battles over ownership and rights as issuers enter financial distress. The recent defaults of Kuwait's Investment Dar and Saudi Arabia's Saad and Algosaibi Groups may provide important insights over the comparative treatment of *sukuk* holders and conventional creditors."[5]

On the retail side, Islamic finance is proving to be quite successful. Interestingly, some large Islamic banks such as Al Rajhi, Maybank Islamic from Malaysia, and Standard Chartered Saadiq are finding that, in some mar-kets, they are attracting more non-Muslim new customers than Muslims, in some cases up to 60 percent. Many banks are now using segmentation, which was explained in Chapter 3.

Despite the cautionary comments above, and the concerns of many experts that there is a lack of innovation in Islamic finance, it is proving to be very attractive among both Muslims and non-Muslims globally. The governments of Muslim-minority countries such as the UK, Singapore, and Hong Kong all have well-developed Islamic finance strategies, aiming for regional hub status in this category. As an industry, Islamic finance is still small despite its rapid growth, and has some way to go in terms of size compared to conventional banking. Product development also appears to be slow.

Islamic Education

While Islamic education has traditionally been under the purview of the mosques and those in charge of them, over the last two to three decades there has been an explosion of Islamic educational institutions, ranging from kindergartens (for example, Qids Kindergarten in Malaysia) and primary and secondary schools, through to tertiary education (for example, Al-Azhar University in Egypt). Such institutions often teach conventional as well as Islamic subjects, and there is now considerable competition in this sector.

Strong brands survive. Al-Azhar, located in Cairo, is probably the most important university in the Muslim world. It was established in the year 969, and is regarded by many as the oldest university in the world. It has produced countless eminent Islamic scholars over its 1,051-year history. Al-Azhar University continues to teach traditional Islamic subjects, as well as modern medicine, engineering, languages, commerce, agriculture, and science. Its library is said to contain over 99,000 books and 595,668 precious manuscripts and rare books, some dating to the 8th century.[6] The university has around 90,000 students enrolled at any one time.

There are now many good Islamic universities, such as the International Islamic University of Islamabad (Pakistan), the International Islamic University (Malaysia), the Islamic University Rotterdam (the Netherlands), Islamic American University (the US), and many more. Islamic education is also experiencing tremendous growth at the pre-tertiary level, with schools such as Ah-lul Bayt (Canada), Al-Hidayah Islamic School (Australia), and Andalusia Academy Bristol (the UK). Islamic schools exist in Muslim-minority countries also, an example being the Madrasah Al-Junied School in Singapore, which was established in 1927 with its vision of "Nurturing Generations of Islamic Scholars and Leaders." As Islamic education becomes more commercialized and enters into the mainstream of educational services, this is an area of growth with good prospects for new market entrants.

Islamic Entertainment and "Edutainment" ▬

Entertainment

Art, sports, and entertainment can be enjoyed by anyone. There are hundreds of television channels throughout the world dedicated to the Muslim consumer, varying in content usually but not always by country. Even in Muslim-minority countries, entertainment brands are doing well—for instance, Islam Channel in the UK. As all brand and marketing managers know, brands are not confined to companies; personalities and celebrities are also often managed as "brands." The case of Sami Yusuf, the Muslim pop star, demonstrates the success that can be attained.

CASE STUDY 8: SAMI YUSUF

"King of Muslim Pop"

Sami Yusuf is one of the biggest names in the growing genre of Muslim pop. A British Muslim artist, Sami is one of the most popular singers in the Arab world and among Muslims in the West. In 2006, *Time* magazine called him "Islam's biggest rock star," and the BBC has dubbed him "The King of Muslim pop." Sami Yusuf debuted in 2003 with the album *al-Mu'allim*. Together with his second album, *My Ummah*, he has achieved sales of over five million copies worldwide. He has since released a third album.

Sami Yusuf's songs have revolutionized the traditional *nasheed* industry (Islamic tunes in praise of God and the Prophet Mohammed) and given birth to a new genre of modern Islamic music that appeals to the large Muslim youth population. He has sold millions of records and played to hundreds of thousands of fans across the globe. His 2009 single, "You Came to Me," had received over three million YouTube views by January 2011.

By carefully crafting a branded identity for the new generation of Muslims, and reflecting every aspect of Islamic values in his "brand," Sami Yusuf has opened up a new Muslim lifestyle market for many others to tap into. From a branding and marketing perspective, Sami is a savvy new media marketer, appealing to the young with an active presence on Facebook (approximately 1.3 million fans in January 2011), Twitter, and YouTube. His carefully branded identity is enhanced by quality packaging of music, high-quality choreographed concerts, and industry-leading creative videos. He has a multi-ethnic appeal, with his website available in Arabic, English, Turkish, French, and Farsi. Many of his songs incorporate different languages, and his videos reflect global Muslim locations. In Istanbul, Turkey, in 2007 he performed before a staggering 250,000 fans.

Source: www.samiyusufofficial.com/main/sami-yusuf.

The new wave of entertainment in the media exists in both offline and online forms, but a shift is now occurring to more online brands and websites, such as the online arts and entertainment journal www.muslimentertainment.com, which provides an insight into the world of Islamic music and entertainment. The digital world provides huge opportunities for developing Islamic brands, and this is dealt with separately below.

"Edutainment"

Sitting between education and entertainment is an interesting development that marketers call "edutainment," a good example of which is provided by *THE 99*.

CASE STUDY 9: *THE 99*

Superheroes Based on Islamic Culture

Like kids the world over, Muslim children have long fantasized about superheroes such as Superman, Batman, and the like. In 2003, they got some superheroes hailing from places closer to their homes when

Kuwait-born businessman Dr. Naif Al-Mutawa created a new breed of superheroes packed with Muslim traits and virtues. The THE 99 comic book series is based on superhero characters who each personify one of the 99 qualities that the Qur'an attributes to God.

The superheroes—such as Jabbar, The Powerful and Noora, The Light—are intended to appeal to a wide universal audience by reflecting the virtues of generosity, wisdom, and faithfulness—all encouraged by a number of faiths. World-famous DC Comics has revealed it is planning a crossover mini-series of the Justice League (Superman, Batman, Wonder Woman, and so on.) and THE 99. The success of the THE 99 comic books has already translated to a theme park, merchandise deals (for example, with Nestlé), and an animation series.

The success of THE 99 is a great example of projecting the values that drive Islam, and it has garnered widespread media attention globally. US President Barack Obama acknowledged THE 99 as a highly innovative response to the building of a bridge between the Muslim world and the West.[7]

THE 99 is owned by Teshkeel Media Group, a Kuwait company with offices in New York and Cairo that is focused on creating, re-engineering, and exploiting all forms of children's media based on or infused with localized culture, beginning with a proprietary superhero concept. It has both an online and offline branding and marketing strategy, with geographical distribution through regional distributors, and a strong digital presence with a website packed with features, including downloadable copies of the comics.

Teshkeel's mandate is to mine local culture for themes that will resonate with our staple segments. Our core focus is to maintain international industry standards that produce a rewarding and entertaining experience for a younger audience. In short—we are in the field of localizable edutainment. Teshkeel plans to cultivate and harvest those themes intrinsic in our regional culture that will speak equally to children both in and outside of the Middle East. Drawing upon our own history, culture and traditions, we aim to provide positive and inspirational images for children by creating properties that they can relate to.

The Company's intent is to create a strong brand through the reinforcement of our main characters and to then delve into the many lucrative opportunities that present themselves through this. To achieve our objective, Teshkeel Media Group functions as a licensing company on a global scale. Not only are Teshkeel's original concepts licensable, we are also in the process of adding to our arsenal of properties pending negotiations to acquire the rights to rethink others' intellectual properties to better suit a localized audience. Teshkeel's long-term goal remains an unwavering commitment to delivering a unique multimedia customer experience to children wherever they are from.[8]

Islamic Travel, Tourism, and Leisure

Islamic travel, tourism, and leisure is another segment of the Islamic market that offers products and services to Muslims and non-Muslims. From tourist destinations in the Middle East to *halal* airlines and fully *halal* hotels and resorts, there is something for everyone, and most countries are trying to cash in on the growth of tourism and tourism-related travel. For example, Al Jawhara Group of Hotels and Apartments complies with *Shariah* rules throughout its operations, as does the 55-story Tamani deluxe serviced apartment hotel in the Dubai Marina that opened in 2008.

Muslim travelers can look to Islamic service companies for travel planning assistance—for example, www.Irhal.com. ("*Irhal*" means "go away" in Arabic, and the company's tagline is: "Go Away. . . . Soon!") Another interesting service is that offered by CrescentRating.com (www.crescentrating .com), as discussed in Case Study 10.

There is also some growth in Islamic medical tourism, a relatively new marketing field, and this leads us to the next category.

CASE STUDY 10: CRESCENTRATING.COM

Halal-friendly Travel Guide

As a world-traveling executive for a multinational corporation and an observant Muslim, Fazal Bahardeen found the experience of traveling frustrating in terms of meeting his basic needs as a Muslim, such as access to *halal* dining and facilities to perform prayers. In 2006, he wrote a paper on the latent needs of Muslim business and recreational travelers globally, and devised a "*halal*-friendly" hotel rating system to serve as a guide for hotels. In 2009 he created a web-based solution for Muslim travelers called CrescentRating.com, where his services rated and evaluated hotels globally based on their own ratings system.

Crescent Rating allows hotels to adjust to this new demand for the *halal*-conscious traveler by amending or upgrading their services as they see fit. Crescent Rating generally looks at six salient "*halal*-friendly" areas, namely: prayer facilities, *halal* food services, guest bathroom facilities, Ramadan facilities, recreation facilities and services, and non-*halal* activities. CrescentRating.com is another pioneer in the growing global Muslim lifestyle offerings, paving the way for recognition and awareness of this segment of Muslim needs.

Sources: www.crescentrating.com; with some material reproduced with permission from www.dinarstandard.com.

Islamic Medical, Pharmaceutical, and Beauty Products and Services ▬▬▬▬▬

This category promises to be the next huge growth area in Islamic markets. For many Muslims who want to comply with *Shariah* law and ingest only what is *halal*, there is a growing industry in generic medical, pharmaceutical, and healthcare products that don't contain non-compliant substances such as certain animal-based gelatines. Organically made products, such as the European skincare brand Saaf Pure Skincare, contain highly concentrated healing botanicals, anti-inflammatory seed oils, shea butter, and other ingredients that offer an alternative not just to Muslims but to anyone interested in using natural, as opposed to animal, ingredients.

The growth of this category, spurred on by new standards and *halal* accreditation availability, has meant that some countries such as Malaysia are strategically earmarking companies manufacturing medicines, and pharmaceutical and cosmetics products, for special assistance. Brunei is another country that has already produced accreditation standards in this area.

According to various estimates, cosmetic and personal care products form an increasingly significant part of the growing market for *halal* products in the Muslim world. "While the hospitality, food, packaging, banking and finance industries are already devoting a lot of attention to the development and delivery of *halal* or *Shariah*-compliant products and services, the demand for *halal* cosmetics and beauty products has been relatively slower to take off," said Mr. Ahmed Pau-wels, CEO of Epoc Messe Frankfurt, organizers of Beautyworld Middle East 2010, which is the largest networking platform for the beauty and wellness industry in the region. "But this trend is rapidly changing, with growing consumer awareness and the drive for quality ingredients, making the market for *halal* and *Shariah*-compliant personal care products a high-growth segment with tremendous potential," he added. Exhibitors from across the world displayed a range of *halal* and *Shariah*-compliant cosmetics and beauty products at Beautyworld Middle East 2010, which has been acknowledged as the definitive trade event for the beauty, wellness, and spa industry for 14 years.

The event was held on June 1–3 at the Dubai International Convention and Exhibition Centre. "Consumers in Asia, especially Malaysia and Indonesia, have been the first in driving demand for *Shariah*-compliant health and beauty products, with Malaysia last year drafting a *halal* certification standard that evaluates the content, modes of production, storage, handling and packaging for cosmetics and beauty products," Ms. Elaine O'Connell, senior show manager, Beautyworld Middle East pointed out. "Customers in the prosperous and high-growth markets of the Middle East are becoming increasingly selective of the quality and content of the products they use, and this is reflected in the surge in demand for *halal*-certified beauty products."[9]

Further significant comment is given by another media article, as follows:

Recent research conducted by AMEinfo.com, a Dubai-based online business website, reported that the market for halal cosmetics in the Middle East is now booming at 12 percent growth per annum. In 2008, the segment recorded a sales value of USD2.1 billion in the region that holds only one-fifth out of a total population of 1.57 billion Muslims around the world. A survey conducted by KasehDia Consulting revealed that approximately 57.6 percent of Muslims in Southeast Asian countries are aware of and will purchase halal cosmetics if the products are available. However, more than half admitted to having difficulties finding halal cosmetics products on local retailers' shelves.

Indeed what is really driving the industry's demand is the fact that the Muslim population is now dominated by a demographic of young, adherent and dynamic professionals. They are a new generation that embrace their Islamic lifestyle and are generally knowledgeable when it comes to preserving halal as part of daily life. In France, home to international cosmetic brands such as Estee Lauder and L'Oréal Group, a new young affluent middle class of Muslims was reported to have spending power worth an estimated USD6.7 billion a year.

. . . Analysts already predict that halal cosmetics will be the next thing in the Islamic economy after halal food and finance. Interestingly, halal cosmetics are also gaining momentum amongst modern consumers of an eco-ethical consciousness, that is those willing to pay a premium for organic, natural and earthy cosmetics products to suit their modern lifestyle.

What is progressing now will be the emergence of Muslim home brands that are already making waves through online distribution, marketing halal cosmetics as the choice of purity, safety and cleanliness. This new development certainly heralds a significant potential boost in the halal cosmetics market signalling a rapid change in consumers' preference in making their decision when buying beauty products. In Europe, the world's biggest cosmetics producer, the revenue for natural cosmetic sales is forecast to approach USD2.4 billion in 2010.[10]

Further:

> *The* halal *cosmetics business—estimated to be worth 560 million dollars globally—is seen by analysts as next in line for growth after the lucrative* halal *food and Islamic finance sectors.*
>
> *Mah Hussain-Gambles, founder of the first* halal *cosmetics company in Europe, Saaf Pure Skincare, said the industry has also benefitted from a "green wave" and that 75 percent of her customers are non-Muslims. "The principles are the same—they want something that doesn't harm the body, the purity and that is exactly the same as the* halal *movement," she said. "I create an eco-ethical brand which is organic, vegetarian and* halal*—they are all important elements to me," she said, adding that demand "is getting out of control."*
>
> *Abdalhamid David Evans, a British expert on the* halal *business, said more manufacturers will jump on the bandwagon as Muslims choose* halal *products to reinforce their identity while others become more eco-conscious. "People are becoming increasingly concerned about those things and they become a marketing issue," said Evans, of Imarat Consultants.*[11]

From the above articles and commentaries we can see that the opportunities for Islamic brands are huge in this industry, and that the major Western brands have yet to move into the *Shariah*-compliant space in any significant way. It is not without its challenges, though. A good case to consider with respect to challenges and opportunities is OnePure Halal Beauty, a brand that is making significant headway in the beauty industry, and which is discussed in more detail in Chapter 9.

Islamic Fashion and Products for Women ▬

In addition to the categories of lifestyle media magazines and beauty products, the world of Islamic clothing and fashion has started to blossom globally, offering women a vast array of products that combine *haute couture* with Islamic principles. There are also new products that are more recrea-tional in nature, such as the "Bodykini" and "Burquini" swimwear.

Another example in the area of women's fashion is the clothing brand Aab, which was formed on the premise of designing fashionable and bespoke Islamic clothing for the modern British Muslim.

The brand follows three essential guidelines: comfort, luxury, and mod-esty. Aab has already caused quite a stir within the Islamic fashion industry, and is rivaling some of the celebrated, luxury brands. It has now made its clothes available worldwide via its website, www.aabuk.com.

Aab's clothing collection is entirely handcrafted. The company uses only high-end fabrics that reach the designers' own high standards, and each collection redefines the style of traditional clothing and fuses it with mod-ern, stylish patterns. This more contemporary approach to design is attract-ing a younger, chic demographic to Islamic clothing.

Islamic Internet, Media, and Digital Products

This subject is covered in depth in Chapter 7. I will provide just a brief introduction here to the many opportunities for brands in this category.

The Internet, media, and digital products are plentiful, and Muslims can easily find digital libraries, digital art and photography, digital Islamic clock widgets, and a whole host of other products. Non-Islamic brands can also see the market potential in digital products. For example, giant consumer electronics phone manufacturer LG launched mobile phones in August 2009 with "a number of special features, including a *Qiblah* indicator that uses an inbuilt longitude and latitude orientation or city references that, when used in comparison to the magnetic north, indicates the direction of the *Qiblah*. The two phones also come complete with *Adhan* and *Salah* prayer time alarm functions as well as *Qur'an* software, the *Hijiri* calendar and a Zakat calculator. Whenever Ramadan approaches, the features will be a welcomed benefit during the holy month."[12]

Pure e-brands also are increasing in number, such as the Internet portal www.halalapalooza.com, which is a guide to the world of Islamic e-commerce. In the area of social networking, brands such as Muxlim.com are also rapidly growing. Muxlim claims to be the world's largest Muslim lifestyle media company. It says:

> *Our vision is to connect the world's Muslim communities to each other, and to the wider world, through shared online experiences. Tens of millions of users visit the Muxlim Network every year to enhance their Muslim lifestyle and enjoy content including music, entertainment, fashion, food, sport, science, news, culture and more. Muxlim.com is the company's flagship social media service combining interactive video, audio, blogs, polls and images. Muxlim is focused on the Muslim lifestyle as part of a diverse, all-inclusive world which recognizes and welcomes people of all faiths and backgrounds who want to share, learn and have fun.*[13]

Vast Opportunities; No Big Brands

This brief excursion into the world of Islamic products shows that huge opportunities and potential exist in all categories for those companies that really understand Muslim consumers and their needs and wants. The question is: *Why are there so few brands from the Muslim world of any notoriety in these categories to date?*

More Strong Islamic Brands Are Needed

This chapter has revealed the main sources of and opportunities for brands that are aimed at Muslim audiences, while the previous chapter examined the extent of the market. However, the opportunities lie largely untapped and the potential remains. It is interesting to note, for example, that there are no OIC (Organization of Islamic Conference, an international organization with 57 predominantly Muslim-majority member states) companies among the top 100 brands as listed by *BusinessWeek* magazine in conjunction with Interbrand's rankings. Nor are there any from OIC countries in the 50 most innovative companies in the world as determined by *BusinessWeek* and Boston Consulting Group. And few make the list of Fortune 500 companies.

Table 6.1 lists the top 100 companies in the Muslim world. As can be seen, seven of the top 10 are oil and gas companies. As more countries see the need for diversification, we can expect to see more brands from this list, and others, emerging. Indeed, if the Muslim world is to become richer and the quality of life of Muslims is to be improved, then more brands are needed. Brands bring jobs and wealth to countries, and can represent as much as 70 percent of the value of stock exchanges, as they tend to do in the developed world. They are intangible assets of huge proportions and can bring in sustainable flows of revenue over decades. Table 6.2 shows the DinarStandard leading brands list of the top one hundred companies of OIC countries.

According to Rafi-uddin Shikoh, CEO of DinarStandard, there have been few innovative Islamic brands in the last few years. In a major talk at the Inaugural Oxford Islamic Branding and Marketing Forum held in July 2010, he said: "Although a rich diversity of exciting brands is emerging from across the Muslim lifestyle, Islamic finance and OIC markets, as yet they are far from their potential or global impact." He pointed to the fact that "there is no Google yet, and there is no Silicon valley as yet, and there is no values-driven truly global Islamic brand." The cause of this, he said, was the tendency of companies in the Muslim world to develop corporate cultures that foster "fear of failure" at all levels, "small thinking" by executive leadership, and "corporate cultures that discourage critical thinking at all levels." The major gaps in these companies' approach to branding and marketing compared to Western brands were, he said, "firstly, a disingenuous brand soul/identity and secondly, a relative lack of marketing investment."

The answer, Rafi-uddin said, is to:

- develop products and brands with a unique soul, based on Islam-driven core values and purpose;
- "rehabilitate" an innovation culture; and
- develop competitive marketing and innovation practices.

Rafi-uddin says that these top 100 companies are not found in the lists of the World's Most Admired Companies (*Fortune*), the Top 100 Brands (*BusinessWeek*), The World's Most Innovative Companies (*BusinessWeek*), or The Most Reputable Companies in the World (Reputation Institute). This is not a list of brands, but many of these companies do own brands.

Table 6.1   The 2010 DS100: Top 100 Companies of the Muslim World

COMPANY	RANK	COUNTRY	REVENUE 2009* US$ (mln)	GROWTH	TYPE	SECTOR	INDUSTRY
Saudi Arabian Oil Co. (Saudi Aramco)[1]	1	Saudi Arabia	$182,396	−42.48%	Government	Energy	Oil & Gas - Integrated
National Iranian Oil Company[1]	2	Iran	$79,277	−43.30%	Government	Energy	Oil & Gas - Integrated
Petroliam Nasional Bhd. (Petronas)	3	Malaysia	$70,869	−18.09%	Government	Energy	Oil & Gas - Integrated
Kuwait Petroleum Corp.[1]	4	Kuwait	$50,404	−45.36%	Government	Energy	Oil & Gas - Integrated
Sonatrach	5	Algeria	$47,980	−32.30%	Government	Energy	Oil & Gas - Integrated
PT Pertamina (Persero)[1]	6	Indonesia	$34,678	−37.43%	Government	Energy	Oil & Gas - Integrated
Qatar Petroleum	7	Qatar	$32,421	−29.88%	Government	Energy	Oil & Gas - Integrated
Nigerian National Petroleum Corp.[1]	8	Nigeria	$30,890	−30.86%	Government	Energy	Oil & Gas - Integrated
Abu Dhabi National Oil Co.[1]	9	UAE	$30,849	−43.66%	Government	Energy	Oil & Gas - Integrated
Koc Holding A.S.	10	Turkey	$28,978	−19.32%	Listed	Diversified	Auto, Consumer goods, Energy, Finance, others
Saudi Basic Industries Corporation (SABIC)	11	Saudi Arabia	$27,488	−31.66%	Listed	Basic Materials	Chemical Manufacturing
National Oil Company (NOC)[1]	12	Libya	$24,636	−44.65%	Government	Energy	Oil & Gas - Integrated
Saudi Telecom Company	13	Saudi Arabia	$13,544	6.97%	Listed	Services	Telecommunications
KazMunayGas	14	Kazakhstan	$13,441	−21.04%	Government	Energy	Oil & Gas - Integrated
The Emirates Group	15	UAE	$12,362	0.38%	Government	Transportation	Airline
Sabanci Holding	16	Turkey	$12,181	−15.27%	Private	Diversified	Financial, Retail, Auto, Chemicals, others
Astra International	17	Indonesia	$10,935	1.51%	Listed	Diversified	Auto, Finance, Heavy Equipment, Agri others
Yildiz Holding/ Ülker	18	Turkey	$10,900		Listed	Consumer Non-Cyclical	Food Processing

Table 6.1   (Continued)

COMPANY	RANK	COUNTRY	REVENUE 2009* US$ (mln)	GROWTH	TYPE	SECTOR	INDUSTRY
Isbank	19	Turkey	$10,897	2.66%	Listed	Finance	Commercial Banking
Pakistan State Oil Co.	20	Pakistan	$10,208	21.48%	Listed	Energy	Oil & Gas - Integrated
Sime Darby Bhd	21	Malaysia	$10,019	−8.90%	Government	Diversified	Plantations, Heavy equipment, Auto, others
Perusahaan Listrik Negara, PT	22	Indonesia	$10,002	6.97%	Government	Utilities	Electric Utilities
Iranian Mining Industries (IMIDRO)[2]	23	Iran	$9,811		Government	Basic Materials	Steel, Aluminum, Copper, Cement, others
Ziraat Bank	24	Turkey	$9,805	5.84%	Listed	Finance	Commercial Banking
Tenaga Nasional Bhd	25	Malaysia	$9,798	5.35%	Listed	Utilities	Electric Utilities
Iran Khodro plc	26	Iran	$9,089	14.02%	Listed	Consumer Cyclical	Automotive Manufacturing
Emirates Telecom (Etisalat)	27	UAE	$8,394	5.01%	Listed	Services	Telecommunications
(Zain) Mobile Telecommunications Co.	28	Kuwait	$8,056	8.27%	Listed	Services	Telecommunications
Saudi Oger Co.	29	Saudi Arabia	$8,000		Private	Capital Goods	Construction Services
Egyptian General Petroleum Co. (EGPC)[1]	30	Egypt	$7,738	−37.95%	Government	Energy	Oil & Gas - Integrated
Akbank	31	Turkey	$7,441	3.66%	Listed	Finance	Commercial Banking
Petroleum Development Oman (PDO)[1]	32	Oman	$7,385	−35.86%	Government	Energy	Oil & Gas - Integrated
Telkom Indonesia	33	Indonesia	$7,203	6.93%	Government	Services	Telecommunications
National Iranian Petrochemical Company	34	Iran	$7,192	4.27%	Government	Basic Materials	Chemical Manufacturing
Dogan Holding	35	Turkey	$6,607	−17.44%	Listed	Diversified	Finance, Energy, Media, others
Saudi Electric Company	36	Saudi Arabia	$6,360	7.01%	Listed	Utilities	Electric Utilities

(*Continued*)

Table 6.1 (Continued)

COMPANY	RANK	COUNTRY	REVENUE 2009* US$ (mln)	GROWTH	TYPE	SECTOR	INDUSTRY
Maybank Group	37	Malaysia	$5,999	5.54%	Listed	Finance	Commercial Banking
Agility	38	Kuwait	$5,723	−7.58%	Listed	Transportation	General Freight Trucking
ETA - Ascon Group	39	UAE	$5,690		Private	Diversified	Engineering, Construction, Other
TurkCell	40	Turkey	$5,492	2.89%	Listed	Services	Telecommunications
Saipa Corporation[2]	41	Iran	$5,462		Listed	Consumer Cyclical	Automotive Manufacturing
YTL Corporation Berhad	42	Malaysia	$5,373	85.48%	Listed	Diversified	Electric Utilities, Construction Services, Real Estate
SOCAR (State Oil Company of the Azerbaijan Republic)	43	Azerbaijan	$5,260	−10.93%	Government	Energy	Oil & Gas - Integrated
Dallah Albaraka Group[2]	44	Saudi Arabia	$5,204		Private	Diversified	Finance, Media, others
Enka Holdings	45	Turkey	$5,124	−26.33%	Listed	Capital Goods	Construction Services
Orascom Telecom	46	Egypt	$5,065	−4.92%	Listed	Services	Telecommunications
DOGUS Holding Co.	47	Turkey	$5,011	12.51%	Private	Diversified	Finance, Automotive, Retail, Construction
Halkbank	48	Turkey	$5,010	4.58%	Listed	Finance	Commercial Banking
Saudi Binladin Group[2]	49	Saudi Arabia	$5,000		Private	Diversified	Construction Services, Telecom, Mining
The Lion Group	50	Malaysia	$4,907		Listed	Diversified	Steel, Retail, Agriculture, Real Estate, others
Vakif Bank	51	Turkey	$4,802	1.01%	Government	Finance	Commercial Banking
Savola Group	52	Saudi Arabia	$4,778	29.64%	Listed	Consumer Non-Cyclical	Food Processing
Emirates National Bank of Dubai (NBD)	53	UAE	$4,734	10.75%	Listed	Finance	Commercial Banking
Consolidated Contractors International Co.	54	Saudi Arabia	$4,608	9.87%	Private	Capital Goods	Construction Services

Table 6.1   (Continued)

COMPANY	RANK	COUNTRY	REVENUE 2009* US$ (mln	GROWTH	TYPE	SECTOR	INDUSTRY
Abu Dhabi National Energy Company (TAQA)	55	UAE	$4,589	0.29%	Listed	Utilities	Electric & Water Utilities
Turkish Airlines	56	Turkey	$4,508	14.91%	Government	Transportation	Airline
Bank Melli Iran[2]	57	Iran	$4,473		Government	Finance	Commercial Banking
Group ONA	58	Morocco	$4,445	1.90%	Listed	Diversified	Mining/Construction Materials, Agri, Tourism, Finance, others
Saad Group of Companies[2]	59	Saudi Arabia	$4,352		Private	Diversified	Construction, Health-care, Information Technology
M.A. Kharafi & Sons[2]	60	Kuwait	$4,300		Private	Diversified	Engineering, construction, others
Bank Rakyat Indonesia	61	Indonesia	$4,299	26.02%	Listed	Finance	Commercial Banking
Suez Canal Authority	62	Egypt	$4,280	−20.45%	Government	Transportation	Misc. Transport
Axiata Group Berhad	63	Malaysia	$4,278	15.49%	Listed	Services	Telecommunications
Electricity Generation Company Inc. (EUAS)	64	Turkey	$4,199		Government	Utilities	Electric Utilities
Bank Mandiri	65	Indonesia	$4,141	16.69%	Listed	Finance	Commercial Banking
Indofood	66	Indonesia	$4,122	−4.27%	Listed	Consumer Non-Cyclical	Food Processing
Syrian Petroleum Company[1]	67	Syria	$4,101	−39.00%	Government	Energy	Oil & Gas - Integrated
Sapco[2]	68	Iran	$4,071		Government	Consumer Cyclical	Motor Vehicle Parts
IOI Group	69	Malaysia	$4,054	−14.07%	Listed	Consumer Non-Cyclical	Palm Oil
Felda Holdings Bhd	70	Malaysia	$3,865	−22.96%	Private	Consumer Non-Cyclical	Agriculture, Forestry, Fishing, others

(Continued)

Table 6.1 (Continued)

COMPANY	RANK	COUNTRY	REVENUE 2009* US$ (mln)	GROWTH	TYPE	SECTOR	INDUSTRY
Orascom Construction Industries	71	Egypt	$3,830	3.03%	Listed	Capital Goods	Construction Services
Bumiputra-Commerce Holdings Bhd	72	Malaysia	$3,720	13.97%	Listed	Finance	Commercial Banking
National Commercial Bank	73	Saudi Arabia	$3,681	−5.27%	Government	Finance	Commercial Banking
Malaysian Airline System Bhd	74	Malaysia	$3,655	−24.78%	Listed	Transportation	Airline
Saud Bahwan Group[2]	75	Oman	$3,500		Private	Services	Auto Merchant Wholesalers
UMW Holdings Bhd	76	Malaysia	$3,464	−16.04%	Listed	Diversified	Auto, Manufacturing & Engineering, Oil & Gas
BIM Birlesik Magazalar A.S.	77	Turkey	$3,442	25.48%	Listed	Services	Retailing
Brunei Petroleum[1]	78	Brunei	$3,441	−36.62%	Government	Energy	Oil & Gas - Integrated
Eregli Iron And Steel Works Co. (Erdemir)	79	Turkey	$3,355	−23.00%	Listed	Basic Materials	Iron and Steel
Samir Sa	80	Morocco	$3,323	−31.80%	Listed	Energy	Petroleum Refining
Independent Petroleum Group	81	Kuwait	$3,291	−32.40%	Listed	Energy	Petroleum/Coal Products
Mobile Communications Company of Iran	82	Iran	$3,272		Government	Services	Telecommunications
Selçuk Ecza Deposu	83	Turkey	$3,250	24.28%	Listed	Services	Pharmaceutical Distributor
PT Bumi Resources Tbk	84	Indonesia	$3,219	−4.71%	Listed	Basic Materials	Coal Mining
Al Rajhi Banking and Investment Corp.	85	Saudi Arabia	$3,187	3.91%	Listed	Finance	Commercial Banking
Public Bank Bhd.	86	Malaysia	$3,090	24.30%	Listed	Finance	Commercial Banking
Bank Central Asia Tbk	87	Indonesia	$3,085	19.26%	Listed	Finance	Commercial Banking

Table 6.1 (Continued)

COMPANY	RANK	COUNTRY	REVENUE 2009* US$ (mln)	GROWTH	TYPE	SECTOR	INDUSTRY
Eczacibasi Holdings[3]	88	Turkey	$3,015	20.17%	Private	Diversified	Pharmaceuticals, Building materials, Consumer products
PT Adaro Energy Tbk	89	Indonesia	$2,980	48.89%	Listed	Basic Materials	Coal Mining
Vestel[4]	90	Turkey	$2,977	−1.04%	Listed	Consumer Cyclical	Appliance & Tools
Gudang Garam Tbk PT	91	Indonesia	$2,964	9.00%	Listed	Consumer Non-Cyclical	Tobacco
Etihad Airways	92	UAE	$2,951	29.15%	Government	Transportation	Airline
DP World	93	UAE	$2,929	−10.78%	Listed	Transportation	Marine Cargo Handling
Tasnee (National Industrialization Company)	94	Saudi Arabia	$2,897	8.23%	Listed	Basic Materials	Chemical Manufacturing
Genting Berhad	95	Malaysia	$2,873	−2.08%	Listed	Diversified	Leisure & Hospitality, Plantations, Property, Power, others
Telekom Malaysia Bhd	96	Malaysia	$2,780	−0.79%	Listed	Services	Telecommunications
Arab Bank plc	97	Jordan	$2,727	1.12%	Listed	Finance	International Trade Financing
Ciner Group[2]	98	Turkey	$2,680		Private	Diversified	Textile, Energy, Mining
Perusahaan Otomobil Nasional Bhd (Proton)	99	Malaysia	$2,676	26.20%	Listed	Consumer Cyclical	Automotive Manufacturing
Kuwait Finance House	100	Kuwait	$2,672	−13.35%	Listed	Finance	Commercial Banking

Showing 1 to 100 of 100 entries

2010 Ranking is based on end of 2009 revenue data of OIC (Organization of Islamic Conference) member-based companies.

Notes:

1. Revenue figures are estimates based on 2009 crude oil production only (OPEC data).
2. Based on End of Fiscal Year 2008 revenue or earliest available (EOY 2009 could not be obtained)
3. Group's major subsidiary is listed.
4. Owned by Zorlu Holding, Turkey.

Source: www.dinarstandard.com as at January 27, 2011. Reproduced with permission.

Table 6.2 Leading Brands of the 2010 DS 100: Top 100 Companies of OIC Countries (listed alphabetically)

NAME	COUNTRY	SECTOR	DS 100 RANK
Afia	Saudi Arabia	Food	#52 (Part of Savola Group)
Al Rajhi	Saudi Arabia	Banking	#85
Arab Bank	Jordan	Finance	#97
Arcelik	Turkey	Consumer Electronics	#10 (Part of Koc Holding)
Beko	Turkey	Consumer Electronics	#10 (Part of Koc Holding)
BIM	Turkey	Retail	#77
CIMB	Malaysia	Finance	#72
Emirates	UAE	Airline	#15
Etihad	UAE	Airline	#92
Etisalat	UAE	Telecom	# 27
Hurriyet	Turkey	Media	#35 (Part of Dogan Holding)
Indomie	Indonesia	Food	#66 (Part of Indofood)
IsBankasi	Turkey	Banking	#19
Kuwait Finance House	Kuwait	Banking	#100
Malaysia Airlines	Malaysia	Airline	#74
Petrol Ofisi	Turkey	Energy	#35 (Part of Dogan Holding)
Petronas	Malaysia	Energy	#3
Proton	Malaysia	Automotive	#99
Samand	Iran	Automotive	#25 (Part of Iran Khodro)
Sime Darby Property	Malaysia	Real Estate	#20 (Part of Sime Darby)
Tat	Turkey	Food	#10 (Part of Koc Holding)
Turkish Airline	Turkey	Airline	#56
Ülker	Turkey	Food	#18
Vestel	Turkey	Consumer Electronics	#90
VitrA	Turkey	Home Products/ Retail	#88 (Part of Eczacibasi Group)
Zain	Kuwait	Telecom	#28

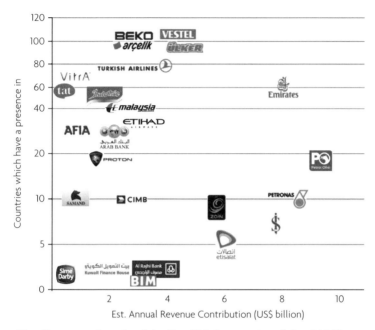

Figure 6.1 Consumer Brands of the Top 100 Companies of the OIC (from DinarStandard's DS 100 Ranking)

Source: www.dinarstandard.com.

Finally, Figure 6.1, from the DinarStandard, shows some examples of consumer brands that are doing well plotted on two dimensions: the number of countries/markets they are in, and their contribution to their group's revenues. The figure illustrates that brands from the Muslim world are beginning to make their presence felt.

The DinarStandard provides the best-available picture of the Muslim brand world to date. I agree with Rafi-uddin that, as the Muslim lifestyle markets begin to flourish, it is inevitable that companies from the Muslim world will begin to make their presence felt, although to develop great brands they will need to heed the points mentioned earlier. The remainder of this book is designed to provide information and strategies that will help Islamic companies to build better brands.

Summary ━━━━━━━━━━━━━━━━━━━━━━━━━━━━━━━━━━

This chapter has explored the range of global categories into which Islamic brands fall and which are beginning to grow very rapidly. National or country brand images are very important, as they bring with them many associations that may be positive or negative in nature, and which may reflect similarly on the brands under them, such as ministries and companies. Sometimes there are conflicts between national brands and their sub-brands and product brands. Countries must therefore try to manage outside perceptions and generate the best possible image for their nations, as country-of-origin influences buying behavior. Countries in the Muslim world also need more brands if they are to generate employment, intangible asset value, wealth, and a sustainable and better quality of life.

Despite the fact that opportunities abound in every category, companies from the Muslim world in general have been slow to catch on to the idea of creating brands, and they have failed largely because they have not been innovative in their thinking, and have not used the range of Islamic values to create and develop emotionally driven brands. However, it seems they are now beginning to explore many global categories that offer brand development potential. We have seen some examples of this trend in this chapter, and later chapters will offer additional examples.

In Chapter 7, we will look at the digital world, which represents arguably one of the most interesting and open categories for growth, before considering in Chapter 8 the challenges that face brands originating from the Muslim world.

Notes ━━━━━━━━━━━━━━━━━━━━━━━━━━━━━━━━━━━━

1. "The Global *Halal* Food Industry Revisited," *The Halal Journal*, May/June 2009.
2. *The Banker*, November 2008.
3. *The Banker*, October 2009.
4. *Ibid*.
5. *Ibid*.

6. www.sacred-destinations.com/egypt/cairo-al-azhar-university.
7. Presidential Summit on Entrepreneurship, Washington, DC, March 2010.
8. www.the99.org/.
9. www.ameinfo.com/232308.html.
10. www.in-cosmeticsasia.com/page.cfm/link=65.
11. *The Independent*, May 9, 2010.
12. www.experientia.com/blog/lg-launches-islamic-phone/.
13. www.muxlim.com.

The Future: Opportunities in the Internet, Media, and Digital World

This chapter specifically addresses opportunities in the Internet, media, and the digital world. Global branding is heading rapidly into the era of digitalization, both strategically and in terms of brand management, and developments such as social media networking are transforming the way in which people and brands interact. These developments offer a wealth of opportunities for Muslim brands, and the chapter looks at a number of companies that are seizing those opportunities successfully. The important thing about these opportunities is that the timescale required to establish digital brands is much shorter than for normal offline brands, such as those in manufacturing, and so on.

Nevertheless, brand and marketing managers are increasingly finding that even those brands that are not producing Internet-based products require online strategies if they are to encounter consumers. No one can escape the demands presented by consumers via the Internet.

I am grateful to Mohamed El-Fatatry, founder and CEO, and Stephen Lee, COO, of Muxlim Inc., for their assistance in writing this chapter. The sections on the impact of Internet developments on marketing, social media branding, and the Muslim lifestyle consumer, and their implications, draw heavily on two unpublished papers written by them, and others, cited at the end of this chapter.[1]

Introduction

There is no doubt that the advent of the digital world has transformed the world of media. While the traditional media are still alive and kicking, they are rapidly being overtaken by digital alternatives powered by the Internet. Despite the fact that there remain opportunities in the traditional media, as will be seen later in this chapter, I believe that more significant opportunities for Islamic brands lie in the digital space.

Less than 10 years ago, the Internet was just starting to be used as a small part of the brand manager's touchpoint analysis and development. Today, we are firmly in a digital world, where sophisticated online brand strategies are an accepted part of the brand manager's toolkit.

There is no longer a digital divide. The gap between those who used the Internet frequently and those who had little access, skill, or willingness to use it, has largely disappeared. Now nearly all age groups are computer literate and Internet savvy, from children as young as four, to adults in their golden years.

The most fundamental change in how we use the Internet relates to the fact that it is becoming much more "real time." Some of its applications enable users to know what is happening *now*—not several hours or a day or so ago. This huge step forward has empowered people who use the Internet for social, as well as business, purposes, and has enfranchised many who previously didn't use it. We have witnessed the birth and development of a number of Web-based relationship brands, and you will read some case studies on these in this chapter.

The above changes are a direct result of the new digital world—or "Web 2.0," as some call it. The rise of this "new world" has spawned many brands that exist to facilitate relationships between consumers, a bit like hosting a continuous party for friends. Traditional brands not only have to harness the power of these brands as strategic alliance partners in their online strategies; they also must manage their relationships with customers in every way.

The Internet and its applications have revolutionized the way in which humanity communicates and does business. I don't know of a company that doesn't have a website now, and many are using "podcasts" as a means of promoting their brands. I also know of several individuals who now have their own personal websites, and there are vast numbers of people who have their own blogs (web logs, or diaries). But for hundreds of millions of individuals who use the Internet, social networking sites such as Facebook do the job just as well, telling the world who they are, and allowing everyone to join or create a "club" that enables them potentially to communicate with millions of others. Privacy settings allow users to choose who can see their details or contact them. An increasing number of sites, and not just social networking sites, enable users to post vlogs (video blogs, often taken with a mobile phone camera). Reality programming can be carried out by anyone via their own chosen channels, and reality TV no longer has a monopoly on instant viewing. This isn't just a one-time digital revolution that has taken place; it is ongoing, with more and more sophisticated services emerging that make life easier and enable us to do things faster.

Symptomatic of the swiftness of the change that is taking place is the rapidity with which Coca-Cola, for decades the world's most valuable brand, has been displaced by the Internet search engine Google. As of April 2010, Google was the world's most valuable brand for the fourth year running, valued at US$114,260 million, an increase of 14 percent from 2009.[2] Brands such as Google, YouTube, MySpace, and Facebook have become legendary in less than eight years, and are transforming everything from politics to personal relationships, from finding things to finalizing deals, as we will see in the case studies in this chapter. Companies that have not embraced the Internet will find themselves at an increasing disadvantage, as nowadays an online brand strategy is just as important as an offline one.

The Speed Factor

It took 89 years for telephones to reach 150 million users, television 38 years, mobile phones 14 years, the iPod 7 years, and Facebook just 4 years. Facebook is often now referred to as the world's third-largest nation, as it has over 500 million members, and is still growing at around 5 million members per week. Facebook can reach any audience across the globe, and Facebook (Muslim Groups) is evidence of this. Muslims represent a fragmented audience of approximately a quarter of the world's population that has never previously been strategically engaged by the media, because until recently the technology has not been available to enable that to happen. YouTube (Muslim Channels) is another example of the ubiquitous consumption of media in this way by Muslims worldwide.

This new digital world is characterized by enormous and increasing speed; not just marketing speed, but the speed of innovation and availability. The development of the Internet has accelerated commercialization to the point where it is hard to keep up. It's both a brand manager's dream and nightmare: you can become a star overnight, but a has-been a short while thereafter. And for some, the idea may be good, but the time required to make a profit is too long, and the idea becomes obsolete or is superceded by new players. Whatever happened to WordPerfect and boo.com?

Fundamental Change

Technological innovation of the kind referred to above is producing game-changers in all areas of the digital world. In the case studies that follow, we will see how this fundamental change is playing out. We will see how social networking, in a relatively short time since its entrance, has totally changed the global communications landscape, and how new channels are providing everyone with the opportunity and ability to know what is happening around the world, and to get involved, *instantly*, rather than a day or hours later. The new digital world allows users to be interactive with anyone, anywhere, and at any time in *real time*.

The Impact of Internet Developments on Marketing

Marketing has taken a huge shift in this digital and Internet-driven world. No longer do companies dominate the channels and dictate what a consumer can and will hear. Now, consumers have a choice. They use search services to find what they are looking for. They listen to their friends and digital communities. They talk to people en masse in a very personal way. Today, you can communicate with hundreds, thousands, or even millions of your "friends" at a click of a button. The viral opportunity presented by the Internet may be the boom or bust for a company's marketing. Digital and social media are the cost-efficient key to attracting new customers and keeping old ones. But the new dynamics of this situation have made it clear that, if companies want new customers, they need to have a relationship with them; a strong relationship built over time. That means knowing them, understanding them, and providing them with real value, even before they expect consumers to buy from them directly.

Digital communications have made it easier to reach different audiences that were previously difficult to contact. No longer is a customer's geographic location a problem in talking to them. Location has simply become a part of their overall demographic. By understanding and grouping people by a deeper demographic set, combined with location-independent digital delivery, marketers can understand and sell to more specific niche groups. These groups may reflect consumers' ethnicity, culture, or lifestyle.

Diversity is fast becoming an important marketing opportunity. If knowing one's customers and creating this relationship is important, one key opportunity for reaching them is honest recognition and celebration of their culture, ethnicity, and lifestyle. As fragmented niches are brought together using digital tools, there is no better way to reach diverse and multicultural audiences than through digital and social media.

This revolution hasn't escaped the attention of the Muslim world, and Muslims are as eager as any other population group to make the digital world a part of their modern lifestyle. The Muslim consumer market is in line with other multicultural marketing efforts in its increasing digital and integrated marketing focus. In particular, digital choices for marketers have helped make the Muslim consumer easier to reach and addressable as a single market segment. Muslim social media and other Muslim-specific digital channels are emerging as a new gateway to building relationships and loyalty. Additionally, one of the most attractive facts about this market is that it feels ignored by brands and is highly perceptive to marketing that addresses consumers as being Muslim. This situation is now changing rapidly, as we will see.

Muslims and Social Media

Like the rest of the world's population, millions of Muslims are going online each day. For instance, the largest Muslim Facebook group—called "I'm a Muslim, And I'm Proud"—has over a million fans. Muslims utilize the Internet to share and enrich all aspects of their lifestyle. Entertainment, food, fashion, and education are just some of the topics Muslims discuss, share, and explore online. Muslims use online networks such as Facebook.com, Youtube.com, and Twitter.com, as well as specialized Muslim networks such as Muxlim.com. It is the Internet that has made it possible for this geographically fragmented segment to be addressed as a unified consumer market. Muslim women are also very active online, which allows marketers to reach them in ways that are not possible using traditional media or offline.

Companies such as Vodafone (UK), Shoes.com (US), Nokia (Finland), Mobily (Saudi Arabia), and others are connecting with Muslims digitally. Brands such as these have chosen the digital route to access the Muslim market as Muslim communities are a cross-section of all socioeconomic classes, age groups, nationalities, and races; a fact that makes the community harder and more expensive to target and reach as a mass market.

Digital media is able to maneuver around the segregation between different Muslim sub-communities (Arab, Asian, etc.), and allows for new ways of communicating with Muslims as a group that is not necessarily attracted by the same messages as the mass market. It enables brands to reach all sub-communities simultaneously, where marketers can easily deliver messages to each community in its own language and style. Traditional media has never been able to deliver this capability.

The case studies in this chapter describe how new brands are embracing the opportunities to grow quickly in the Islamic world. Later in the chapter we will look at traditional media successes.

Social Media Branding and the Muslim Lifestyle Consumer

The New Age of Advertising

Does advertising still work? In the Internet age dominated by Google, Facebook, TiVo, and other brands, how can a company get its message heard by its potential customers? Has traditional advertising become a billboard that people just drive by every day without noticing, or does it still have a role?

The short answer is that advertising can still work, but the way companies use advertising has a new dimension.[3] No longer is it a one-way path from the company through media buys. Today, the only messages that are absorbed are those that the consumer has sought out or developed a relationship with. This is not to say that banner ads, print, billboards, and TV commercials cannot be effective, but a new supporting base, a relationship, needs to be built; a sustained relationship built over time that involves trust and real value to the customer. Sometimes this value needs to be established even before the customer buys the company's product. In addition, measurement of trends and consumption is key to the understanding and creation of relevant advertising. In short, without knowing the customer, advertising is often a waste.

The Customer is in Control

The age of Google and other major Internet brands has put more power in the hands of the consumer. Where messages could be channeled through a select group of medias in the past, the ability to search for what one is looking for has caused power to shift away from marketers. Consumers now have the ability to completely ignore messages from marketers, and Muslim consumers are no different in this respect. They want to be addressed, entertained, and informed by the media they watch. As a result, marketers are becoming content producers.

Strategically creating content for the Muslim consumer is a key relationship-building tool that brand managers have no option but to develop, as the consumer now has the ultimate power to ignore anything and everything a company might say.[4] Choice has now put the power of message consumption in the hands of the consumer, and brands are desperately trying to harness and maintain the opportunity that can be found as the chosen favorite of the consumer. They struggle because the control of their brand's image and message has fallen out of their hands.[5] They are forced to do something that marketing departments haven't been set up to do: have a dialog with customers and learn from their consumption of things that are not their products. The Internet offers companies a new opportunity. If companies know what digital content their users like to consume and can find a way to provide that, they can, step by step, create a relationship with their customers and even make those customers excited enough to tell their friends. In effect, sharing among friends is the best marketing a company could buy. Herein lies the opportunity with digital social media.

Social Media: A Relationship-building Tool

When social media first began, companies jumped into media sites such as Facebook and YouTube, but tried to sell their brands by telling their old messages in the same way they had always advertised. It was like having a stranger come into one's bedroom and tell you of their undying love for you.

This is the age of what many are calling "earned media."[6] To earn lifetime customer value—a long-term customer's love—companies need to be able to listen and have a dialog and emotional relationship with the customer. Brands without a good connection to their fan base are often very good at talking, but very bad at listening. They don't really know what is important to their customers. They only know their own message. So, the media they produce follows the old push media model. No one, if they have a choice, likes to hang out for very long with someone who just talks about himself or herself constantly. The difference today is that customers can easily avoid or walk away from these brand messages.

It can also be argued that communications for big brands was designed for a different kind of mass communication. Social media is born out of individual needs and niche communication. It wasn't designed for those who want to push out advertising messages, which is why it very often fails in this capacity. It does, however, make it cheap and easy to tailor the right messages to specific audiences. These are messages that were designed around what people are looking for and want to be told. Rather than putting out the same message en masse, companies that use social media successfully are now starting to build the right content and using trusted channels for specific target audiences to create a more powerful and memorable impact.[7] They are observing content interaction and sharing in the discussion. They are learning to be an integrated part of the conversation by providing value-added information,[8] services, and entertainment that may or may not be directly related to their products. This helps customers and potential customers to draw closer to the brand, and simply shows consumers that the company understands who they are and is ready to engage with their lives.

After a brand establishes association with relevant content or services, companies can establish ways to actually become a valued and trusted supplier of portions of that content. Done well and over time, eventually the conversation includes more organic references about the company within the conversations across media and postings beyond the company's own work. At this point, social media has been used as a tool to successfully integrate a brand into the social conversations in a particular area and has developed an appetite in the market for successful advertising.

Interactive Consumer Touchpoints

Television and print are still the primary media for advertising, but the growth of the Internet and the digital world promises to give companies more opportunities for targeted and one-to-one advertising. The power brand companies are now developing interactive strategies that cover all possible consumer communications touchpoints.

For example, as well as carrying out all the traditional means of advertising and promoting its watches, Swatch has its own club, with an online community for whom it provides social networking opportunities and a means to share common interests and photos, and to engage in discussion forums. It has blog features where Swatch club members can share their brand experiences and opinions. Through this experience, Swatch generates many more touchpoints with consumers and ensures that its brand communications is a two-way street and not a one-way dead end.

If we compare the traditional methods of advertising and promotions with the new methods that take advantage of digital innovations, we see differences like those shown in Figures 7.1 and 7.2. Over the last half-decade, there has been an increasing shift toward the use of digital as well as traditional media to ensure that all possible touchpoints with the consumer are covered and that the brand receives maximum exposure. Such interactive strategies also ensure that consumers are involved with the brand and can communicate with it.

The inevitability of brands having multiple touchpoints in the digital world, because consumers do, means that they have to develop multiple platforms for attending to consumer interactions.

Brands Using Multiple Digital Media

Many of the big brands are now paying a lot more attention to digital branding and marketing strategies, and are creating multiple online presences. For instance, Coca-Cola uses several platforms, as shown in Figure 7.3.

Figure 7.1 Brand Touchpoint Wheel: Traditional

Figure 7.2 Brand Touchpoint Wheel: Digital Age

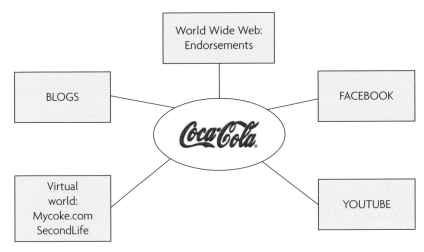

Figure 7.3   Coca-Cola: Branding in Digital Space

Coca-Cola has a MyCoke website and a virtual world called Second Life, and endorses on their websites other major brands relevant to its target market, such as *American Idol*. It has its own corporate blog site and one for fan blogs, plus a social networking page on Facebook, where members can exchange pictures and videos, and conduct discussions. Coca-Cola also features on YouTube. The company clearly sees social networking as a major part of its online brand strategy.

Many other companies haven't got this far but are experimenting with social media. For example, Carphone Warehouse, Comcast, and Virgin Media have used Twitter to respond to customer service questions, and Dell offers discounts to people who follow it on Twitter. Nokia has used LinkedIn to assist in reaching over 5,000 professionals; and H&M, Reebok, and Prada have all used Facebook.

In China, online games are offered by website operators such as social networking site Kaixin001, which lets people who play the game "park" cars in virtual car garages. Volvo, BMW, Shanghai General Motors Co., and Shanghai Automotive Industry Corp. are all represented. By clicking on a particular car brand model, users can see features and information about their choice. Shanghai General Motors vice president, Terry Johnsson, was quoted in *The Wall Street Journal* of April 9–13, 2009 as saying: "We will definitely do more on social-networking sites." In 2009, he said 10 percent of the company's overall media budget is allocated to the Internet. This trend is apparent in most industries, with many companies shifting budgets away from traditional media and toward new media.

In the battle to promote smaller cars, Ford is also using new ways of marketing on the Internet. According to the same *Wall Street Journal* article, 100 young drivers who are frequent users of the Internet were selected from more than 4,000 video submissions viewed more than 640,000 times online. The company rated applicants on their "social vibrancy" (how much they were followed online across a number of platforms) and on their creativity, video skills, and ability to hook a viewer within 5–10 seconds. Successful applicants were asked to drive the new Ford Fiesta subcompact model for six months, and to post their views on social networking sites YouTube, Twitter, and Flickr. Ford hopes that these 100 people will be "opinion leaders" and build a "collective of digital storytellers."

These are examples from the Western world, where the global brands are usually the first to react to changing consumer behavioral trends, but they demonstrate what Islamic brands need to be doing if they are to compete successfully in the digital world.

Many more companies are turning to these new and exciting ways of developing relationships with existing and potential customers, and are using the experience to understand how consumers react with each other. Some are still trying to work out how to use social networking to their advantage without alienating consumers by being too intrusive. It is important to note, however, that social media are still only a part of the quest to really understand what motivates people, and should be used in conjunction with other ways of developing consumer insight, such as those discussed in Chapter 5.

Diversity and Multicultural Opportunities

Since culture is a core part of many people's lives, recognition and celebration of diversity has become one way for companies to establish a direct connection with consumers. Companies can demonstrate true understanding of the customer by providing honest, value-based information, services, and entertainment. These opportunities built through the facilitation of content development and distribution can create the building blocks for a long-term relationship with the multicultural customer.

One of the best opportunities for reaching diverse markets is ethnic- and lifestyle-based marketing through social media,[9] which provide a proactive recognition and celebration of the customer's culture. Very often it results in the release of untapped excitement toward a brand[10] that takes the step of engaging with the community through social media sharing and recommendations.

The Value of Measurement and Analytics

To know the multicultural customer is to address and understand his or her needs and consumption trends. Digital technology makes it possible for constant analysis of content activity on the Internet. Combined with demographic data, this provides a window into the kinds of ideas, needs, and products consumers within niche markets will respond to. The opportunity for companies within social media is not only to efficiently build the relationship with multicultural customers, but also to help strengthen that relationship through these analytics. In effect, this is the new way to listen to the customer. The proof of that listening is the response of better content or services from the company, which becomes the dialog that cultivates the strengthening of the relationship with the consumer over time.

Implications for Islamic Branding and Marketing

Marketers who use digital channels have the great advantage of directly addressing potential Muslim consumers through trusted Muslim-focused or ethnic media. This type of media allows marketers to communicate messages directly toward the Muslim consumer. These actions help not only to gain the trust of Muslim consumers and create a reputation-safe scenario, but also target the message to those who would best understand and value it. Digital channels also make it easy to hone the message and interact in a direct manner with all those engaging with the brand over the long term. This allows brands to directly manage their relationship and have continuous communication with their loyal and potential customers.

The combination of the above factors that make digital channels easy and low-cost platforms for marketers can result in oversaturated digital marketing environments. To gain consumers' attention and trust in such conditions, many marketers find it necessary to be increasingly open, honest, and even intimate in their marketing communications, and to listen very carefully to the consumers' response. Corporate blogs, or blogs maintained by company members, micro-blogs, profiles on social networking sites, and other so-called social media applications are some of the most commonly used tools that marketers use to develop intimacy with online consumers.

But there is a challenge here. Given the rapid take-up by consumers, brand managers have to think how they can build their brand communities, and this means generating emotional relationships with them. There are challenges for the brand owner here, because in the world of social media brands are not invited into the conversations consumers are having, and yet people using the social networks may well be talking about their brands. There is a need to enter the digital social media space and find ways of attracting consumers to their sites. This will not be accomplished by merely posting advertisements on the social media sites—there is a need to engage the consumer in a much more entertaining way. Moreover, brands cannot rely on one particular medium or site; they have to develop multi-channel digital relationships and manage all possible touchpoints on the Internet.

As regards specific target audiences, Muxlim.com notes that there are two Muslim sub-segments that are particularly difficult to reach via traditional channels: Muslim women and Muslims in emerging market countries. The women's market in general has been ignored for many years and is finally getting some of its due share, but it is still far from being fully explored. Several research projects have evidently shown and validated that the majority of buying decisions in the developing as well as the emerging world are made or influenced by women, but the majority of the marketing efforts are still targeted toward men. The role of Muslim women, in particular, is becoming more interesting, especially with the digital-generation consumer. Brands that will connect with this growing segment may experience a long-term beneficial relationship. Muslim women today are demanding, vocal, and brand conscious. Also, mobile penetration is growing rapidly in emerging markets, many of which are Muslim countries, suggesting that one unique use for digital mobile marketing in Islamic marketing is to reach emerging market consumers who have little access to any other media.

One of the most effective types of marketing is word of mouth. Hence, the goal for many marketers is to have an established relationship with customers and to get those customers to talk about their products with their friends. These relationships, however, need to be initiated and maintained by marketers for the effect to last. Because the digital world is a place where people seek both companionship and answers, brands have an opportunity to engage with consumers and provide them with information, services, and entertainment that enhances their lives. This generates valuable brand exposure, develops a positive relationship with consumers, and maximizes the chances of word of mouth. Therefore, developing a solid relationship with members of an online community and allowing them to be the mouthpiece for the company is an effective way to generate brand exposure. Consumers are changing rapidly and are becoming very vocal about their opinions and preferences (both positive and negative). Easy ways to share interesting information help create a word-of-mouth snowball effect that spreads to both online and offline consumers.

Digital media has created an opportunity for marketers to develop a genuine conversation and relationship with the Muslim consumer that is partially shaped by interactions with the brand's messages. By taking a single common entry point (the lowest common denominator) and then listening carefully to how consumers react to it and shape it, marketers can understand and cater to all sub-identities in their marketing messages, thus maximizing their appeal among Muslim consumers.

The use of digital channels by brands also allows marketers to carefully target Muslim consumers without over-using their "religious" identity to attract their attention. Consumers may feel that their identity is being over-used if marketers single them out in mass marketing, whereas digital media can subtly integrate brand messaging among lifestyle content. This takes into account consumers' sub-identities from sports to fashion, technology, entertainment, and more, providing instant value to the consumer, which initiates and cultivates a relationship at a very low cost. Accordingly, consumers can socially endorse the brand or capture their friends' attention (who may not be necessarily interested at first) by interacting with a brand digitally.

Muxlim.com, owned by Muxlim Inc., is firmly in the midst of this Muslim lifestyle social networking revolution. The following case study outlines not only what Muxlim has done and is doing, but also how it can help other brands enhance their market presence and sales to the Muslim world though digital research.

CASE STUDY 11: MUXLIM INC.: I

Gateway to the Muslim Consumer Market

ABOUT MUXLIM

Muxlim was created by Mohamed El-Fatatry, an Egyptian student who grew up in the UAE and moved to Finland as a teenager to complete his university studies in media technology. The instantly global service tapped into a unique need of people both inside and outside the Muslim community. Initially, it appealed especially to Muslims living in Muslim-minority countries such as the United States. These people, like Mohamed El-Fatatry, were looking for information and relationships beyond the daily politics and religion that dominated the mainstream media channels. Over time, the network grew and more services were launched. Muxlim found itself as both a neutral brand for Muslim lifestyle and, increasingly, a data source for trends and consumption within the Muslim consumer market.

Muxlim is now an integrated media company that helps brands understand and market to the US$1 trillion global Muslim lifestyle consumer market using market intelligence, data analysis, and social media.

The company has evolved from its roots in social networking to using its data and expertise to offer social media advisory services in an integrated media approach toward the multicultural consumer. Muxlim has a wide portfolio of clients, including some of the biggest global brands, and a number of strategic partnerships that enforce the company's market leadership. The power of the Muxlim community and the advantage of the Muxlim brand has provided a gateway for mainstream consumer product companies to enter this market. For example, during 2009 and 2010 Muxlim provided services for brands including Vodafone, Wilson Basketball, Lufthansa, and one of the largest publicly listed footwear companies in the US, Brown Shoe Corporation.

Muxlim Inc. has evolved into an integrated marketing company that specializes in helping companies understand and reach the Muslim lifestyle consumer. The company also owns the world's largest Muslim lifestyle network, Muxlim.com, which provides lifestyle content across a number of categories such as news, entertainment, fashion, music, and sports. The company cohesively integrates Muslim lifestyle content and context across multiple platforms, such as web, print, mobile, TV, live events, and so on. and reaches tens of millions of people in 190 countries. The network includes syndicated and user-generated content, branding, branded content, storytelling, advertising, and more. The Muxlim brand is now recognized and trusted as a communication path by both the Muslim lifestyle community and global brands.

With its lifestyle focus, Muxlim is the first company to make this market approachable and attractive to mainstream advertisers, as well as to provide an effective marketing channel to reach the fragmented Muslim lifestyle consumer market. Addressing the Muslim consumer market is part of the wider trend as companies work to attract more consumers to their brand and products through diversity. Since Muxlim reaches a wide range of multicultural markets, the company has also partnered closely with the firm Global Diversity Marketing, based in New York, to offer its expertise across other ethnic and lifestyle segments, including African American, Hispanic, Asian, and women.

Muxlim Inc. is now maximizing opportunities for brands and companies that want to reach this market, having the unique advantage of developing in parallel with this market opportunity. Recently, at the US Presidential Summit on Entrepreneurship, Muxlim Inc. was cited on National Public Radio (NPR) in the US, by Thom Ruhe of the Kauffman Foundation, as the most significant opportunity for US companies to engage with Muslim consumers.[11]

Muxlim has emerged as the unrivalled gateway to the global Muslim lifestyle market. The company continues to further strengthen its market dominance through a diverse product portfolio, market evangelism, brand building, and network growth, providing market access to non-traditional customers at a lower cost with a higher return on investment, and offering integrated media marketing services through Muxlim Advisory. These services are supported and strengthened by the growing Muxlim Network, which includes Muxlim.com and its extended social media reach beyond the Muxlim site itself.

B2B PRODUCTS AND SERVICES: ABCD

Muxlim has four main business-to-business (B2B) product offerings designed for global consumer goods and services companies whose chief marketing officers are at different stages in their effort to reach the multicultural consumer. The products are under a service called Muxlim Advisory (http://advisory.muxlim.com), which helps make strategy and implement social communication with Muslim lifestyle users. The four Muxlim Advisory products are Analyze™, Bridge™, Channel™, and Deliver™ services (ABCD). The company describes these as follows:

- **Analyze™**: Muxlim Advisory Analyze™ is a product targeted at companies researching the lucrative revenue opportunities in the multicultural consumer market. It is a market intelligence and information report that provides strategic options and validation of a company's opportunity within segments such as the Muslim consumer market. Unlike generic high-level reports that don't include any company- or industry-specific customization, this product provides companies with customized market intelligence and strategic options to help them immediately tap into the buying power of the market.

  Product Goal: Understanding the opportunity and steps needed to reach the consumer.

  Product Components: 1. Analyze report. 2. Strategic options analysis. 3. Pilot.

- **Bridge™**: Muxlim Analyze Bridge™ is a product for companies that have realized the importance of growing multicultural markets and need a strategic approach to take advantage of the opportunities. It provides strategic and creative development, resulting in a complete executable marketing solution designed to reach the consumers.

  Product Goal: Helping companies develop specific options and the corresponding strategic plan to address the consumer.

  Product Components: 1. Integrated marketing communications strategy. 2. Social media marketing development. 3. Content development. 4. Execution plan.

- **Channel™**: Muxlim Channel™ provides strategic execution of a company's integrated marketing plan through the best digital and appropriate offline channels. The product is designed to develop and maintain a long-term relationship with the multicultural customer while maximizing advertising opportunities across all planned media. Data and reporting are critical mechanisms that provide the information used to instantly recognize trends and constantly tailor messages and content to the customer's needs. Social media provides the core components for word-of-mouth sharing of content, brand messages, and associated advertising.

  Product Goal: Helping brands develop product and brand loyalty among multicultural consumers through social media engagement, digital media, and traditional channels.

  Product Components: 1. Distribution. 2. Channel management. 3. Reporting. 4. Evaluation.

- **Diagnose™**: Muxlim Diagnose™ is a product designed to help companies monitor their marketing investment, channel growth, and digital campaign performance across the Web. It uses online diagnostic tools to examine trends, results, and conversations that help grow and build better engagement with multicultural customers. It also provides baseline and return on investment (ROI), while defining customer acquisition and retention cost.

  Product Goal: Provide feedback from across the Web; used for constantly improving marketing efforts toward multicultural customers.

  Product Components: 1. Campaign report. 2. Brand- and industry-specific trend report. 3. Expert analysis.

In addition to the B2B products offered, Muxlim also has a business-to-consumer (B2C) capability with Muxlim.com.

B2C PRODUCTS AND SERVICES: MUXLIM.COM

Muxlim is a big player in the B2C marketplace through Muxlim. com, a lifestyle content-centric social media website. It is designed to give individuals and companies the ability to share information, with content activities including viewing, sharing, commenting, voting, and more. Companies and professional publishers are given special customization features and extended publishing services to gain loyalty for their content or brand. (Muxlim.com becomes B2B in measuring trends and being a place where a company can pay to provide value-added content, and by being an advertising platform.)

■ ■ ■

Muxlim has reacted very quickly to the increasing reach of social media in the lives of Muslims and has gained a first mover advantage as a result. By providing a crucial link between brands and consumers, it occupies a leading role in all three areas of B2B, B2C, and customer-to-customer (C2C) marketing.

MARKET LEADERSHIP AND AWARDS

As a consequence of its speed and innovation, Muxlim has won numerous awards, including:

- 2009 Internationalization Awards of the President of Finland Tarja Halonen;
- Nordic Winner of Grand One Best Startup, SIME Rising Stars of the North;
- Helsinki MIT Entrepreneurial Marketing Competition Winner;
- UK Trade & Investment Nordic Business Award Finalist;
- The official Finland Nominee to the World Summit Awards;
- Muxlim CEO named among the world's "500 Most Influential Muslims" (2009 and 2010) by The Royal Islamic Strategic Studies Center & Georgetown University;
- Muxlim CEO named among Finland's "Sampo Laureates," an award given to 10 innovators under the age of 29, every 100 years;
- Muxlim CEO named among 200 business leaders invited to the "Presidential Summit on Entreprenuership";
- Muxlim CEO named "Business Man of the Month," January 2011, by NewzGlobe; and
- Muxlim CEO named among *Chief Executive* magazine's "Leaders of Tomorrow," the youngest leader on the list.

Muxlim has carried out some interesting work in helping other brands, including non-Muslim companies, to interact with the Muslim population in their countries, and to grow their business in this important segment. Case Study 12 examines how Muxlim helped Wilson, the American global brand and sporting goods producer.

CASE STUDY 12: MUXLIM INC.: II

Muxlim Helps Western Brand Wilson Basketball Find and Engage Muslim Consumers

WILSON BASKETBALL TAPS INTO A HIDDEN NEW CUSTOMER MARKET

Mike Kuehne, general manager—Wilson Team Sports, Basketball, Soccer & Volleyball, commented:

> We are interested in the market potential that could be realized by connecting with basketball players and parents in the Muxlim.com *online community. Wilson's goal is to connect with people who really play the game and provide them with the best equipment for their sport. Today, we are using more and more social media to take our already solid relationships with teams and players and digitally extend that loyalty. Muxlim.com, Facebook and Twitter are just a few of those places we are extending our reach.*

Wilson is the world's leading manufacturer of sporting goods equipment. Wilson's sporting focuses are tennis, baseball, American football, golf, basketball, softball, badminton, and squash. As a global brand, Wilson enjoys strong distribution and channel relationships. The company was incorporated in 1913 as Ashland Manufacturing Company, and is now a fully owned subsidiary of Finland-based Amer Sports. Headquartered in Chicago, in the US, Wilson employed 1,919 people at the end of 2006, and serves customers in over 100 countries. Its business is structured into three areas: racquet sports, team sports, and golf.

In early 2010, Wilson Basketball launched a campaign called the "Dream Team" on Muxlim.com. The campaign focused on understanding, participating in, and observing trends in online conversations about basketball within the community across the Internet. The result not only provided valuable information about how to reach this lucrative potential market, but also had the effect of raising the percentage of "share of voice" for the Wilson brand of online communication among Muslim consumers interested in basketball.

CHALLENGE

Like most consumer brand companies in recessionary times, Wilson Team Sports was looking for more customers both around the globe and within the US, their main market. They were also very new at using social media to complement their business, with less-than-desired success from their Facebook and other online efforts. They decided to look into multicultural and lifestyle markets to see if they could find a way to draw new consumers and loyalty to their products. A pitch from Muxlim Inc. caught their interest as a low-cost and low-risk opportunity to approach a high-value multicultural consumer segment: The Muslim Lifestyle consumer.

SOLUTION

Muxlim Inc. first took two months to examine, analyze, and report on the market revenue potential of the Muslim community in the area of sports and recreation. The study estimated that Muslim consumers spend hundreds of millions of dollars (exact numbers are kept confidential by Wilson) on sporting equipment every year as individuals and organizations dedicated to sport within the community. It also found that in a survey of millions of Internet sites, including blogs, Facebook posts, Tweets, and other online media, within the context of basketball, the online "share of voice," or mentions of Wilson in the context of basketball, was 0.016 percent for the month preceding the "Dream Team" campaign. The best brand performance was Nike at 2.76 percent. Overall, the total untapped conversations online (with no brand mentions) were over 95 percent.

Muxlim then used this data to create and deliver a campaign specifically designed not only to build awareness of the Wilson brand, but also to catalyze engagement from the ground up.

The campaign was designed to be the first in a three-step process of engagement to add real value to potential customers' online experience:

1. Associate with content and activities that the users currently engage with.
2. Provide information, services, or entertainment that are original and turn the brand into the "go to" resource for a particular need or opportunity.
3. Become the one they talk about in their own conversations, due to successful content, services, and the establishment of ongoing dialog with key customer influencers.

The "Dream Team" project didn't try to push Wilson's advertising messages to the customer directly. It was specifically not religious in tone or action. The campaign focused on celebrating stories about Muslims playing in the NCAA basketball tournament and around the league as news. The Wilson brand was seen with each post and share of the post to other networks such as Facebook. During the month of the initial campaign, it started to become the easy place to find where the often-buried stories about Muslim players were being highlighted. It became a positive destination for Muslim basketball lovers who both play and watch the game.

Posts of different types (including video, blogs, and polls) were created. Some posts contained generic reporting, and others had Muslim-specific highlights, such as Muslim players who had contributed in a win. As expected, posts with Muslim references received sometimes 20 times more views than generic items.

Most exciting among the results was an increase in "share of voice" for the Wilson brand to 3.82 percent in one month. Muxlim operated as a launch pad for the content, but most of this increase was seen in sharing of the articles across networks and among friends on Facebook and Twitter.

As with any relationship, Wilson will need to continue to engage with the community in order to continue to influence and be a part of the conversation. All the gains won in the project can also be lost without continuous engagement with the community and regular management based on analytics. The next phase of the project will be to move to directly creating content, such as player profiles, schools that promote diversity, or videos that highlight positive sports activities or contributors. The project has also prepared the appetite for on-the-ground marketing, advertising, and sales at events and through organizational leadership.

Source: Information provided by Stephen Lee, chief operating officer of Muxlim Inc. Helsinki, Finland; http://advisory.muxlim.com. Case reproduced with permission of Muxlim Inc.

This case is a somewhat unique and good example of how a Western brand was assisted by a Muslim brand in order to understand and connect with the Muslim-minority market.

Other Internet Brands

In addition to Muxlim.com, there are other examples of Islamic Internet brands that have done well in this fast-growing market. These include Yahoo Maktoob and Naseem.com. Both brands are described briefly below.

Yahoo Maktoob

Maktoob.com was founded in 2000 by Samih Toukan and Hussam Khoury as the world's first free Arabic/English web-based email service. It has since grown to be the leading online community in the Arab region. According to ComScore (a global leader in measuring the digital world and the preferred source of digital marketing intelligence), Maktoob has seen very impressive growth: 21.8 million unique visitors in June 2009, up from 6 million in June 2008. Its page views have grown in number from 406 million to 1.1 billion over the same time frame.

In August 2009, Yahoo! announced that it had entered into a definitive agreement to acquire Maktoob.com, which at that time had more than 16.5 million unique users. "This acquisition will accelerate Yahoo!'s strategy of expanding in high-growth emerging markets where we believe Yahoo! has unparalleled opportunity to become the destination of choice for consumers," said Yahoo! CEO Carol Bartz.

Instead of expanding its current portal with Arabic content and features, Yahoo! felt that acquiring Maktoob.com was a better option. The acquisition would enable Yahoo! to leverage on the brand name and equity of Maktoob, which had developed an affinity and familiarity with its user base in the Middle East. On this basis, Yahoo! decided to use a sub-branding approach to integrating the Maktoob brand into its own brand, as shown below.

Yahoo! initiated this strategic move in a bid to fill what it perceived as a significant gap in the web portal space with Arabic content that caters to an Arabic-speaking audience. While Internet usage in the Middle East has grown more than 10-fold since 2000, most markets are still in the early stages of adoption. According to the World Bank, there are more than 320 million Arabic speakers worldwide, while less than 1 percent of all online content is in Arabic.

Naseeb.com

Naseeb.com is a Muslim social network service—similar to Friendster.com or Facebook—that allows Muslims around the world to interact for reasons such as sharing views, finding a soul mate or activity partners, or establish-ing friendships with individuals they may encounter on the website.

Naseeb.com has also introduced *Naseebvibes*, an online magazine (e-zine) that features interviews with over 500 influential Muslim figures, including Islamic scholars such as Imam Faisal Rauf, Dr. M. Nejatullah Siddiqi, Dr. Javed Ghamidi, and Omid Safi, and other renowned figures in the Muslim world.

It is clear that the Internet is providing many opportunities for digital Islamic brands, but does this mean that the traditional forms of media are on the decline? This doesn't appear to be the case.

Opportunities in Traditional Media

Muslims have the same access as people in any country to the traditional media, such as news, television, and radio. However, often there is insuffi-cient local content, as people seek to explore new offerings and, in particu-lar, content to do with lifestyles that are relevant to them.

Given the huge growth of digital media, does this mean that there are no opportunities for Islamic brands in traditional media? In a word: no. Opportunities still abound, as this has been a relatively unexplored mar-ket, and people still rely a great deal on traditional ways of receiving news and communications. Thus, there is still a need for traditional channels to provide television and print media to Muslim audiences, as the cases below reveal.

Television

Up until the 1990s, most TV channels in Muslim-majority countries were state-owned monopolies with limited reach outside their native country. In the GCC countries, where the audiences are both Muslim nationals and expatriates from diverse backgrounds, terrestrial channels operated by the government were predominant, where the local English channels showed Western programs and the Arabic channels produced local content. Since 1991, however, the liberalization of broadcasting rules and the proliferation of media zones has led to the explosive growth of free-to-air (FTA) and subscription-based TV channels.

Privately owned satellite channels include MBC, a pan-Arab FTA channel that went to air in 1991, followed by Future TV in 1995, Al-Jazeera in 1996, Al Manar in 2000, Zayn TV and Dream TV in 2001, and Al Arabiya in 2003.

According to researchers Arab Advisors Group, there are now more than 470 FTA channels in the Arab world alone. Mazen Hayek, MBC's group director of marketing, says that TV is extremely popular with an average consumption of four hours a day and a satellite penetration exceeding 95 percent. For marketers interested in the *halal* consumer, mainstream channels such as MBC offer a large audience, although not an exclusively Muslim one. "Clearly, we are living in the heart of the marketing segmentation and customization era, but when we talk about Muslims in the Arab world, the mainstream approach [is] the norm, with few exceptions when it comes to non-Muslim Arabs or expats," says Hayek. "The *halal* lifestyle is a given in the Arab world. . . . Being culturally relevant and sensitive to tradition is key—at all times."

Regional TV programming has created many choices for marketers. There are opportunities to broadcast the *halal* lifestyle to more liberal-minded audiences, such as those tuning into the Al Resala channel and the 4Shabab "Islamic" music channel; as well as to the more orthodox channels that don't accept any advertising, such as the Al Majd channels in Saudi Arabia; and to others that don't air programs or accept ads that contain music. Advertisers wishing to reach the audience served by Al Majd need to adhere to the channel's Islamic guidelines, which don't allow music or female models but do allow natural sounds and female voiceovers. Advertisers whose music-free "*halal*" ads can be seen on Al Majd channels include General Motors, Kraft, P&G, Reckitt Benckiser, and Unilever.

Although there are now hundreds of Arabic channels, the Arab world represents only 20 percent of the world's total Muslim population. New TV channels targeting specific Muslim ethnic segments are being set up, opening new avenues for marketers to consider.[12] One Islamic channel that produces its own content and enjoys a strong viewership and good advertiser support is London-based Islam Channel (see Case Study 13).

CASE STUDY 13: ISLAM CHANNEL

With headquarters in Central London, Islam Channel provides alternative news, current affairs, and entertainment programming from an Islamic perspective. Since its launch in 2004, Islam Channel has developed into a platform for ingenious and practical television. Broadcast in English, Islam Channel aims for its programming to appeal to both Muslims and non-Muslims, conveying Islam in its true form to curious non-Muslims and to further educate Muslims. Consequently, it has established itself as the leading 24-hour, FTA, English-language, Islamic-focused satellite channel available globally in 132 countries. In the UK, Islam Channel is available on SKY Channel 813. It can also be viewed on its website, www.islamchannel.tv.

Islam Channel aims to be "an informative channel and to abolish misconceptions about Islam with the aspiration to portray Islam in its true form through a vital tool that sits in almost everyone's living room." It has a religious-sounding name but represents a growing trend among broadcasters to Muslims, including conventional theological and religious content mixed with varied lifestyle programming.

Its programming covers a wide range of topics appealing to many different types of audience, covering religious education, children's programs, a women's issues program called "City Sisters," news, politics (featuring debates from the British Parliament), and legal and health shows. The hot spots for paid sponsorship, however, are the five calls to prayer broadcasted daily—*Fajr, Zuhr, Asr, Maghrib*, and *Isha*—and thousands of viewers tune in to Islam Channel at these times.

Islam Channel has gained a great deal of reputational support for conforming to international standards and quality, having gained certificates and accreditation from the Institute of Directors, Commonwealth Broadcasting Association, and The Association of International Broadcasting.

With television media, it looks like any other sector of any *halal* industry, serving a global Muslim market that shares common values and the *halal* lifestyle, and it is increasingly gaining the attention of the world's top brands. It seems certain that television will continue to offer and reflect the *halal* lifestyle in a variety of ways.

Source: www.Islamchannel.tv.

Another excellent example of a company that has seized an opportunity in the Muslim media industry is *emel*, the UK Muslim Lifestyle magazine.

CASE STUDY 14: *EMEL*

The Muslim Lifestyle Magazine

emel, the Muslim Lifestyle magazine, was envisioned in 1999 and brought to realization by its founders, Mahmud Al-Rashid and Sarah Joseph, in 2003. The brand was the first to form and articulate the concept of *Muslim Lifestyle*, and its name is derived from that concept—M (*em*) and L (*el*) = *Muslim Lifestyle*. The word "*emel*" has its roots in the Arabic and Turkish language and means "hope" and "aspiration." Since its inception, the brand has attempted to articulate the broad and varied hopes and aspirations of Muslims.

The recognition by Mahmud and Sarah—husband and wife—that Muslims don't spend their time talking just about religious dogma or politics was counter-intuitive to the two-dimensional presentations of Muslims within mainstream media. Simultaneously, within the Muslim communities the desire for a normalized imagery and narrative of Muslim lifestyles meant that the brand sparked huge excitement. This positive community reception was matched by media coverage from the likes of BBC World and CNN, and although *emel* is a UK-based brand, this international attention meant that it quickly gained global exposure.

When *emel* was launched in September 2003, there was almost no marketing activity directed toward Muslims outside of the Muslim-majority countries, bar some small-scale government or health messaging. *emel* was one of the first media packs to be put together that focused on data pertaining to Muslims. Sarah Joseph, *emel*'s editor and CEO, puts it thus:

> Up until emel, *Muslims outside of Muslim-majority countries were not being marketed to on account of their lifestyle choices based on their faith. This was bizarre because all research that we conducted*

*showed that faith-based lifestyle was the single biggest influence on
their lives and impacted far more than just prayer and politics. If
you're teetotal as a lifestyle choice it makes sense that soft drinks
companies should be beating a trail to your door; but in 2003 that
was just not happening.*

Advertisers in *emel* now include the likes of Shloer, British Airways,
HSBC, Malaysia Tourism, BMW, and Mercedes.

emel was launched as a bi-monthly magazine, but by 2005 readership
surveys showed the desire for greater frequency. In September 2005, the
magazine went monthly and mainstream, becoming the first Muslim
publication to be available through mainstream newsagents and
supermarkets, including the large retailers such as W.H. Smith, Borders,
Tesco, and ASDA. Media coverage around the mainstream launch of
emel again generated global coverage and further consolidated *emel's*
brand strength, as well as its global reach. The media coverage included
features in *The Times, Sunday Times, Wall Street Journal,* and *London
Evening Standard,* and in leading Turkish, Malaysian, Dutch, Swiss,
Iranian, and Japanese newspapers. While still focusing its attention
on the UK, *emel* now has distribution in the US, Middle East, and
Southeast Asia. In addition, it has subscribers in over 60 countries.

Sarah Joseph believes that the brand has benefitted from the
increasing recognition of the Muslim market, but feels that marketers
have still not quite got it: "Messaging has to reflect the community
you're trying to market to. There is no point just buying space." Joseph
is concerned that it is too easy for those in the Muslim media to take the
advertisement and say nothing about inappropriate campaigns. "This
will be detrimental to the long-term health of the industry," she says.

*Marketers have to think through their campaigns. How is your
message going to be received by the end consumer? We say to our
clients, "It's our responsibility as a brand which has spent years
getting to know that consumer to take you through that journey." We
don't just want an advertisement; we want marketers to ENGAGE
with the end consumer.*

With readers from Royalty and Downing Street to schools and media pundits, *emel* is reaching way beyond the Muslim community and taking the Muslim community to the mainstream. The magazine has had an outstanding beginning. The Oxford University academic Timothy Garton Ash wrote in the *Guardian* that *emel* "not only informs wider society about Muslims, but also makes a point about wider society itself." Joseph feels this enhances, rather than dilutes, its position as a Muslim market brand leader. "The Muslim market is complex. It's engaging with the mainstream, but the question has to be, 'Is the Muslim market engaged BY the mainstream?' And we don't think it is."

While some Muslim brands have chosen to say the Muslim market is whatever Muslims decide it is, Joseph is more circumspect. "Muslim Lifestyle doesn't exist in a vacuum. It has values, and it would be foolish and counterproductive to ignore those. Rather, I think that a sensible marketer will take the lead by highlighting those values." For Joseph, it's important that ethical, organic, free-range, environmentally friendly products make it to the Muslim marketplace.

> There is tremendous synergy between what I call the Green Pound/Dollar—namely, the Muslim market—and what others call the Green Pound/Dollar—namely, the Environmentally Aware Market. Over 75 percent of those we surveyed had strong connections to environmentally friendly products. I think the marketers who highlight best practice in areas such as the environment and CSR will have the edge in the Muslim marketplace.

Joseph is also keen to point out not just the complexity of the market, but also its seeming contradictions.

> You have people driving £80,000 cars and walking round with £1,000 handbags, but they live within the community and shop in Tesco. When you really get to know the market you recognize that these things are not contradictory—they're pragmatic.

In 2009, *emel* launched its online brand, emel.com. It had only had a small brochure site up until this point. Given that all the content for the magazine is produced by *emel*, emel.com is content rich. It also gives the *emel* brand an opportunity to create media other than just print. emel.com has given value-added content to the magazine. They have begun making short films, which are then picked up by the social network sites. Indeed, the social networks of Twitter and Facebook have become tools to engage the reader in an extended conversation. "Magazines, unlike newspapers, fall almost within the inner circle of trust for consumers. Facebook falls within that inner circle. When people engage with the *emel* brand via the social network sites, they do so as friends, not simply as fans," says Joseph.

emel's content is diverse, catering to every segment of the concept of Muslim Lifestyle. It has features, a comment section, and big-name interviews—interviewing personalities such as David Cameron and the Archbishop of Canterbury (making global headlines with the latter). A "Life Forum" section covers health, the environment, finance, ethics, and education. The very popular "Real Lives" section contains first person accounts of marriage, relationships, trials and tribulations, as well as humorous diaries. However, the most popular section deals with lifestyle: food, fashion, gardening, travel, gadgets, and motoring—all with a Muslim twist. "It's more than just a *hijab* here and a piece of calligraphy there," Joseph cautions. "It's a lot more profound than just that. The lifestyle is about drawing on a rich history and culture and translating that for a contemporary Western Muslim Lifestyle. That's no mean feat."

In the summer of 2009, *emel* launched *embox*, a Muslim Lifestyle proposition geared toward the student market. While the target market for *emel* is 25- to 40-year-old professionals, *embox* targets the 18- to 24-year-old student segment. The Muslim demographic makes *embox* "an obvious brand extension," says Joseph. And given that 1 in 10 further education students in the UK is a Muslim, and that 50 percent of Muslims in the UK are under 25, she is probably right. *embox* is distributed free, unlike *emel* which is paid for. Although 72 percent of students surveyed said they would pay for *embox*, it is not looking to change the free distribution model at the present time.

Joseph has a number of plans in the pipeline for other *emel* brand extensions, but she is not giving too much away just yet. "The Muslim Lifestyle Market has a long way to go," she says. "*emel* created the concept of Muslim Lifestyle, and we want to take it all the way to its maximum potential."

Source: Sarah Joseph and *emel*.

emel is an example of a successful Muslim-focused, traditional-format lifestyle publication produced in a Muslim-minority country. Another example is Singapore-published *Aquila* (which means "sensible and intelligent" in Arabic).

CASE STUDY 15: AQUILA

Aquila, a bi-monthly women's magazine, was launched in 2010 by founder and publisher Liana Rosnita Redwan-Beer. It was the first Asian magazine to cater to young, educated Muslim women with a worldly outlook who also want to remain true to their faith. "Modest and fabulous" is the magazine's strap line. In competing against many women's magazines across the Middle East and Asia, *Aquila*'s point of differentiation is that it is published in English and targets women who would normally read Western-style staples such as *Cosmopolitan*, *Vogue*, and *Marie Claire*, but who really want something that covers topics that are more relevant to them and their Islamic values.

"This is a magazine for someone like me, like my sisters, women who have careers, who wear suits, jeans, gladiator sandals, who may or may not wear the *hijab* headscarf, who may or may not look like what a Muslim women is supposed to look like, but who are very much Muslims," said Redwan-Beer, a Singaporean now based in Indonesia, the world's most populous Muslim nation, in an interview with Reuters.

"We're not a magazine that preaches. We don't tell our readers what is right or wrong; but we help them live their lives to the fullest by including information about Islam in the context of modern living," Redwan-Beer said. The idea for the magazine came after her husband asked her why there wasn't a publication for modern Muslims like her.

"We looked into potential markets and we asked all our friends in Europe, Asia, and around the world to see if there was a similar venture. We came up with nothing," she said.

The first issue of the magazine was published in March 2010 in the Muslim-majority countries of Malaysia, Indonesia, and Brunei, as well as in Muslim-minority Singapore. Feedback has evidently been positive, although readership will take time to build.

A MIXTURE OF OLD AND NEW

Aquila is not just going to rely on print media, and is covering a mixture of content that is both modern and driven by Islamic values. For example, it doesn't accept advertisements from businesses considered "*haram*," or unlawful, such as wine and beer firms, and articles on travel include a list of *halal* restaurants and mosques. It also has a page on Facebook which is receiving many posts from Europe and Asia and expects to strengthen its online presence.

The content in the first issue also reflects both a conservative and more modern mix of topics. A fashion section featured a heavily made-up model in tight-fitting clothes with a headscarf that still shows off a lot of her hair; another featured the all-covering burqini swimsuit. There was an article on premarital sex and virginity, and an opinion piece on what to do if your daughter dates a non-Muslim.

This might be considered by some Muslims to be a little on the edge of respectability, but Redwan-Beer says that this type of content is found in most women's magazines, and emphasizes that religious references are checked by a Singapore-based Muslim cleric and legislator. "What we're doing is not bold; it's no more daring than any other women's magazines out there. We're just tending to the needs of Muslims. We talk in the language of cosmopolitan Muslims. If we happen to be able to explain, or educate, a little bit about Islam or Muslims, we think that's cool," she said.

Source: Miral Fahmy, April 22, 2010, http://in.reuters.com/.

Summary

The Muslim media world is open for business and represents almost a blank canvas of opportunities for Islamic and non-Islamic companies. The future is digital and first mover advantage is on offer. There will be many more brands such as Muxlim.com that will give 1.57 billion Muslims a values-driven choice that fits with their needs. As the youth proportion of the total Muslim population continues to grow, this will provide even more opportunities in the next few decades.

Digital media has enabled the most fragmented of markets to be crafted into lucrative opportunities, including the Muslim consumer market. The world is rapidly becoming digital, and nearly 25 percent of the world's population is Muslim. Since Muslim consumers have not previously been strategically engaged, brands can build loyalty and gain competitive advantage within this emerging market by utilizing the emotional powers of digital media. They can easily become the clear choice for Muslim consumers in their own segment by taking the lead within this market.

Despite the rising power of digital brands, Muslim markets still hold many opportunities for more traditional media brands, and so the broad media category is likely to grow extremely quickly over the next 10 years.

In the next chapter, I will review some of the challenges that Islamic brands face when reaching out to new markets and striving for success.

Notes

1. "It Feels Funny When Brands Say, 'I Love You!'," unpublished paper by Stephen Lee, COO of Muxlim Inc., 2010; and "A Digital Media Approach to Islamic Marketing," unpublished article by Mohamed El-Fatatry, Tariq Khan, Stephen Lee, and Violi Lehdonvirta, 2010.
2. www.millwardbrown.com/mboptimor.
3. http://gmj.gallup.com/content/12232/can-advertising-still-contribute. aspx.
4. http://blogs.wsj.com/digits/2010/03/15/web-users-take-dim-view-of-paywalls-study-confirms/.
5. www.jmorganmarketing.com/do-companies-have-control-over-their-brands/.
6. www.avc.com/a_vc/2009/04/earning-your-media.html.
7. http://moblogsmoproblems.blogspot.com/2009/03/being-successful-with-social-media.html.

8. www.marketingpilgrim.com/2008/03/successful-social-media-marketing-requires-personal-involvement.html.

9. "What Social Media Can Learn from Multicultural Marketing," http://adage.com/bigtent/post?article_id=138864.

10. "Halal McNuggets a Hit in Detroit. Sales are so Good, McDonald's Expands the Idea to Other Restaurants," http://islam.about.com/od/dietarylaw/a/halalmcd.htm.

11. http://marketplace.publicradio.org/display/web/2010/04/26/am-us-promotes-muslim-entrepreneurship/.

12. Farruk Naeem, "The Rise of 'Halal' TV," *Gulf Marketing Review*, March 31, 2010.

8 Challenges Facing Islamic Brands

Introduction

It is worthwhile to remember that, while the overall Muslim global market is huge, it is not a homogeneous market in its behavior. As illustrated in Chapter 3, there are both similarities and differences in practically every country where Muslims live.

What this means is that any brand wishing to serve multiple Muslim markets cannot rely on one brand strategy. Arising from these variations in markets are some specific challenges that need to be dealt with in formulating multiple marketing strategies. Before we move on to consider the strategies that are available, we will look at the main challenges facing Islamic companies wishing to acquire a good foothold in both Muslim and non-Muslim markets and to build strong brands.

Key Challenges for Aspiring Muslim Brands: The Six A's

Islamic brands attempting to break into and progressively gain a share in their chosen markets, especially where Western brands are already in dominant positions, will have to overcome a variety of challenges, the most important of which fall into six main areas:

1. **Awareness**: Gaining brand awareness
2. **Accessibility**: Ensuring accessibility
3. **Acceptability**: Gaining acceptability
4. **Adequacy**: Achieving suitable and consistent standards and quality
5. **Affinity**: Gaining trust
6. **Attack**: Attack from brand competitors

Gaining Brand Awareness

One of the most fundamental obstacles to the growth of Islamic brands is achieving brand awareness when entering already crowded markets dominated by other, often Western, brands, especially if the product category isn't targeted specifically at Muslim audiences. In particular, there are strategic questions that must be answered, such as: How can a breakthrough be achieved in terms of consumer trial, purchase, and preference when there is already some loyalty toward existing established brands?

This is no easy task, and even existing players may face difficulties if there is a powerful leader of the pack, which often happens in consumer markets. For example, in the sports shoes and apparel market, Nike has around a 40 percent global market share, with Adidas and the others falling way behind. Similarly, in the global mobile phone market, Nokia for many years enjoyed a nearly 40 percent market share annually, and even the nearest competitors—such as Samsung and LG—struggled to keep anywhere near the leader, while former leaders and well-known brands such as Motorola now have a very small piece of the market. This is a major issue for any brand that is not well known.

It is a daunting task to gain awareness and entry into such markets, but it can be done. For example, although not an Islamic brand, in around 10 years HTC has transformed itself from an OEM (Original Equipment Manufacturer) of mobile phones into a fast-growing global brand with revenues in excess of US$3 billion in 2008. It hasn't lost its OEM business either, as it now makes essential elements of Nexus One, Google's new smartphone. Also, Apple and Blackberry are brand names that have taken advantage of Nokia's inability to keep up with new technologies and have rapidly taken market share.

The media provides a good example of how a niche market can be created without directly challenging the global giants. While CNN is probably the world leader in news, followed by the BBC, Al-Jazeera is well on its way to becoming a global brand, targeted at Muslim audiences and people who want a different view of news about the Muslim world and world news from a different, and not necessarily Muslim perspective. Cleverly, Al-Jazeera has a good strategy that downplays its Islamic heritage and adopts a very Western style of global news presentation. It employs some well-known former Western news anchors and presenters to gain the attention of global audiences and avoid Islamic stereotyping. In just a few years it has grown in stature and respect. The lesson here is that there is always room for an alternative choice, but not *too many* alternative choices. Al-Jazeera has provided such a choice, not just for the Arabic-speaking population; it also broadcasts its programs in English for anyone in the Muslim and non-Muslim world who wants a different choice, providing all the news and sports items that the global media need to offer to global citizens.

Ensuring Accessibility

A second challenge to Islamic companies wishing to build their brands is the issue of how to gain access in these sometimes crowded markets. In order to become successful as an international brand, especially in fast-moving consumer and retail goods, it is important to get critical mass in terms of distribution. In established markets, this can be difficult. For example, gaining shelf space in supermarkets in major cities is tremendously difficult for smaller brands, where the major players dominate consumer "eyeballs." This is the case even in major categories, as we can see in the United States where *halal* food products are outnumbered by *kosher* products in supermarkets by a ratio of 86:1. As a consequence, 16 percent of Muslims in the US buy *kosher* foods, as they cannot gain access to their preferred *halal* products. And in other Muslim-minority markets such as the United Kingdom and France, *halal* food brands have difficulty getting the shelf space in large retailers such as Tesco, Asda, and Carrefour.

Therefore, gaining a foothold in the market requires not just a broad range of products with mass appeal to consumers, but, most importantly, the capability to distribute the brand and make it accessible to consumers.

There are two ways to solve this problem: first, create an alliance or strategic partnership with the big retailers, as several companies have done with Tesco in countries such as Malaysia; and second, go for a niche target market with carefully planned distribution to avoid competing against the established brands, and perhaps tempt them into giving you space once you have made a market impact, as shown in the case study on Ummah Foods in the next chapter.

Gaining Acceptability

Many factors impinge on a brand's acceptability by consumers, not the least of which is its country of origin. In the absence of powerful branding, consumers are very risk-averse, and don't like to buy products from countries about which they have any doubts or prejudices. This is the "Made in China" quality syndrome, where the truth or otherwise of the perceived poor quality of Chinese-made products is irrelevant; in the world of branding, *perception is reality.*

Prejudice against a brand that might be perceived as being from an "Islamic" country can take many forms. For example, companies that try to penetrate the US market under a "Made in Iran" label may not find this too helpful in marketing their products, whereas a "Made in Malaysia" product may not come up against such barriers. Conversely, a "Made in Iran" label marketed in a Muslim country that is more orthodox or conservative, such as Yemen or Afghanistan, may be just as acceptable or even more so than a product from Malaysia.

The issue here isn't so much about religion; it is about how the country from which a brand originates is perceived. What are the mental associations for the consumer when a product is associated with a particular country? Brand owners have to decide whether to play up—or play down—the country of origin, and market research can be particularly useful in determining what associations the country of origin will have that will transfer to the image of the brand.

However, even a negative nation brand effect can be successfully overcome. For example, Haier, the second-largest white goods manufacturer in the world, disposed of the "Made in China" issue by setting up a factory in the US and producing goods labelled "Made in USA." It employed American workers and operated just as an American company would do, and so it was never viewed by the public as a Chinese company. It won many awards and even had a street in America named after it! Toyota employed the same strategy with its Lexus brand to avoid being associated with the mid- to low-level image of the Japanese parent company, with no mention of any links with Toyota USA.

Thus, care should be taken to understand how the market feels about the country of origin of your brand, and whether attaching this association to your brand is likely to have any positive or negative benefits for short- and long-term brand and market development.

Complete avoidance of any links to the country of origin is one strategy that has proved to be successful if executed well in international markets. Another positive strategy that can be used by Islamic brands is to attract non-Muslim audiences through careful use of brand communications. In the case of *halal* food, educational communications might be one way to persuade people of the health benefits of *halal* products, as mentioned under "Educating Consumers" in the next section.

Finally, many Islamic companies may want to attract both Muslim and non-Muslim audiences, and so will have to be very selective in the way they build their brands (especially with respect to the values they use and how these are communicated) and in the messages they project. This comes down to skillful brand and market communications, which can deliver key messages that can be seen as relevant to either or both Muslim and non-Muslim consumers. This topic will be discussed in more detail in the next chapter. However, all of the aforementioned necessities for developing a strong Islamic brand will be of little use if the brand is inadequate.

Achieving Suitable and Consistent Standards and Quality (Adequacy)

By "adequacy," I mean the capability of a company to produce branded products and services that are of top quality and are acceptable to those markets where they intend to sell them. It is impossible to build and sustain a strong brand in the absence of a top-class product and service quality. There are no exceptions to this rule. Making products of lesser quality than those of your competitors, or that give users a disappointing experience, will prevent your brand becoming a power brand and may even threaten the survival of your business in the medium to long run. If you want to do well in *halal* markets, you have to ensure that you have the correct accreditation in place from the relevant authorities.

The issue of *halal* accreditation and quality standards is worth commenting on again briefly here. Despite much government support, many Muslim companies don't make it to the international stage because they satisfy only the local part of the criteria—the accreditation side. But even this can pose problems, as there is no one globally acknowledged accreditation system. As a consequence, some *halal*-accredited brands are not accepted in other Muslim countries that have their own accreditation systems with different standards. Further, whatever *halal* accreditation a brand has obtained, this will not enable it to reach some developed markets where the quality standards are high. In other words, *halal* accreditiation in many countries doesn't link into quality standards.

Halal *Standards*

The *halal* accreditation standardization issue has been debated intensely over many years, but the differing standards between countries remain. This situation makes it difficult for any player to be a global or multinational leader in *halal* foods. The need to standardize accreditation—and labeling, in particular—is agreed at all the usual *halal* forums and conferences, but the Organization of the Islamic Conference (OIC) countries never seem to be able to agree on what the standards should be. Leaving this larger issue aside, one of the most worrying things is that some Muslim countries that aspire to be leaders in the global *halal* market have industries with their own accreditation standards in place, but they don't align this with quality standards, so product quality is inadequate. I know of several instances where companies have received the local *halal* accreditation standards and recognition in their own country, but cannot export their products to the European Union, or indeed to other Muslim countries, because they don't meet the necessary quality and *halal* standards. So, from a Muslim-to-Muslim marketing perspective, having an accepted *halal* brand is important; but from a Muslim-to-non-Muslim marketing perspective, top quality is an additional imperative.

The IHI (International Integrity Alliance) has been set up to establish common accreditation standards, but it has not yet succeeded in doing so. As its website says:

> The International Halal Integrity Alliance ("IHI Alliance") is an international non-profit organization created to uphold the integrity of the halal *market concept in global trade through certification, collaboration and membership. One of its reasons for existence is that at present, the global* halal *industry is devoid of a significant non-government organization (NGO) presence or position that can provide accreditation to certification bodies. The main reason for this is the absence of a constructive platform for the industries to communicate and network. The absence of a credible reference center for information has resulted in industries and*

> *consumers being bombarded with various interpretations of the meaning and application of halal which often contradict each other. Initial feedback has indicated that there is a significant need for a neutral platform established based on studies carried out worldwide. It was against this backdrop that the IHI Alliance was formed.*[1]

Well, let's hope it succeeds, because it is my view that everyone would be better off if this goal was achieved.

In addition to achieving the right accreditation logos to go on packaging, and so on, if the aim of a brand is to enter Muslim-minority markets where there is an opportunity also to attract non-Muslims, then it is also necessary to educate consumers as to what *halal* actually means.

Educating Consumers

Educating consumers about what *halal* means is also a challenge. Here companies have a dilemma. On the one hand, if they want to reach out to non-Muslim consumers they have to explain what *halal* is. On the other hand, consumers may have misgivings if the concept isn't explained properly. For example, interest groups such as animal rights activists may have misgivings about required methods of slaughter. However, *halal* food is very wholesome and healthy, and could reach wellness-oriented consumers if the concept is communicated in the right way. In fact, it is very similar to *kosher* food—as mentioned, Muslims will eat *kosher* food if *halal* food is not available—and there has never been an issue with *kosher* food generally, so *halal* food brand managers may be able to learn something from this category. They will also learn something from looking at the large retailers in the West who have a presence in some Muslim-majority and minority countries; for example, Tesco is highly skilled at managing food brands from all sources, including ethnic foods.

One implication for brand communications is to keep the *halal* profile low and the brand profile high. By so doing, Muslims who are looking for *halal* accreditation can see a *halal* certification logo in small print on the back of the packaging, and non-Muslims can see the brand more upfront and brand messaging that highlights the rational and emotional attributes of healthy, wellness, organic authenticity, and so on.

Gaining Trust (Affinity)

One "must have" for any aspiring international or global brand is affinity, and by this I mean trust. Without trust there is no loyalty, and customers won't stay with your brand. A good example of great affinity between a brand and its customers is Apple. Once people become a customer of this brand, they hardly ever seem to leave it, despite what the competitors are offering. Most of the global brands have this brand strength. People trust them, like them, and are loyal to them.

One of the elements that go to make up trust is quality, already mentioned above as a requirement for entry into some markets. Once consumers have experienced the quality of a brand's products or services, then they expect the same experience again and again. A slip-up in quality can mean a loss of customers and profits. Product quality is becoming easier with each year to maintain to high levels, especially as technological improvements occur, and people know there are no excuses for poor quality. This was evident in 2009 when Toyota had to recall over eight million cars because of defective parts that caused accidents and injuries. At the time of writing, legal proceedings are still going on, and Toyota is in the midst of spending billions of dollars to replace parts and recapture falling demand for its products in the United States and elsewhere.

Service quality is another element that affects trust in brands. In Asian countries generally, service quality is still variable; it is found to be reliably high only in the more affluent outlets, such as high-class hotels and boutiques. There is no consistency, and this therefore represents an opportunity. Currently in the Middle East Muslim countries, national airlines such as Etihad Airways from Abu Dhabi, Gulf Air from Bahrain, and Qatar Airways, as well as Emirates Airlines from Dubai, are fighting for a share of air travel through the service quality offering.

Attack from Brand Competitors

The last of the six A's is the potential for or actual attack from established and major brand competitors, especially from the global brands. Opportunities in Muslim markets have already attracted non-Muslim companies in large numbers, and the major companies have moved quickly and quite deeply into these markets with powerful positioning, strong brand names, and good value propositions that are already known and respected both globally and in the Muslim world. They have been quick to realize that the Muslim market in its totality accounts for nearly a quarter of the world's population, and is relatively untapped. A good example here is Nestlé, a global corporate brand that is gradually ensuring that its range of 4,600 brands conform to *halal* standards and achieve *halal* accreditation. Other global brand names that are localizing their products to the Muslim market include McDonald's and Subway.

It is very clear from the above that the same Muslim market opportunities attract non-Islamic as well as Islamic companies, and the larger companies already have well-established, trusted brands, needing only to allocate appropriate resources in order to achieve results.

Summary

There are many factors that can pose obstacles to the growth of brands originating from the Muslim world. However, these challenges are not insurmountable if the right strategies are in place. The next chapter looks at those strategies that can be used to build and market Islamic brands. We look at the cases of some companies that are enjoying success by employing these strategies, after which we will consider the challenges and strategies for non-Muslim brands in Muslim markets.

Note

1. www.ihialliance.org/home.php.

9

Key Success Factors and Strategies for Aspiring Islamic Brands

Introduction

The challenges facing Islamic brands in entering both Muslim and non-Muslim markets, as described in the last chapter, may at first seem daunting. This chapter examines a number of strategies for effective brand building and marketing that can be used to overcome these challenges and achieve international success. We will also look at a number of Islamic brands that are taking very positive steps to implement these strategies.

The main strategies for brand building by Islamic companies are:

1. Understand the market clearly.
2. Build your brand based on Islamic values with universal emotional appeal.
3. Position your company and brand on relevance to the market.
4. Communicate the brand appropriately and with Islamic appeal.
5. Gain first mover advantage in new industries and categories.
6. Consider mergers, acquisitions, and partnerships.
7. Develop new and ethical business models using Islamic values and practices.
8. Build an international brand using Western techniques and appeal.
9. Aim for a niche market.
10. Offer a close alternative in a major category.

1. Understand the Market Clearly

The challenge of gaining acceptability was mentioned in the previous chapter. Market acceptability depends to a large extent upon how well a company understands the market for its goods or services, and what consumers really need and want. However, it is surprising how many companies don't conduct market research before attempting to target consumers. By failing to do their homework, they cannot hope to understand the market properly. I discussed market dynamics and segmentation in some detail in Chapter 1, but the following examples are of relevance to this discussion.

Religious interpretations differ by country and culture. Failure to understand these differences could lead to unsuccessful branding and marketing. For example, Islamic swimsuits and headscarves for women probably would not sell in large numbers in either France or Turkey, but for different cultural reasons. In France the wearing of headscarves in schools has been banned, while there is little demand for them in Turkey although they were previously banned. Both of these examples derive from the secular constitutions of the countries concerned.

Muslim consumer behavior and attitudes differ widely across industry sectors. For example, in the luxury goods category, consumers the world over tend to act the same, have the same needs and wants, and buy the same goods and services, whereas in the financial services category there are a variety of behaviors and needs and wants for Islamic and conventional products and services.

Ethics, safety, health, and lifestyle are all drivers for consumer behavior. These are all trends emanating from global citizens that provide opportunities for both Islamic and non-Islamic brands. Non-Muslims are often looking for similar values and product attributes as Muslims. For instance, we see in the financial services market that Islamic banks are gaining just as many non-Muslim customers as conventional banks, as transparency and ethics play a large part in consumer buying behavior. Another opportunity exists for *halal* food producers to educate consumers about the health advantages of their products, and even to position themselves as foods in the wellness/organic category or ethnic foods category, focusing on the country of origin as opposed to their *halal* nature. These strategies capitalize on trends that are on an upswing around the world.

The next strategy concerns the use of brand values, an essential strategy once the market for a brand is clearly understood.

2. Build Your Brand Based on Islamic Values with Universal Emotional Appeal

This strategy is of immense value to Islamic companies. The top brands in the world are built upon emotional values of universal appeal, and Islam as a religion provides many opportunities for brand managers to use such values. Islamic values, some of which are mentioned in Chapter 5, can be drawn from various sources, including the *Qur'an*, the 99 Names of Allah—and the practices of the Prophets—not just Muhammad but also Yusuf, Ibrahim, Ismail, and Idris.

As great brands are always built on emotional values of universal appeal, then to my mind the building of brands based on Islamic values represents a huge opportunity. According to Professor Rodney Wilson, who gave an address at the Middle East Centre, Oxford University, in October 2009, the most profitable Islamic bank in the world is Al Rajhi, of Saudi Arabia. Case Study 16 provides an example of how Al Rajhi Bank has used Islamic values to expand its operations.

CASE STUDY 16: AL RAJHI BANK IN MALAYSIA

When Al Rajhi Bank decided to establish and grow its branch network in Malaysia, it realized that it would have to appeal both to Muslim and non-Muslim audiences. Around 60 percent of the Malaysian population is comprised of Muslim Malays, with the rest being mainly Chinese and Indian. Islamic finance is a growing industry with plenty of opportunities, as explained in Chapter 6, and Islamic financial products can appeal through their basic features to Muslims and non-Muslims alike. Al Rajhi chose to project its brand based on values acceptable to and appreciated by all races and religions, especially Muslims. These values were "truth," "respect," and "honor."

The bank's creative strategy was based on these three core values, and advertising copy was designed to provoke debate on each value. For example, one advertisement read, "Try not to become a man of success, but rather try to become a man of value." Another advertising feature asked: "Moral values—how important are they?" Advertisements such as these drove consumers to the website malaysian-values.com where they could discuss what they valued most. By avoiding regular banking promises and clichéd jargon, Al Rajhi's intention was to develop a long-lasting brand culture that represents Islamic principles and a world-class standard of banking.

These campaigns proved to be very successful, and attracted as many non-Muslim new customers as Muslims. Appealing to the values and beliefs that people hold dear all over the world, without stepping away from the values inherent in the Islamic faith, is the way to build a powerful brand.

The use of powerful values helps enormously in brand development, but the company must also ensure that it positions itself so that it is seen as relevant to consumers in the target market.

3. Position Your Company and Brand on Relevance to the Market

Some brands fail because they become irrelevant to the market; in other words, they no longer satisfy the changing needs of the consumer base. The converse is also true; a brand can become highly successful by being relevant to what consumers actually want and sensitive to their changing lifestyles. The Islamic Bank of Britain uses multilingual employees in its branches and call centers so that *any* customer can feel "at home." Emirates Airlines wants to be the brand that is the "link" between East and West, but it has to compete with huge brands such as British Airways and appeal to multiple markets such as the UK. It has chosen to promote itself in more of a Western style through sponsorship of Arsenal Football Club and the Emirates Stadium. Nevertheless, it serves only *halal* meals on its flights, which are enjoyed by both Muslim and non-Muslim travelers.

Relevance can also be seen in *halal* food. In the UK and other European countries, the trend is toward fusion foods and those that are more "oriental" and spicy. This applies to fast food as well as to mainstream restaurant food. Chicken Cottage Ltd. built a neat, focused *halal* food brand by understanding market changes and tastes in Britain and combining traditional Western fast-food products with the rich, intense flavors of the East.

CASE STUDY 17: CHICKEN COTTAGE LTD.

Here is the story of a small, creative company that saw a gap in the market, as told by Sadaf Kazi (franchise coordinator).

"In 1994 the first Chicken Cottage store was opened in Wembley, North London and it was here that the Chicken Cottage concept began to take shape. Our immediate goal was the creation of a unique taste, closely followed by the conception of a memorable logo and individual brand identity.

We were determined to produce a product that would not only be successful in the UK but also around the world and realized that winning the 'battle of the globals' lay with the novel taste of our product and developing products that were set to become core to the success of Chicken Cottage in our global reach.

These products were fresh, original, and designed around tastes that were for those people who enjoy more spicy dishes. We realized that the well-known brands were like lumbering old dinosaurs, unable to react to the fast-changing pace of consumer trends and demands that were becoming increasingly more sophisticated and fickle.

Initially our menu was a scaled-down version of today's menu and was not representative of our present 'sell all miss none' philosophy— we started small and tested thoroughly.

Importantly, however, it did represent how British society was changing in general, which could only be described in one word: fusion. By combining traditional Western fast-food products with the rich, intense flavors of the East, we were able to create a menu and cuisine unparalleled in the industry by offering fresh ideas loved by diverse communities.

It was this idea of fusing different tastes from a variety of cultures and the use of *halal* meat that guaranteed Chicken Cottage was able to present products to the public that didn't exclude any community, offering those much-loved spicy variants for customers as well as the usual products expected from outlets such as ours.

BRAND IDENTITY

We needed to find a name and a logo that represented our non-exclusionary ethos and would send a strong message to the public about what it means to experience our concept. After much deliberation, 'Chicken Cottage' was chosen as this name embodied not only the main focus of attention— that is chicken—but also conjured up images of home cooking in cozy environments that were non-intimidating and welcoming.

. . . The logo produced was novel, fresh, and ahead of its time, based on an abstract view of two chicken heads. It continues to be the main focus of our brand identity today. The trademark was quickly protected and registered to avoid plagiarism and allowed us to concentrate on promoting our brand and maintaining brand integrity, without fear of dilution with blatant copying.

GROWTH

Since our first outlet opened in Wembley, North London in 1994, we have grown at a rate of one new outlet every month since 1996. Today, in early 2010, we have:

- 93 franchises in England;
- 10 franchises in Scotland; and
- 10 international franchises.

With almost 15 more franchises destined to open this year, we have achieved, in fact exceeded, our goals. Chicken Cottage has taken 'fast' food to a new level and is rapidly becoming a household name, hence our consumer popularity and fast expansion.

We believed people wanted more than just a takeaway curry on a Friday night so we set out to offer a universally available range which was healthy, convenient, and ready-to-hand as and when required or desired. With this belief in mind, the concept of Chicken Cottage was conceived."

Source: Chicken Cottage Ltd. For further information, see www.chickencottage.com.

Having a great product is important, but communicating the brand to consumers is equally valuable in establishing the relationship and building market share.

4. Commmunicate the Brand Appropriately and with Islamic Appeal

If you have created a brand that is both relevant and possesses strong Islamic values, then that brand has to be communicated in the most appropriate way for its target audiences. With Al Rajhi above, the brand is more conservatively communicated, the values coming across strongly and without being ultra-modern; this is appropriate for a financial services company that operates primarily in Muslim countries.

While Zain (see Case Study 19) leans more toward Western branding/emotional advertising techniques with some Islamic touches, Olpers (Case Study 18) focuses much more on Islamic emotional appeal.

CASE STUDY 18: OLPERS

Using Islamic Emotional Appeal

Olpers, a Pakistani milk brand introduced in 2006, has been seeking to compete with Nestlé. Its television commercials for Ramadan in 2008 and 2009, developed with JWT, mention the beverage only briefly at the start and end. Most of the commercials' time is devoted to showing Muslims in prayer at mosques; Muslims at work in countries including Turkey, Pakistan, and Morocco; and Muslims doing good deeds like helping the elderly.

Advertising agency Ogilvy says the commercial aimed to "situate the modern Muslim in the context of the *Ummah*, or the global Muslim community, reminding them of their larger interconnectedness and giving them an enormous sense of belonging." The commercial also emphasizes the ideas that "all are equal in the eyes of God" and "brotherhood is a crucial component of success" by equating the work of, say, a craftsman in Brunei and a scientist in Egypt.

The 2009 spot navigates between tradition and modernity by featuring Atif Aslam, a Pakistani pop singer, and Dawud Wharnsby, a Canadian songsmith who converted to Islam. "We have a message of peace for the earth," they sing.

Such choices reflect research by Ogilvy's Islamic brand building practice Ogilvy Noor, which shows that young Muslim consumers are different from their Western "Generation Y" counterparts in that they believe that by staying true to the core values of their religion, they are more likely to achieve success in the modern world.[1]

Another good example of a company building and communicating a brand emotionally and appropriately, this time to several Muslim-majority and minority markets, is the telcom Zain.

CASE STUDY 19: ZAIN: I

Using the Power of Emotion and Relevance

The telecommunications company Zain was established in 1983 in Kuwait. Originally known as MTC, the company was renamed in 2007 as part of a re-branding exercise aimed at making the brand more meaningful to Muslim and non-Muslim audiences. As of December 31, 2009, Zain's customer base reached 72.5 million active customers across 24 countries in the Middle East and Africa, representing a 14 percent increase compared to December 31, 2008. Zain's turnover in 2008 was US$6 billion, and in the full year of 2009 the group announced consolidated revenues of just over US$8 billion

(US8,056.1 million, an increase of 16 percent over the previous year). Zain aims to become the first telecommunications company to enter the global list of top 100 brands.

BRAND NAME AND VALUES

Zain means "beautiful," "good," or "wonderful" in Arabic. The company's tagline is "A Wonderful World," which is consistent with that meaning, thus underlining its brand name. Zain is built on three emotionally charged brand values:

- *Heart:* courage, resolve, engaging one's spirit.
- *Radiance:* Leading the way with imagination, joy, richness in life.
- *Belonging:* Bringing fellowship and community to all.

Zain's retail outlets are colorful, bright, optimistic, and relevant to the "wonderful world" the brand wants to portray.

TV COMMERCIALS

In a couple of Zain TV ads, the main messages are:

- "Life is a fairytale. And seeing the positive aspect in everything and making the world a better place is what Zain is all about." (This message is essentially meant for the retail consumer.)
- "Zain promises their customers the opportunity to enjoy life to the fullest with easy, practical solutions." (This message is meant for the business consumer.)

The example illustrates that the company is staying true to its core brand message of "A Wonderful World." Case Study 21, further below, highlights Zain's corporate social responsibility initiatives, which also remain fixed on the core brand message.

Zain moved quickly into the telecommunications industry, as it was in the fast growth stage. This is linked to the strategy of gaining first mover advantage, discussed next.

5. Gain First Mover Advantage in New Industries and Categories ━━━━━━━━

New industries are rapidly emerging that are offering a multitude of opportunities for enterprising new and existing companies. Most of these are a direct result of technological advancements that enhance consumer lifestyles. Many examples of the kind of opportunities that technological advancement have made possible can be seen in the digital revolution and the growth of the Internet. Google is now the most valuable brand in the world and one of the largest companies by market capitalization; Apple has revolutionized mobile communications; and Facebook has become the third-largest nation in the world with over 600 million members and is still growing.

Such opportunities are also present in the Muslim world, and Muxlim. com is a very good example. The digital world, including the case study on Muxlim.com, was discussed in detail in Chapter 7. The first company to gain a foothold in a new category tends to keep that number one position, even when competitors enter the market. Google and Facebook are cases in point.

Mergers, acquisitions, and partnerships are a way to fast track a brand's growth, and this strategy is considered next.

6. Consider Mergers, Acquisitions, and Partnerships ━━━━━━━━

If a company wants to fast track its branding and business development efforts, it can do so by entering into agreements with other Muslim or non-Muslim brands, or indeed by acquiring them. Some countries and companies buy brands and their businesses as investments, or indeed they may use the acquisitions or partnerships to learn how to build and manage brands better. Examples of recent brand buys include the acquisition of Aston Martin, which, on March 12, 2007, was purchased from Ford Motor Company by a joint venture company headed by David Richards and co-owned by Investment Dar and Adeem Investment of Kuwait and English businessman John Sinders.. Ford retained a US$77 million stake in Aston

Martin, valuing the company at US$925 million. Another well-known British brand, Manchester City Football Club, was purchased by Abu Dhabi United Group in August 2008.

A further good example of an acquisition that lifts a corporate brand's portfolio and adds global reach is the takeover of Godiva Chocolatier by Ülker Group, a company that had focused mainly on its home market of Turkey throughout its history.

CASE STUDY 20: GODIVA CHOCOLATIER

Godiva Chocolatier is a manufacturer of premium chocolates and related products, and was founded in Belgium in 1926. Godiva began as a small praline-making business run by the Draps family out of their home in Brussels. It was initially called Chocolate Draps until the founder, Joseph Draps, renamed it Godiva. His inspiration came from the well-known Saxon legend of Lady Godiva who rode unclothed through the streets of Coventry to entreat her husband, Leofric the Dane, to lower taxes. Subsequently, Godiva was acquired by Campbell Soup Company in 1967 after it entered the US market in 1966.

Godiva owns and operates more than 450 retail boutiques and shops in the United States, Canada, Europe, and Asia. Its products are distributed through more than 10,000 specialty retailers.

Godiva was acquired by the Ülker Group, a Turkish corporation, in 2007 for US$850 million when Campbell Soup Company decided to divest the brand. Campbell made this decision because, it said, the "premium chocolate business does not fit with Campbell's strategic focus on simple meals." Ülker Group is part of Yildiz Holding in Turkey, a major manufacturer of food products.

Ülker Group is a manufacturer of food products, which are exported internationally to 110 countries. It seems that the Godiva acquisition fits nicely into Ülker's business portfolio since its business focus is related product categories such as cakes, flour, chewing gum, and baby food. Furthermore, Ülker has always taken pride in producing products of the highest quality, and this is reflected in its winning the "Candy Company of the Year in Europe" award from the European Candy Kettle Club in 2004. Ülker's Biscuits, Chocolate and Cake division president Ali Ülker describes the purchase of the world-renowned Godiva brand as a step toward the company becoming a regional power, since it is already dominant in Turkey.

Yildiz Holding CEO Atilla Kurama commented that Yildiz Holdings viewed Godiva as a stand-alone company and would continue to treat it as such. However, it was planned to open the first Godiva boutique in Istanbul soon after the handover, and it is clear that Yildiz hopes to learn a great deal about global branding and marketing via Godiva's experience. The intent to set up a Turkish-American board of directors for Godiva was expected to help the acquisition of such knowledge.

Since the acquisition, Godiva has also modified the communication strategy for the brand. Prior to the 2009 global recession, the essence of the brand was focused on luxurious celebration. According to the senior vice president for global brand development, Lauri Kien Kotcher, this made sense at a time when people had plenty of money with which to indulge themselves. However, she said that when the economic downturn came about, it was decided that the Godiva brand essence needed to change to one that "re-engaged people around its Belgian heritage" and elevated the experiential and emotional appeal of consuming the brand. With this in mind, a new marketing campaign was launched using the theme of "golden moments." Kien Kotcher explained: "The idea is to appeal to consumers in different places and times who want a little piece of chocolate. You can have your own golden moment at home, by yourself."

Godiva also introduced a sub-brand, called "Godiva Gems," in 2009 in the middle of the global economic downturn. This new line extension was intended to help make consumers perceive the premium brand as more affordable or accessible. Godiva Gems are packages of smaller pieces of chocolate, individually wrapped so that they can be shared. The new line had a launch price of US$4.99 and US$9.99 per packet and is sold in Godiva stores, newsstands, duty-free shops and even—in a first for the brand—supermarkets such as Publix, Safeway, and Wegmans. With this new range, Godiva customers can pamper themselves in the comfort of their own homes and experience their own "golden moment" while indulging in deliciously made chocolates.

While acquisition is one way to grow globally, the opportunities to form partnerships with Western or non-Muslim brands are not confined to large companies; indeed, there are many opportunities for smaller companies to do so. For example, Tesco's success in countries all around the world is based on its philosophy of working as much as possible with local businesses (suppliers). For example, *Borneo Post Online* announced on January 7, 2010:

Five small and medium enterprise (SME) suppliers from Malaysia are preparing to ship their halal *food products worth some RM600,000 to the UK to be sold at 180 Tesco plc (Tesco) stores there beginning January 11.*

In a press release yesterday, Tesco Stores (Malaysia) Sdn Bhd (Tesco Malaysia) said the move is seen as a part of its efforts to bring Malaysian products to the world market. The suppliers are Brahim's ready-to-use chicken curry, rendang *and* satay *sauces supplier Dewina Food Industries Sdn Bhd, ready-to-eat fried rice producer Sal's Food Industries Sdn Bhd, instant noodles manufacturer Vit Makanan (KL) Sdn Bhd, as well as chili and garlic-chili sauce maker Kampong Koh Sauce (M) Sdn Bhd.*

"This is the first group of SMEs that Tesco Malaysia is introducing to the British market, and there will be many more. We will continue to help Malaysian SMEs meet global standards and produce consistent and quality products for our consumers," said Tesco's chief executive officer Chris Bush, adding that all the products by the five suppliers have passed the strict "British Retailers Consortium" standards. Tesco is one of the United Kingdom's leading retailers.[2]

Working with big international brands such as Tesco helps small firms not just to grow, but also to learn about quality, packaging, and other essential aspects of business. There is a lot that can be learned, and the impact on a supplier's brand image as a result of working with a global brand is very powerful.

7. Develop New and Ethical Business Models Using Islamic Values and Practices

There are some very interesting new ways of developing businesses in the Islamic world through applying traditional Islamic values and religious practice to corporate life and brand building. For example, corporate social responsibility (CSR) might be considered by many a largely Western invention, but it is in fact one of the foundation stones of the Islamic way of life, and has been for centuries. One of the most successful and intriguing, innovative developments in this area is the creation and implementation of "corporate *waqf*," coupled with "intrapreneurship" and the development of entrepreneurs. Johor Corporation is a role model here in combining social responsibility and practical entrepreneurship (see Case Study 22 later in the chapter). In the next case study, we see how Zain also builds social responsibility into its business and brand development. However, we will first recap on Islamic values and ethics.

Islamic Values and Ethics

Possibly the most important Islamic value is the belief that any worldly resource is a gift from God, and has to be used in the most efficient and productive manner for the benefit of all. Islamic business is thus not for the betterment of any individual alone; it is a matter of obligation of everyone to help others, as in Islam, mankind is merely the steward of God's resources and should look after these so that all may benefit in the present and the future. Connected with this, business activities should serve all of society. Second, there are certain businesses that are not permissible under Islam, such as those involving usury, gambling, pornography, alcoholic products, pork products, and others. (This stipulation can have a significant effect on the marketing of some Islamic products such as finance, where anything to do with the financing of such businesses is *haram*, or not permissible). Third, the Islamic way of doing business promotes cooperation and not conflict, but doesn't exclude competition. Indeed, competition may be welcomed, as the receipt of excessive profits isn't deemed to be acceptable if society doesn't benefit from it. Fourth, the needy and poor should be looked after by the wealthy; a rule that is made real by the *zakat* tax, and one that also influences many companies in their CSR activities, particularly in the application of *waqf* concepts. Fifth, honesty is an imperative, and deception is not acceptable. This has implications for advertising, promotion, pricing, and the value proposition.

As we shall see, these Islamic principles have implications for branding and marketing in Muslim markets, and this "ethical" stance is becoming more important in today's world. It is important to note that the ethical basis of Islamic business is predetermined and cannot be changed, although there is some leeway in terms of scholastic interpretation. Also, although profit maximization is considered to be acceptable, it is not if it doesn't benefit society in general, and so value maximization becomes an important concept. These ethical dimensions are, however, interpreted differently by different organizations and scholars in different countries; they are fashioned to some extent by culture. Nevertheless, it is significant that the sustainability concept is inherent in Islamic business values and practice.

This is, arguably, where capitalism has failed, by allowing businesses to focus on short-term profit at the expense of the welfare of all. There has, as witnessed by the recent global financial failures, been little or no attention paid to sustainable value in the West. Stephen Green has plenty to say about this in his book, *Good Value: Reflections on Money, Morality and an Uncertain World*.[3] I will discuss some of Green's views below, and consider how these values link to the Islamic way of doing business. I will then talk about corporate social responsibility, before looking at the "corporate *waqf*" concept, which has been put into practice most effectively by

Johor Corporation and which I believe to be an area of future growth and development.

Capitalism, Values, and Profitability

Green's argument includes some valid points about today's "global bazaar." One such point is that the *value* of a business is dependent on its *values*. The recent financial meltdown is an example of how capitalism has largely failed to integrate value with values. Indeed, Green comments that a strong culture of values is critical—a *sine qua non*—to the sustainable value of a business. Boards of directors in capitalist countries have failed, he says, to promote and nurture a culture of ethical and purposeful values throughout their organizations.

This argument is very relevant to the world of branding and marketing. The key to effective branding and to creating sustainable value is having the correct combination of values that both customers and employees (*all* stakeholders, for that matter) can accept, buy into, and deliver on. Most corporate brand managers would agree that this is one of their most important roles: to create a value set to which everyone can subscribe. But do they actually do this? In my experience, many companies don't have a great track record in this area, and have been forced into it by the backlash from consumers who have seen too many unscrupulous companies.

But what does "sustainable value" actually mean? Here we must consider, first, whether profit maximization is acceptable; and second, whether it should have a positive impact on society as a whole. I don't believe that any business would deny the acceptability of profit maximization, and Islamic businesses are no different. Profit maximization is quite acceptable for any Muslim business, and this is stated very clearly in the *Qu'ran*. Where the difference of opinion might lie is in the second question; Should sustainable value and profitability only be relevant to the business, or should it benefit the wider community? While Western brands may, sometimes reluctantly, support charitable causes, they tend on the whole to do so in order to appease their customers—that is, CSR isn't a part of the fabric of most businesses. But it *is* a part of the fabric of Islamic businesses, because it is a fundamental part of the faith. Let us now look at the two examples I cited at the beginning of this section—Zain and Johor Corporation.

CASE STUDY 21: ZAIN: II

Corporate Social Responsibility

Zain, the telecommunications company whose brand message is, as we saw earlier, "It's a Wonderful World," has a comprehensive CSR strategy. Dr. Saad Al-Barrack, CEO of the Zain Group, describes how Zain's mission relates back to its core message and values:

> *Our mission is to re-humanize business, to create business romance within our community and among nations, through a commitment to corporate social responsibility. We can do this by championing transparency, the fight against corruption, education and the welfare of the poor. Our CSR initiatives are driven by issues rather than image. Empathy, respect, and participation are what motivate us. And while we see CSR as a worthy social goal, we also believe that it is a sound business proposition, as contributing to social and economic well-being will ultimately benefit all businesses. CSR is simply the new business reality, and at Zain we embrace it, guaranteeing sustainable success and prosperity for all.*

Zain's CSR vision is:

- to be a regional and global CSR entity; and
- to be a true partner in community and environmental development

And its CSR mission is:

- to guide and streamline the company's business processes in a socially and environmentally responsible way;
- to produce a positive impact on society and its stakeholders, now and in the future; and
- to invest in these communities to help fulfill their potential.

It is clear that, for Zain, CSR isn't just a "nice-to-have" but a fundamental value built into the business.

For Johor Corporation, as we can see in Case Study 22, applying CSR values, encouraging "intrapreneurs," and applying the Islamic concept of corporate *waqf* are at the very heart of its business.

CASE STUDY 22: JOHOR CORPORATION (JCORP)

Intrapreneurship, Waqf Practice, and Social Responsibility

JCorp (formerly known as Johor State Economic Development Corporation) is a corporate enterprise established by the state government of Johor, in Malaysia, as the principal instrument for the generation of economic growth in Johor, particularly in the leading economic sectors such as oil palm plantation and property development. From a state agency with RM10 million capital in the form of an oil palm plantation estate in 1979, JCorp has become a highly successful state government-owned organization that strives for economic betterment of society through its business activities. Today, JCorp's core business divisions include agro business, healthcare, timber, industrial development, and property development. The JCorp Group also owns small businesses in a range of industries under its Intrapreneur business division.

Six Islamic values underpin JCorp's corporate values, principles, and beliefs, as stated below:

1. Replacing greed as the core value for economic success.
2. Consistently upholding the fundamental teachings of Islam.
3. Adoption of an internal structure and system embodying the principles and practice of *Shariah*.
4. Internalizing strong work ethics and linking these to the pursuit of life-long learning and continuous acquisition of knowledge.
5. Adoption of a selection process that entrusts leadership responsibilities to the most able and talented.
6. Maintaining a fine balance in attending to staff interests and welfare needs without ignoring the principles of equity, justice, and fairness.

ADOPTION AND ADAPTATION OF THE ISLAMIC CONCEPT OF *WAQF* IN CSR AND BUSINESS DEVELOPMENT

A "*waqf*" can be thought of in English as an "Islamic trust" or a "pious foundation." In its simplest form, a *waqf* is a charitable endowment that allows a person to dedicate his or her property to Allah (God) for the benefit of the public good. The relief of the poor is the ultimate purpose of every *waqf*. What separates *waqf* property from any other charitable asset is that it is dedicated to Allah for all time.

A *waqf* is considered in Islam to be an expression of internal belief in the Creator expressed through philanthropic activity of an individual, group, or organization. *Waqf* founders become well known to the masses. This is in contrast to other forms of pious charity, such as *zakat* or *sadaqah*, which are to a large extent hidden from public recognition. Further, a law considered sacred governs the *waqf*, but this doesn't limit its activities to being purely religious in nature, nor are its benefits necessarily confined exclusively to Muslims.

JCorp's "corporate *waqf*" is aimed at enabling the Muslim community to have access to high-value assets with the aim of mobilizing and managing them through *waqf* for the greater benefit of society, and also to serve the higher cause of Islam. A true corporate *waqf* is also entrusted with responsibility for growing corporate assets over time; it is therefore perceived to have a distinct and unique advantage compared with a conventional *waqf*, in that it allows access to—and thus can benefit from—all the success and profitability of corporate-driven businesses.

JCorp started its *waqf* practice in 1992 via the traditional method of building mosques, and managing and funding their operations. Other forms of traditional *waqf* practice have included the transfer of ownership of two lots of plantation land to the State Islamic Religious Council, the state-authorized custodian. Revenues from the plantation were used to construct and maintain a religious school and orphanage at the plantation.

JCorp moved away from the traditional *waqf* toward a more innovative form in 1998, when it set up a number of *waqf* charity clinics. The objective of the clinics was to provide affordable medical healthcare services to the less privileged and the poor, and they have since become the core of JCorp's community outreach program.

Since 1998, the nine *waqf* clinics (including dialysis centers and a mobile clinic) and a *waqf* hospital have served more than a million patients from various ethnic groups and religious backgrounds throughout the country. This was made possible with the professional and resource support of JCorp's investment arm in healthcare, KPJ Healthcare Berhad.

THE CORPORATE *WAQF*

In 2005, JCorp became the sponsor of corporate *waqf* by dedicating and transferring 75 percent of JCorp-owned equity in a private company to a custodian company that also manages the *waqf* charity clinics. In August 2006, JCorp transferred RM200 million worth of JCorp-owned equities in three public companies (listed on the bourse of Malaysia) to the custodian company, specifying that dividends deriving from the shares were to be allocated as follows:

- 70 percent to JCorp for the purpose of reinvestment to generate more *waqf* assets in future and for the development of companies under corporate *waqf*;
- 25 percent for *fisabilillah*, which refers to religious, charitable purposes, including donations to orphanages, scholarships, financial assistance given to the needy, subsidies paid to the *waqf* charity clinics, social responsibility and community activities, and donations to beneficiaries selected by KWANB (the company set up by JCorp to act as receiver of *waqf* assets and provide governance of the utilization of their profits); and
- 5 percent to the State Islamic Religious Council (SIRC).

The corporate *waqf* activities referred to above can thus be thought of as the Islamic equivalent of true corporate social responsibility. While corporate *waqf* operates very much externally to the organization in terms of the benefits received by the community, JCorp designed an internal program—its "intrapreneurship" scheme—to ensure that people inside the organization also benefited.

JCorp's "intrapreneurship" scheme

As a way to encourage people working in its companies, and Muslims in general, to become more entrepreneurial, JCorp developed the concept of "intrapreneurship," meaning entrepreneurship from within. Development of the concept of entrepreneurship, and inculcation of an entrepreneurship culture and values, has always been one of JCorp's objectives. In fact, JCorp's entrepreneur development program has become a key component of its own corporate growth and expansion strategy.

JCorp's strategic use of the "intrapreneuring" concept helped see it through the worst of the 1997 economic crisis, when it had to fight for survival as a business entity. Forced to downsize and restructure, JCorp used the "intrapreneur" development concept to strategically redefine its organizational structure. Through intrapreneuring, JCorp facilitated the steps of "unbundling" itself and "downloading" its corporate overheads. Long-term corporate growth can only be assured where there is a will to continuously plant new seeds, supplemented by the courage to seize new business opportunities and continue to venture into uncharted waters. This requires that people be enabled by systems and structures, be backed by assets and resources, and be motivated by values and attitudes in such a way that translates into a corporate formula for better managing risks and performance.

This led to the introduction of the JCorp Intrapreneurship Scheme, involving direct share ownership, in 2000, JCorp had realized that companies in the group had, over time, been weakened by the lack of "ownership" commitment on the part of executives/managers. Steps were thus taken to share both the risks and rewards from enterprise development, by offering a maximum 25 percent equity stake to intrapreneurs involved in the scheme (which was subsequently officially referred to as the Intrapreneur SME—Skim Milikan Ekuiti—or Intrapreneur Equity Ownership Scheme). The scheme was a radical departure from the traditional policy, under which JCorp owned 100 percent of the equity in all its businesses.

Subsequent to the launch of the scheme, the companies involved showed tremendous improvement in their performance, both in terms of turnover and profitability. The success of these intrapreneur companies indicated the willingness of the intrapreneurs involved to assume ownership responsibilities, while at the same time underlining the anticipated motivational force derived from a greater legitimization of their corporate authority. The strong entrepreneurial drive among the intrapreneurs translated into better results not only for the companies involved, but also for the group. As part-owner of their respective companies, the intrapreneurs are exposed to a truly business-driven performance climate with the full trimmings of risks and returns. The performance of these companies is shown in Table 9.1.

Table 9.1 Growth in Entrepreneurial Businesses within JCorp, 1999–2009

Year	No. of Companies	Aggregate Revenue (RM)	Aggregate Profit before Tax (RM)
1999	2	18.00	0.40
2000	4	48.30	2.70
2001	6	65.60	4.00
2002	15	134.00	15.00
2003	16	153.00	12.00
2004	24	200.00	18.00
2005	33	310.00	29.00
2006	37	369.00	32.00
2007	48	513.00	47.00
2008	56	585.00	38.00
2009	65	621.10	35.00

Note: Amounts are in Malaysian ringgit.

Source: Johor Corporation.

One of the challenges in developing intrapreneurs has been to establish many small businesses and use them as "incubators" to nurture inexperienced and novice executives, with the aim of developing among them outstanding businessmen with entrepreneurial talent. A core element in JCorp's Intrapreneur Development Program has thus been the coaching and mentoring component, largely done internally and on-the-job as executives carry out their day-to-day functions.

By mid-2010, there were 74 such intrapreneurs managing JCorp-intrapreneur companies engaging in a multi-range of businesses. They are unified under a non-profit company, Johor Intrapreneur Malaysia Berhad (JIMB), an association-like company in which the intrapreneurs become members. The role of JIMB is to provide a platform for these intrapreneurs to share technical knowledge, expertise, and business ideas, to expand their networking, and to explore opportunities for business synergies among each other and external companies.

JCorp has accomplished a great deal, and has become a role model for many Islamic businesses by implementing a very traditional and fundamental part of Islamic ideology, *waqf*, in an innovative way for the benefit of the community, and the development of entrepreneurship to further help individuals and business development. Both of these comprehensive activities have enhanced the brand image of JCorp considerably. It is important to emphasize that whether a company uses conventional Islamic or Western CSR techniques, it must be embraced as a long-term strategy. People need to believe that the philanthropic ideas a company embarks upon are real and not just rhetoric, and this can only be demonstrated over time, through both good and tough business times.

Moving on from this strategy, we come to the opposite end of the spectrum, with brands built using more Western brand-building techniques as described in Chapter 5.

8. Build an International Brand Using Western Techniques and Appeal

Some Islamic companies may not wish to build brands that appeal just to Muslim consumers, as they may be competing on a larger stage for global reach and acceptance. This is not to say they fail to subscribe to CSR and the Islamic values driving it; they do, as our next case demonstrates. The case of Dubai Aluminium, often referred to as DUBAL, is also interesting in that DUBAL is a business-to-business brand, and not a consumer brand. Even in the Western world, many B2B companies don't bother with branding, thinking it is a retail activity. However, enlightened companies know that it is essential, and DUBAL is such a company.

CASE STUDY 23: DUBAI ALUMINIUM (DUBAL)

Developing and Managing a Global B2B Brand

INTRODUCTION

DUBAL is one of the very few brands I have seen in global markets (and whether from a Muslim or non-Muslim country) that has not only conducted a global corporate branding exercise thoroughly and completely, but has also installed and uses a meticulously efficient and effective brand management system.

DUBAL is the brand name of Dubai Aluminium Company Limited. In 2005 the company's management decided to position the company for the global market, given its ambition of becoming one of the top five producers of aluminum in the world. It had made tremendous technological advances, possessed the largest single-site smelter in the world, and had a top-quality product. DUBAL's management knew that without such attributes the prospects of becoming a powerful brand were slim, but once they had achieved these successes it was time to bring branding into play. It was in 2005 that DUBAL began its brand journey, which led to a substantial effort that encompassed the whole of the company and its stakeholders in an initiative that still has momentum today. Before we look at DUBAL's holistic branding program, we will take a brief look at the company's background and history.

BACKGROUND

Entirely state-owned, Dubai Aluminium Company Limited was established in 1979 to aid the diversification of the UAE economy by adding value to the country's oil-rich mineral resources. The company, widely regarded as the industrial flagship of the UAE and one of the largest non-oil contributors to Dubai's economy, proudly celebrated its 30th anniversary in 2009.

The company's roots date back to May 22, 1975, when the late H.H. Sheikh Rashid bin Saeed Al Maktoum (then ruler of Dubai) signed a decree establishing DUBAL as a joint-venture company. The smelter complex would be built on a 480-hectare site near Jebel Ali village, 35 kilometers southwest of Dubai alongside the then two-lane highway to Abu Dhabi. Almost five months later, on October 15, 1975, H.H. Sheikh Rashid laid DUBAL's foundation stone. Construction of the smelter complex began in May 1976. Working under very tough physical conditions in the desert and salt flats of Jebel Ali, it took four years to complete the arduous task. At the time, it was the biggest basic industry development project in the world.

The emerging DUBAL development was one of three major industrial and construction projects taking place simultaneously in the Jebel Ali area, the other two being the Jebel Ali Port—then the largest man-made harbor in the world, where DUBAL would have its own dedicated port facilities; and the Dugas gas plant—which was constructed adjacent to DUBAL. Together, the three projects made the Jebel Ali area, as a whole, the world's biggest building site.

In terms of product, exceptionally high purity of metal is maintained, with the standard-purity cells delivering 99.913 percent and the high-purity cells achieving up to 99.96 percent metal purity levels. The company has the capacity to produce more than a million metric tonnes of high-quality finished aluminum products a year, in three main forms: foundry alloy for automotive applications; extrusion billet for construction, industrial, and transportation purposes; and high-purity aluminum for the electronics and aerospace industries.

The exceptional quality of DUBAL's products is a major strength of the business and the brand. Indeed, many companies that work with DUBAL claim that the experience helps enhance their own quality standards, which is instrumental in helping them to secure new business opportunities elsewhere.

Throughout the three decades, DUBAL has been committed to safeguarding the safety and health of all its employees, protecting the environment, and maintaining the highest quality standards. Substantial, ongoing investments have also been made in recruiting the best talent, then retaining people through a combination of skills training and career development opportunities and competitive remuneration packages. In consequence, more than 40 employees celebrated their 30 years' service anniversary at DUBAL in 2009.

DUBAL actively supports community-based initiatives that fulfill the nation's broader development goals and has a very active CSR and community development program.

THE CORPORATE BRANDING PROCESS

The corporate branding process was started after management decided that, to fulfill its global objectives, the company had to prepare itself in every way, including by creating a brand strategy that would enable it to compete with some of the world's largest companies, such as Alcoa and Alcan. After a great deal of planning, a comprehensive corporate branding process was set in motion, which started with an awareness workshop.

Awareness workshop

Following the decision to create a strong corporate brand strategy and a sustainable desired image, the brand process started with a workshop for all senior staff so that the nature and implications of corporate branding would be fully understood by all, and to ensure that all of the management team would be "speaking the same language."

Brand audit

The first thing that must be done in studying any corporate brand with a view to creating a strategy or repositioning the brand is to find out where the brand is now—that is, what the image of the brand is right now. If a company doesn't know what people think about it now, it is impossible to create a brand strategy that will be successful in generating the desired perceptions of the future. A brand's image is, after all, a summary of the collective perceptions that people have of the company.

A comprehensive brand audit was therefore conducted, which sought the views of all stakeholders, including customers, suppliers, banks, analysts, investors, and employees. The exercise was accomplished mostly through a large number of face-to-face or telephone interviews that covered aspects of image, reputation, corporate performance, competitive analysis, and other relevant topics. Distillation of the results provided very high quality data, which served as food for thought in the next stage of the process, a senior management brand strategy workshop.

Senior management brand strategy workshop

Following the brand audit, a two-day senior management brand strategy workshop was held that involved all the key decision makers in the company, and all those who could have a major impact on the company's brand image. It featured not only the process of deciding on the corporate brand vision, values, and positioning, but entailed much lively and positive debate about how, given where the image was now in the light of audit data, and taking into account what managers wanted the brand identity and image to be like, these decisions could be adequately articulated to cover all eventualities involved in the future implementation of the strategy.

Brand blueprint and implementation

DUBAL embraced the concept that branding is holistic in nature and that any brand strategy must be reflected in every part of the organization. At the end of the above brand strategy process, a blueprint was approved by management that would provide the guidelines for every aspect of brand implementation, including:

- business strategy;
- human resource development;
- customer service;
- centralized brand/marketing department;
- advertising and other forms of communications; and
- brand management and guardianship.

In true DUBAL style, no stone was left unturned in communicating and internalizing the brand. In-house trainers were developed that trained the whole workforce to "live" the brand, and every form of internal and external communications was changed to reflect the new brand and its values.

The importance of having an organizational structure to manage the brand was noted, and DUBAL set up a Brand Management Committee (BMC) to deal with all decisions of a strategic nature concerning the brand, and a Brand Working Committee (BWC) to ensure that every possible idea for brand development was elicited from the workforce, that action plans were scheduled after BMC approval, and that everyone contributed to their achievement.

DUBAL is a company that knows there are no shortcuts to brand success. The company is a splendid example of brand building carried out in a holistic manner, carefully and thoughtfully, over a two-year period. Getting the brand strategy right is very important, and a company has only one chance to get it right. DUBAL is, in my opinion, one of the Islamic world's leading examples of how to create, build, and manage a powerful global brand.

Source: Dubai Aluminium, www.dubal.ae

DUBAL operates in a substantial global market. Other smaller brands often have to start by aiming for a niche market.

9. Aim for a Niche Market

Aiming for a niche market is a good strategy, as it tends to play away from the competition, especially the global brands, and in Muslim-minority markets, where the target audience is much smaller.

Two good examples of Islamic brands following a niche marketing strategy are Ummah Foods, which has built a niche brand in the UK where the Muslim population is less than two million, and Bateel, a date producer and retailer.

CASE STUDY 24: UMMAH FOODS

A Niche Category Player in a Big-brand Market

In the Muslim-minority market of the UK, a *halal* chocolate brand owned by Ummah Foods has avoided unnecessary competition and the associated expense of trying to access all stores across the country, taking on giants such as Cadbury's and Hershey (who literally dominate the supermarket shelves by focusing on areas of high population). The Ummah brand is distributed to high-density Muslim cities and districts such as Birmingham, Bradford, Batley, and parts of London, where supermarkets and convenience stores are more likely to stock them to meet local Muslim consumer needs. Khalid Sharif, managing director of Ummah Foods, explains: "Muslim consumers are looking for specific products tailored to meet their religious and community needs. Mainstream supermarkets must embrace and reach out to this growing community which unequivocally defines itself by faith."[4] Tesco, Morrison's, and other supermarkets did indeed start to sell them in 2006. Ummah Foods has added value to the giant retailers such as Tesco, as they like to work with ethnic foods that demonstrate an understanding of the consumer and embrace social responsibility.

The lesson here is that if you are careful in targeting your desired consumer market, not only are you likely to be successful, but you are likely to attract other distributors to sell your product, too.

The next case, Bateel, also proves how developing a niche strategy can be very fruitful.

CASE STUDY 25: BATEEL

"The world's only gourmet date experience. Delighting connoisseurs around the world"

The case study headline is the company's sign-off slogan. Bateel, a Saudi Arabian company headquartered in Riyadh, was founded in 1992. It is a fast-growing gourmet confectionery brand that taps into a unique ingredient of Muslim lifestyle—dates. Bateel offers more than 20 varieties of high-quality dates sourced from its own date groves in Al-Ghat, Saudi Arabia. Today, it has grown its branded retail presence with more than 25 outlets in Dubai, Riyadh, Amman, Mumbai, Delhi, Kuala Lumpur, London, Jakarta, and more, in 14 countries and employs over 550 people.

As stated on Bateel's website:

From time immemorial the date palm has been a pillar of life, the desert oasis. This legendary fruit has been the source of nutrition, a symbol of hospitality, an emblem of a traditional and proud culture. Poets have praised its virtues, Bedouins relied on dates for sustenance and generations were nurtured with its blessing. Dates are rich in vitamins and minerals, full of natural energy, perfect for an active and healthy modern lifestyle. Celebrating its glorious past and harnessing its healthy nutritional value, Bateel has transformed this noble fruit into a world class luxury brand. The ancient fruit is now an exotic gourmet experience. A modern expression of traditional hospitality. Choose from a lavish assortment of premium quality dates, date truffles, chocolate pralines, pastries and other gourmet delicacies such as our refreshing sparkling date drink, nutritious date bar and delightful date jams. All made with the finest Bateel dates and other natural ingredients.

This gourmet confectionery product range is fast becoming a favorite unique business and personal gift item for locals and tourists and, interestingly, is finding a market in corporate gifts. Summing this up, Bateel says it has

. . . given new meaning to the art of gift-giving. Each gift bearing the Bateel name brings with it an age-old tradition of gift offering. A gift from Bateel is a reflection not only of a rich tradition of hospitality but also of impeccable taste. Our wide selection of luxurious and traditional packages offers a variety of suitable choices for any occasion, whether for family, friends or for a business associate. Our corporate marketing representative will be glad to assist you in selecting just the right Bateel gift for your next corporate function or special occasion.

Having fully established itself in the gourmet confectionery industry, Bateel has now expanded to introduce a new concept in casual dining called Café Bateel, which offers a unique range of gourmet foods and beverages that embodies the ancient Umbrian culinary heritage and rich tradition of Arabian hospitality. It also is offering retail franchises.

Bateel has a unique, original, and high-quality brand-building program with high-end gourmet confectionery retail outlets, sophisticated packaging, and a range of communications activities, including print, online advertising, and social media use. (Its Facebook page has more than 1,000 fans.) It complements these with special packages for occasions such as Eid, Ramadan, and Easter, and promotional events such as gourmet confectionery competitions.

Source: Bateel Foods, www.bateel.com. www.DinarStandard.com

Niche strategies are often employed when it is difficult to reach a mass market, and even then it is a strategy that is limiting. Sometimes online sales can represent an alternative opportunity, and smaller or fewer retail outlets can be used, but these possibilities only exist for non-perishable items. Strategic opportunities for Internet branding and marketing are explained in more detail in Chapter 7.

The two cases above relate to brands that are unique. Another way to develop the uniqueness that a good brand needs is to offer a close alternative to consumers' current brand choices.

10. Offer a Close Alternative in a Major Category

When there are major brand categories that are tilted firmly at one single consumer group, there may be an opportunity for an alternative product, especially if the proposed target audience is similar in terms of what it is looking for in the product but different enough in terms of another attribute to justify entry. This is the case with Fulla, the alternative to Mattel's Barbie Doll.

CASE STUDY 26: FULLA

Barbie's Close, but Not Too Close, Friend

The opening remarks on the Fulla website read, "Fulla—the little girl that wears modest outfits. Her top priorities are respect for herself and all around her and being kind to friends and peers. We take pride in promoting virtues to help girls be the very best today so they will grow up to be the women who make a difference tomorrow."

According to *USA Today*:

Fulla, with dark eyes and long brown hair, looks a lot like Barbie, but she is very different. For one thing, Fulla's breasts are modestly smaller. The major detail, though—she's Muslim, wearing the Islamic hijab, or head scarf, with a long flowing gown, or abaya. Fulla even comes with her own prayer rug.

In a world facing greater economic globalization, Fulla represents a growing trend toward the commercializing of Islam. The creators of Fulla, NewBoy Design Studio in Damascus, Syria, say the doll represents Arab and Islamic values such as modesty, respect and piety. Indeed, Fulla symbolizes the ideal Muslim woman in a conservative Middle East. Arab children are now choosing Fulla over Barbie.[5]

NewBoy FZCO, a major distributor for branded toys in the Middle East, is the exclusive owner of the Fulla doll brand. NewBoy is headquartered in Dubai, UAE. The company's business lines include toys, stationery, textiles, food, and publications.

Fulla was introduced to toy stores in the Middle East in 2003. Within two years of its introduction, approximately 1.5 million dolls had been sold. It is now a global product.

The success of Fulla has been attributed to the characteristics that its creator endowed upon the doll. Fawaz Abidin, the Fulla brand manager for NewBoy, says that this is because NewBoy understands the Arab market in a way that its competitors don't. He states that Fulla's "character," as developed in the company's product advertising, is one that parents and children will want to relate to. Her personality is honest, loving, and caring, and she respects her father and mother. These are the characteristics and personality that resonate well with the social values of Muslims. Fulla is also dressed in fashionable yet conservative clothes according to Islamic values, and this also tends to appeal to Muslim children and their parents.

Fulla's popularity has been extended beyond just a toy doll. The character has spawned cartoon programs, children's accessories (e.g. prayer rug), snacks, children's bicycles, children's apparel, story books, and more.

Fulla isn't an exclusively Middle Eastern doll. She has been successfully marketed all over the Middle East, Asia, and Europe. There are Fulla variations for India, for example, who wear *saris*, while the Malaysian Fulla wears traditional Malaysian dress. By the time Fulla arrived in the US and Canada, she was being presented as a young, educated woman working to make the world a better place. (Prior to the launch of the brand in the United States in 2007, families with relatives in the Middle East had been receiving the doll as gifts since 2003.)

Named after a fragrant flower, the Fulla line goes beyond the external fashion and beauty focus. She is a doctor and teacher who respects her parents and likes to read and play sports. "The message that Fulla brings . . . is promoting good virtues for little girls," said Basel Kanawati, chief technology officer for NewBoy. "It's asking girls to take pride in themselves and not dress for boys and be the sex symbols that other dolls tend to be."

Kanawati said the doll fills a void for parents and girls who want a doll that looks like them and represents their values. The father of four daughters said he sees the pressures girls face. "They feel they need to imitate other people to be accepted in society. The message [of Fulla] is [that] you can be proud of yourself and function in society."

Sources: Katherine Zoepf, "Bestseller in Mideast: Barbie With a Prayer Mat," *The New York Times*, September 22, 2005; R. Hussain, "A Doll Fulla Fun," *Khaleej Times Online*, March 4, 2009, www.khaleejtimes.com/DisplayArticle. asp?xfile=data/diversions/2009/March/diversions_March4.xml&section =diversions&col; P. Ebrahimzadeh, "Syrian Barbie," *Forbes.com*, March 5, 2009, www.forbes.com/2009/03/05/fulla-versus-barbie-business_barbie_ban_print.html; *USA Today*, December 13, 2005, www.usatoday.com/news/opinion/editorials/2005-12-13-arab-barbie-edit_x.htm; www.fulla.us, accessed May 5, 2010.

Another example of the entrepreneurial strategy that offers a close alternative is the case of Beurger King Muslim in France.

CASE STUDY 27: BEURGER KING MUSLIM (BKM)

Beurger King Muslim (BKM) is a fast-food restaurant launched in July 2005 in Paris. Its aim is to give Muslim consumers food that is like American fast food but with *halal* acceptability. The brand name is interesting: the word "*Beur*" means "Arab" and is often used by the French to refer to the second generation of North Africans living in France; but, of course, it is also very close to the global brand name Burger King.

The first branch, located in the suburb of Clichy-sous-Bois, where many locals are first- or second-generation Muslim immigrants from former French colonies, offers hamburgers, french fries, sundaes, cola, and doughnuts, but the beef and chicken used in the burgers are *halal* made with meat slaughtered according to Islamic dietary laws. The restaurant also serves specialties such as the Double Koull Cheeseburger ("*koull*" is a play on the American word "cool" and can also mean "to eat" in Arabic), the BKM Burger (a burger similar to McDonald's Big Mac), and several other types of "*koull*" burgers.

Representatives from an independent certification service visit the restaurant weekly to ensure that the restaurant uses *halal* ingredients. More than 80 percent of the restaurant's customers are Muslim. In an area of high unemployment, the provision of over 20 jobs has been a contribution in economic as well as social terms.

The final case study in this chapter examines a brand from the fast-growing category of beauty products and cosmetics.

CASE STUDY 28: ONE PURE BEAUTY

Halal Beauty

INTRODUCTION

OnePure is a brand that provides Muslims with an alternative to the *haram* ingredients found in most body-care products. Providing *halal*-certified products for discerning Muslims who value excellence and desire peace of mind has been key to the creation and building of the OnePure brand.

OnePure was created in 2007 and is still, to a certain extent, an embryonic brand; however, it is rapidly gaining recognition in many parts of the world. It currently sells in Dubai, Egypt, the United States, France, and Russia, but it has had many approaches from potential franchisees across the globe.

In 2008 the research and development phase of the brand's retail line and travel collection was completed. This included product development for the Middle East and Asian skin types, for which products were launched in 2009.

The *halal* beauty and cosmetics industry is still in its infancy. A parallel could perhaps be drawn with the Islamic financial services industry when it was in its early stages and which is now growing at around 15–20 percent per annum. OnePure has therefore established a first mover advantage in an industry set to grow at similar enormous rates.

Founder and CEO Layla Mandi says:

> *I developed OnePure Halal Beauty because there were no* halal-*certified beauty products on the market and wanted chic and effective beauty products that were certified* halal *by an authorized* halal *certification body, not a consultancy or simply the term* "halal" *applied to a label. I wanted Muslims to have the choice of* halal-*certified products globally.*

THE *HALAL* CHALLENGES

The main challenge in developing a *halal* beauty range is that in the production of modern cosmetics and beauty products, there are potentially and often actually used non-*halal* ingredients, such as oleic acid, lauric acid, allantoin, collagen, keratin, palmitic acid, gelatin, stearic acid and stearic alcohol, glycerin and glycerol, and sodium lauryl sulfate. Many products such as skin cleansers, moisturizers, aftershave, toners, masques, exfoliants, and cosmetics contain one or more of these ingredients. For *halal* beauty products, alternatives have to be found. In addition, the journey along the whole value chain—banking, R&D, sourcing, production, logistics, and sales and marketing—also has to be *halal*.

OnePure meets these challenges by:

- *Banking:* Using financial products and services from Emirates Islamic Bank.
- *R&D:* Designing and formulating products in Canada using only acceptable raw materials that conform to *halal* requirements.
- *Sourcing:* Sourcing *halal* raw materials and ensuring that the processes used by suppliers are *halal*.
- *Production:* Ensuring the products don't come in contact with non-*halal* products or processes, such as machinery cleaned with substances containing alcohol.
- *Logistics:* Using *halal*-compliant transportation and storage throughout the supply chain.
- *Sales and marketing:* Gaining certification from Malaysian *halal* accreditation authorities; in retail outlets, making sure female sales personnel wear *abayas*.

Having met these challenges the brand can deliver on its *halal* promise of being "pure." However, this enterprise shows that, with determination, Islamic brands can penetrate every market and attract non-Muslim consumers as well—for example, people who are interested in organic, eco-friendly, ethical, and authentic beauty products.

BRAND DEVELOPMENT

One of the first things that needs to be done in creating and developing any new brand is to gain an understanding of the target audience for the brand, and of how the brand is to position itself against its competitors. OnePure looked carefully at the Muslim consumers of beauty products and gained some interesting insights.

Knowing the extent of the total Muslim market, OnePure decided to start in the GCC countries, where there is one of the fastest Muslim growth rates in the world—around 6.6 percent—and a young and vibrant population, with almost 60 percent below 25 years of age. Cultivating a younger audience, which tends to increase its spending power with age, was one of the initial decisions made. OnePure's research team identified a 19 percent annual growth rate in the purchase of beauty products. The GCC industry growth rate from 2007 to 2009 was 43 percent for skin-care products and 33 percent for makeup. In 2007, there was an average spend per month per woman on beauty products of between US$100 and US$200. The presence of all the major international cosmetics companies in the GCC confirmed that the GCC market was indeed a lucrative route for expansion.

The luxury consumer

Having settled on a target market of the more affluent consumers with heavy and growing spending power, OnePure set about profiling that market more closely. It found certain needs states for a smart, savvy, and discerning luxury brand consumer.

- They are highly demanding: This means that experts need to know in advance what they want.
- They have strong values and principles: these consumers desire to be associated with brands that share their moral values.
- They are largely young, have new access to money and credit, have families supportive of buying *halal* goods, and have easy access to travel, which has given them international exposure to, and a desire for, Western brands while respecting their roots.
- They are keen to buy luxury brands that define and accentuate the type of person they are, or would like to be, that project a real or aspirational identity that reflects their personality and lifestyle, and that assist in communicating these factors to others.

Brand strategy and personality

Having determined who their potential customers would be, where to find them, and the key factors that drive their behavior, a strategy was designed to provide for:

- innovative, creative, unique, and appealing products;
- consistent delivery of premium quality;
- tightly controlled distribution;
- a distinct brand personality and identity;
- a global reputation;
- emotional appeal;
- premium pricing; and
- high visibility.

OnePure's brand personality was built to mirror that of its target audience, and was based on two characteristics of "modern" and "chic."

Brand positioning

The positioning of the brand has to be, as with any luxury brand, that of a premium product, and careful attention was given to potential competitors such as Clinique, Lancôme, Chanel, Laneige, Nude, and SK11. Layla Mandi says, "OnePure strives to offer competitive pricing in line with Clinique, but with a superior product, packaging, and marketing in line with Chanel." In terms of other well-known brands, she says: "OnePure sits across La Prairie and Clarins, with a price point competitive with Clarins."

The real emotional benefit accruing to Muslim consumers is the "peace of mind" provided by the *halal* nature of the product range.

Product range

To be competitive with other luxury beauty brands, OnePure has to have a comprehensive range of products, and this includes the following (with product descriptions from OnePure). As the following descriptions illustrate, both emotional and rational benefits are used to attract the consumer to the brand, while at the same time hinting at the technology behind the products. This is very similar to the practice followed by global brands.

Essentials
The Perfect Toner, 100% Luxe Eye Crème

AcneTreatments
Target Serum, 12-Hour Night Repair Treatment and Multi-Vitamin Repair Mask.

PRODUCT INTEGRITY, LABELING, AND PACKAGING

To ensure maximum security for consumers, OnePure labeling provides barcodes and information on the product formula, and indicates how long the product may be used once opened. The labeling information is provided in multiple languages to ensure compliance with local legislation of the countries where the products are distributed. OnePure products are formulated in Canada by a team of dermatologists following the strictest ingredient laws. OnePure caters for Muslim consumers by manufacturing its products under the strict supervision of OnePure in Malaysia, a country globally respected as a center for certification of *halal* beauty products.

DISTRIBUTION (SALES AND MARKETING) CHANNELS

The main distribution channels used include:

- perfumeries (integrated stores, franchise stores, boutiques);
- department stores;
- upscale pharmacies;
- online sales—e-commerce websites;

- OnePure-branded kiosks;
- luxury hotels;
- airlines; and
- OnePure-branded spas.

FRANCHISING

Of particular interest in terms of trying to grow the brand's distribution as quickly as possible, the brand is developing a worldwide franchising network with OnePure-branded kiosks, which have the benefits of being:

- able to be used anywhere, including markets where luxury points of sale don't yet exist;
- educational;
- direct in terms of client interaction; and
- cost-effective.

MARKETING COMMUNICATIONS

The marketing department develops communications plans adapted to the characteristics of the Muslim target market and conveys the values that constitute an integral part of OnePure's *halal* brand. OnePure favors feature articles and advertisements in the print media, which are intended to educate Muslim consumers about the brand's *halal* products. A proposed monthly newsletter will be used to announce promotions, and to provide product and company updates. Significant sampling programs offering advice on application methods will be conducted to target the maximum number of potential customers.

It is also intended that the corporate website will provide an online beauty consultation service and that this will facilitate dialog with customers, allowing them to enjoy personalized experiences. Exchanges between beauty advisors and customers at points of sale also facilitate this process.

OTHER BRAND AND MARKETING INITIATIVES

Training is required by any luxury brand, and OnePure conducts its own training and hopes to develop its own training centers in future. It is extremely important that specialists who come into contact with customers learn about the *halal* concept and the brand's values and products. All staff are supplied with hand-made *abayas* in OnePure's corporate color to support the brand's luxury image.

OnePure is currently developing a long-term corporate citizen plan that will align the brand with charities and organizations that support women and family causes and promote Islamic values.

Sources: OnePure Beauty; www.onepurebeauty.com.

OnePure is an interesting example of how a new brand can be created by a new company with a small budget to fill a gap in the market for a specific target audience. It shows that *halal* products are well accepted in this growing industry, and that developing a luxury brand is by no means impossible despite fierce competition from giant established companies.

OnePure also reminds us that there are no shortcuts to brand creation and development, and that research and product development, together will all the other aspects of brand management, have to be meticulously carried out.

Summary

This chapter has shown that there are many strategies available to companies wanting to create Islamic brands. As mentioned at the beginning of this book, Islam is a lifestyle; thus, all lifestyle categories represent such opportunities.

In the next chapter, we identify the strategies Western brands are using to enter Muslim markets and see how they have fared.

Notes

1. Liz Gooch, "Advertisers Seek to Speak to Muslim Consumers," *The New York Times*, August 11, 2010.
2. "Malaysia *Halal* Food Products to Hit 180 Tesco Stores in UK," *Borneo Post Online*, January 7, 2010, www.theborneopost.com.
3. Stephen Green, *Good Value: Reflections on Money, Morality and an Uncertain World* (Penguin Books, 2009).
4. www.newtoislam.co.uk/forum/2007/05/, accessed May 1, 2010.
5. *USA Today*, December 13, 2005, www.usatoday.com/news/opinion/editorials/2005-12-13-arab-barbie-edit_x.htm.

Challenges and Key Strategies for the Building and Marketing of Non-Muslim Brands to Muslim Markets

Introduction

We have seen the challenges and strategies that are applicable to Muslim brands. In this chapter, we will look briefly at those that apply to non-Muslim brands wishing to break into Muslim markets or which are already engaged with them and growing their market share.

Some of the challenges that face non-Muslim brands are similar to those facing Muslim brands, but they may have to be approached from a different perspective, especially with respect to Islamic values and practices, and the need for *halal* understanding and accreditation. While Western brands have a great deal of strategic brand management and marketing capability, they may need to be reminded of some of the fundamentals and nuances pertaining to the Muslim market.

The main challenges are as follows.

- gaining brand awareness;
- ensuring accessibility;
- gaining acceptability;
- achieving suitable and consistent standards and quality (adequacy);
- understanding the culture;
- gaining trust (affinity); and
- attack from brand competitors.

Gaining Brand Awareness

This is a challenge faced by any brand in any market if they are relatively new to that market, and the same rules apply: You have to get yourself known by your potential consumers. However, this isn't a challenge normally faced by the established global and international brands. If a brand is already very well established in the non-Muslim world, it is highly likely that awareness of it exists in the Muslim world, such is the ready availability of information and the transparency across markets that come with a globalized world. Thus, we see brands such as Apple, Nestlé, HSBC, Nokia, Toyota, and practically all the luxury brands and brand leaders in most categories, enjoying substantial awareness. As a consequence of this, they don't have to use up valuable resources to build up awareness and can instead focus on the other challenges.

Ensuring Accessibility

Accessibility can be an issue for non-Muslim brands. In financial services, for example, it is not easy in Muslim countries for foreign brands to obtain a license to operate or to establish wide branch networks. In telecommunications, it is also difficult to break in without a partner network. But in general the top global brands usually don't encounter many problems regarding market entry—they are usually welcomed if they understand the culture of the country or market they want to access and are prepared to show that they will adapt to the necessary requirements of the host country.

However, while getting into the market may not be too difficult, distribution may be. We know, for instance, that there are approximately 161 million Muslims in India. There is a lot of bureaucracy involved, but foreign firms can set up in India, and barriers to entry are gradually being reduced, but the challenge is finding the Muslim population all over India, when there is no valid data as to where they are located. And even if they are able to be located, there is the issue of how a company distributes its brand to various groups of Muslims in what is essentially a highly fragmented market with millions of small shops. Below is a case where an understanding of the market and a clear focus can help in meeting these challenges.

CASE STUDY 29: QSR BRANDS BERHAD
AND YUM! BRANDS

Western and Muslim Partners Access India

QSR Brands Berhad has enjoyed a great deal of success as the KFC brand franchise holder in parts of Asia. QSR, via its associated company KFC Holdings (Malaysia) Bhd, operates over 523 KFC restaurants in Malaysia, Singapore, Brunei, and Cambodia, as well as 37 Rasamas restaurants in Malaysia. KFC is among the best-established global brands in the Western Quick Service Restaurants market. It is by far the most popular restaurant chain in Malaysia, commanding a market share of over 35 percent.

In 2010, QSR Brands entered the Indian fast-food market with a KFC Indian venture that was initiated by Jamaludin Md Ali, CEO and managing director, KFC Holdings Malaysia Bhd. Operationally, the business is driven by Hezal Ahmad, CEO, Indian operations, with P. Ragupathy as director of operations. To ensure that the India operations receive the benefit of QSR's established experience in Malaysia, three senior QSR managers oversee the expansion within the state of Maharasthra and several Indian staff members underwent months of training in Malaysia.

Market operations for QSR are also supported by KFC brand owner Yum! Brands, a company that already has around 70 outlets for its products in India, by way of supply chain support such as centralized global procurement of food inputs.

QSR opened two stores—in Mumbai and Pune—in May 2010 and has already been successful in reaching the top three performing stores in India (in sales terms). This success has been challenging. As Ragapathy says, "There's no doubt, India is a challenging market. We never said it was easy—but we have learned a lot with the opening of our first two stores, and we are backed by a solid 37 years' experience in running KFC back in Malaysia." QSR was faced with store opening delays due to construction and licensing delays (14 licenses are necessary per outlet), but lessons learned are likely to speed up further openings, according to the company's management.

The other apparent marketing challenge is that India has the bulk of the world's vegetarians (60 percent of 1.18 billion people), so at first sight the success of the two stores to date may seem surprising. But the 40 percent of Indians who eat meat occasionally or frequently still comprises a good number to attract. The consumers that QSR targets in Mumbai and Pune are non-vegetarians who live in cities and towns, and who eat meat for reasons such as social status, health benefits, and to match the lifestyles of people in developed countries. The Mumbai store is located in Korum Mall, Thane, a suburb with a population of 1.8 million people and a desired residential area for middle-income earners; while the Pune outlet, in Deccan Mall, is located close to colleges and the young working population in the IT sector.

The opportunity may be very large, as there is an increasing food and beverage demand arising from the young population and rising incomes in India. Taking into account also the fact that Indian poultry consumption is growing faster than any other meat type, the future looks bright for QSR Brands and the KFC brand in India.

Source: QSR Brands Berhad, www.qsrbrands.com.

Clearly, QSR had looked carefully into the opportunities in the market and found both the opportunity and the accessibility viable.

A third issue, of course, is whether the market is worth accessing at all. Tesco, a global retailing giant, is trying out sales of *halal* food products in the UK market. However, there are only around 1.8 million Muslims in Britain and this individual market doesn't yet have the volume required for a major retailer. Tesco will only treat the Muslim *halal* market seriously if it can learn from this experience and see that the numbers of consumers globally are not only large but accessible. It is interesting to note that Tesco is beginning to see the growth potential here, as it has extended its trialing in a significant way.

[Tesco] already offers more than 100 fresh halal products to cater for its Muslim customers. Now with the market worth an estimated £2.8 billion a year, Tesco believes it has spotted another gap in the market. The supermarket giant is today launching a halal barbeque food range. It will sell seven frozen chicken and lamb barbeque dishes with plans to add more to the range next year. Only last month Tesco opened its fourth halal meat counter at its Hodge Hill store in Birmingham. Tesco ethnic food buying manager Steve Ewels said: "It's estimated there are two million Muslims living in the UK but until now there's never been a dedicated halal barbeque range. Now we've put that right. We know there is a growing demand for halal food so for us it is a natural move to offer a barbeque range." The launch is in line with a general move by restaurant chains such as McDonald's, KFC, and Nando's plus sandwich specialists Subway to offer halal food.[1]

Gaining Acceptability

Acceptability of a brand is connected in part to its country of origin. Non-Muslim brands that have already gained awareness are not often faced with acceptability problems, and nor do they have quality issues in terms of acceptance into Muslim markets.

Where they *may* encounter a challenge is in gaining acceptance with respect to adaptation of products and the values they portray. In Muslim markets, the main consideration in categories such as food, cosmetics, pharmaceuticals, entertainment, and other such categories is whether they are *halal* or not. To be able to gain market entry in a category such as food and beverage, *halal* accreditation is essential. The challenge here is that there is no one single form of accreditation that all Muslim countries accept. There are dozens, if not more, forms of accreditation in different parts of the world, but none represents a key to open the door to the market in all the different Muslim countries. This means that, in marketing branded products to different countries, you may have to employ different accreditation endorsements, and this can take time and money, and may include modification of factories, products and services, work practices, food security and logistics, and other issues.

Even then, the market entry may not be successful, as Domino's Pizza found out in the UK when it tried a *halal*-only menu at three of its branches. In 2009 it was one of the first fast-food chains to completely remove pork from its pizza menus and to serve *halal*-only meat in its outlets in Birmingham, Bradford, and Blackburn, cities where there are sizable Muslim populations. By August 2010, it had reversed this move and returned to its original recipes, including non-*halal* items such as pepperoni, due to poor sales and some criticism from non-Muslim customers.

According to a statement issued by the company in Birmingham:

> *Domino's Pizza Group decided to trial a Halal menu in Hall Green and two other stores in 2009, but it hasn't had the impact expected and the company has reluctantly decided to return to a conventional Domino's menu in all three stores. This has not been an easy decision for us and we are sorry for any inconvenience.*[2]

A Domino's spokesperson said:

> *As a company we are always trying new things, but on this occasion the response didn't justify keeping it going so we have reverted back to the original menu. The decision has been a completely commercial one in line with the launch of our new lunch campaign. The timing of the decision has tied in with that campaign.*[3]

From a marketing perspective, there are times when a brand manager's conviction that it is the right time to enter a new market segment turns out to be a wrong decision. Whether Domino's carried out its market research adequately is not known, but sometimes there is a risk of alienating existing customers by taking away the products they are used to. And if the new segment of potential customers doesn't "bite," so to speak, it can be double trouble.

Connected with the above is the issue of adequacy.

Achieving Suitable and Consistent Standards and Quality (Adequacy) ▬▬▬

The issue of consistent suitability, and consistent standards and quality, is normally not problematic for non-Muslim brands, especially from Western and some Asian countries where standards are very high. The issue here is local relevancy. Unlike the issue facing Muslim brands, which may have *halal* accreditation but sometimes lack the quality required to move into Western markets, non-Muslim brands may have high quality but may fail to gain an acceptable standard for *halal* accreditation from the Muslim countries to which they are marketing products. It is essential that you work with the different authorities in each individual market to ensure that your products have accreditation that is adequate and accepted. (As mentioned previously, accreditation approval standards may differ between Muslim countries.) It may be adequate to have one *halal* accreditation but better to have another, so care should be taken to understand the nuances of the particular market.

This leads us to another challenge, which is to understand the culture of the particular Muslim market you are aiming at.

We can understand this issue better by taking a look at Colgate's *halal* toothpaste, which is sold in Malaysia and other countries. Apparently, Colgate toothpaste sold in Malaysia is, and has always been, *halal*. According to the company's website: "Colgate Toothpaste is manufactured to *halal* standards and does not contain animal ingredients or alcohol."[4] Proof is required for adequacy purposes, however, and Colgate has received certification from the Malaysian *halal* accreditation agency, JAKIM. According to the website, "JAKIM acknowledges that Colgate Toothpaste is certified *halal* by Islamic bodies recognized by JAKIM as follows: Central Islamic Committee of Thailand, The Islamic Community of Ho Chi Minh City (Vietnam), China Islamic Association (China) and Federation of Muslim Associations of Brazil (Brazil). By receiving this approval from JAKIM, Colgate Toothpaste packs display the Halal seal."

Previously, it had not been a requirement that Colgate display the seal. "Colgate toothpaste was classified as a pharmaceutical product by the Malaysia Ministry of Health and therefore had not been permitted by MOH to display the Halal seal. Realizing that this was causing consumer confusion, Colgate petitioned for, and was granted, special approval to place the seal on the pack. So after 50 years of being *halal* in Malaysia, Colgate toothpaste will now display the seal."

The company goes on to say that "current JAKIM policy allows only products produced in Malaysia to carry the JAKIM seal. There is no standard seal for products produced outside Malaysia. Colgate Toothpaste will either carry the seal of the JAKIM recognized Islamic Body from its country of origin or a generic seal; all of which have been shared with JAKIM prior to use." To further add credibility to the issue, Colgate says that "both the Ministry of Trade and Consumer Affairs and JAKIM have independently tested Colgate Toothpaste and confirmed that the products do not contain animal DNA or alcohol. The calcium in Colgate toothpaste is sourced from minerals and the glycerin in Colgate toothpaste is sourced from plants."

It is imperative that, whether or not your brand is from an Islamic or non-Islamic company, clear approval and the accreditation seal from a recognized authority is gained and is shown clearly on the labeling. And it is worth remembering that gaining accreditation from one Muslim country doesn't automatically mean that your product can be sold in another country. It is thus imperative to check the required accreditation in all prospective national markets.

Understanding the Culture

Non-Muslim brands must not only modify products and services to suit Muslim requirements, but also demonstrate that they understand Islamic values. What is acceptable in Turkey may not be so in Saudi Arabia. As we have seen, Muslim countries differ in their degree of religiosity, so you may need to communicate more clearly the "Islamic values" of your company and its products in those countries that are more conservative.

For example, in Turkey many women don't tend to wear headscarves, but in Malaysia most Malay women do. This fact, together with its long presence in the Malaysian market and its understanding of Malaysian Muslims, gave Unilever the opportunity to create a brand extension. According to a recent article in the *New York Times*:

> *Unilever says the Sunsilk Lively Clean & Fresh shampoo, which is sold in Malaysia and Singapore, was created for people who suffer from oily scalps after wearing any head covering, be it a baseball hat or head scarf. After company research showed that many women who wear the* tudung *complained of oily scalps, it introduced the television commercial aimed at them. The ad begins with a young woman saying that now she can do what she wants because she no longer has to worry about itchiness, before she goes on to kick a goal in a coed soccer game.[5]*

Nokia is another global brand that understands Islamic culture:

> *The company made a concerted effort to appeal to Muslims starting in 2007, when it introduced a phone for the Middle East and North Africa markets that came loaded with a number of applications, including an Islamic Organizer with alarms for the five daily prayers, two Islamic e-books and an e-card application that lets people send SMS greeting cards for Ramadan. Starting this year, the company has been giving customers the choice of which applications they want, rather than loading them all on the phone.[6]*

In its Noor Global Brand Index 2010, described in Chapter 3, Ogilvy & Mather Worldwide said that it found Nokia to be rated favorably by Muslims. Citing one Egyptian respondent, Ogilvy's John Goodman said Nokia had "Islamic values" and offered products to suit the Egyptian consumer. Goodman said that the reason for this was that "Nokia is seen as being a very good corporate citizen and very sensitive to the local market."

If properly executed, demonstrating your knowledge of and sensitivity toward cultural issues will give you a great start in gaining trust.

Gaining Trust (Affinity)

The following example shows how easy it is to offend markets unless adequate research is carried out, and how even the world's top brands can make mistakes. A huge brand like Nike can recover from such an unfortunate incident, but brands of lesser stature and strength that are relatively unknown won't be able to do so.

CASE STUDY 30: NIKE

The Nike Launch that Offended Islam

In 1997, Nike was forced to recall a range of sports shoes carrying a logo that offended Muslims in America, and had to agree not to sell the new line in Britain. The Council on American–Islamic Relations (CAIR) asked Muslims around the world not to boycott Nike products after the company put the ban into effect and apologized to the Muslim world. Nike also agreed to donate a US$50,000 playground to an Islamic elementary school in the United States.

The issue arose when Nike used a logo that was meant to look like flames on a line of basketball shoes with the names "Air Bakin," "Air Melt," "Air Grill," and "Air B-Que." Some Muslims claimed that the logo resembled the word "Allah" written in Arabic script. CNN reported on November 21, 1998:

> *Nike and the Council on American–Islamic Relations completed an agreement last week, officially resolving a problem that began in April 1997 when CAIR objected to a shoe with a design on the heel similar to the Arabic word for God or Allah.*

> *As part of the final agreement, Nike is building three playgrounds for Islamic communities in the United States, said Roy Agostino, communications manager for Nike. CAIR will decide where the playgrounds will be, Agostino said.*

> *The first playground will be at Dar AlHijrah Islamic Center, Falls Church, Virginia, where representatives from Nike and CAIR held a groundbreaking ceremony Saturday. Children from the center's school drew pictures of what they would like in their new play-ground. Nike distributed balloons and T-shirts.[7]*

Nike adjusted the logo, but Islamic leaders said it was still offensive to their religion when the shoes were launched in America. Nike had to withdraw 38,000 pairs of the shoes worldwide.

Nihad Awas, CAIR's executive director, said: "We wanted to reinstate confidence in our community that whenever they see something offensive, there could be something done about it." Roy Agostino, for Nike, said the company immediately diverted supplies away from Islamic states and discontinued production. In addition, it introduced a review panel into its development process to prevent similar problems arising in future. "We have, through this process, developed a deeper understanding of Islamic concerns and Islamic issues," he said. "As our brand continues to expand, we have to deepen our awareness of other world communities."[8]

The lesson here is never to underestimate how a market might react, and to carry out market research in those countries where you expect to market your products. Well-known examples of mistakes being made include when GM launched its world car—NOVA—only to find that in Spanish the word literally meant "won't go," and when Coca-Cola had to change its transliteration of its name in China after the initial rendering translated as "bite the wax tadpole." If a company can't be bothered to really understand a nation's culture and language, it will never really be trusted and is more likely to fail.

If you have a well-recognized and trusted brand, then apart from offering the right *Shariah* products in the right way, it is best to keep the brand that is recognized well to the fore. HSBC aligns its Amanah brand closely with the HSBC global brand in all advertising and promotional materials, including employee name cards. HSBC does this because, through its global brand name, it is pledging its trustworthiness, honesty, reliability, and integrity. As a result, the Amanah brand leverages on the strong brand equity of the mother brand and imports those key attributes, while the association enables HSBC clients to choose Islamic solutions in key markets internationally from a bank they trust.

Trust can also be strengthened by brands that respect Islam and its values. There is no better expression of this than in the holy month of Ramadan (Muslim month of fasting). Many global brands, including

Coca-Cola, Burger King, HSBC, Ikea, Nestlé, Pepsi, Starbucks and more, are experienced in advertising in Muslim markets from Turkey to Malaysia, using messaging and customization that caters to Muslim needs and attitudes. The following are examples of some brands that have incorporated seamlessly the Ramadan and two Eid holidays within their local marketing campaigns.

Walmart

In 2008, Walmart opened a store in Dearborn, Michigan designed specifically for the Muslim and Middle Eastern consumer. The store offers over 550 items targeted at Middle Eastern shoppers, in addition to its standard products. The entrance area was set up to represent a farmers market in Beirut. Tables were stacked high with fresh produce such as *kusa* and *batenjan*, squash and eggplant used in Middle Eastern dishes. A walled-off area of the meat section was devoted to *halal* meats, and in the freezer case was frozen *falafel*. There were also Middle Eastern pop music CDs available, as well as Muslim greeting cards. Two years prior to the opening, Walmart executives started meeting with *imams* and mothers, and conducting focus groups at Middle Eastern restaurants.

CASE STUDY 31: MONEYGRAM INTERNATIONAL

MoneyGram International is a leading global payment services company providing consumers with affordable, reliable, and convenient payment services. The diverse array of products and services enables consumers, most of whom are not fully served by traditional financial institutions, to make payments and to transfer money around the world, helping them meet the financial demands of their daily lives.

The nature of the transaction business positions MoneyGram as an important natural connection between many people in different countries and cultures. Over the years, the company has recognized that the Muslim community represents one of the key customer segments using their services. The Muslim population has immigrated globally.

Millions live in the US, Europe, and around the world, but maintain their connection with friends and family in their mother country through traditions and holidays. As a result, MoneyGram explored and launched strategic marketing efforts aimed at these consumers, particularly during the religious celebrations of Ramadan and Eid.

"We see a large increase of remittances from the USA and Canada to South Asia and the Middle East during the time of Ramadan," said Zainab Ali, senior marketing manager at MoneyGram. "With our more than 203,000 locations across the world, we are able to meet the needs of Muslims everywhere who want to send funds to family."

During Ramadan 2010, MoneyGram combined promotion and social media as it launched a global Ramadan and Eid initiative across Asia-Pacific, Canada, Europe and the United States in which customers had a chance to win US$1,000 per week. Customers who sent money with MoneyGram were given a chance to win with every transaction.

The goal of the campaign was to increase transaction volumes and create awareness of the MoneyGram brand among Muslim consumers. With many alternatives in the market, the company needed to engage and interact with customers to reach its goals. Joining in the celebration of these important traditions provided an opportunity to show appreciation of and share with customers, continuing the development of a long-term connection with the community.

In line with these goals, and in order to increase the visibility of the campaign, MoneyGram looked to connect with users through social media. The company launched an effort that encouraged people to share stories of kindness across the Muslim community with a social media campaign called "Ramadan Kindness." Muxlim.com, Twitter, and Facebook were primarily used to develop and spread heartwarming stories highlighting Muslims doing extraordinary acts for others. Information sharing was catalyzed through daily posting to the different channels to draw more people to the pages and encourage them to post their own stories. MoneyGram banner ads were also posted on a series of high-traffic Muslim sites as part of the campaign. The campaign results encompassed a series of social media metrics, including "likes," fans, comments, sharing, and views. It also provided insight into the click performance of banners associated with the campaign on sites directly tied to the social media campaign and those with no exposure to social media.

To launch and feed the social media activity, 20 professionally written stories with MoneyGram branding were originally posted to Muxlim.com over the course of the Ramadan holy month. The "Ramadan Kindness" social media campaign resulted in thousands of views and "likes" on Facebook and Muxlim.com. In its first five weeks, the MoneyGram "Ramadan Kindness" Facebook page surpassed the company's own fan page by 57 percent, with currently over 2,500 "likes." (The MoneyGram company Facebook page has been up for more than a year.) There were 40,894 content views directly via Facebook and Muxlim.com, 919 comments, and 31,078 shares and "likes," as of September 7, 2010. These didn't include the many thousands of "likes" and shares of the content on other fan pages such as "I Love Allah," which, for example, alone received 5,603 "likes" and 163 positive comments on the MoneyGram "Ramadan Kindness" post for August 24, 2010.

In addition, banner ads that were combined with the social media campaign had a 0.31 percent click-through rate (CTR) versus an average 0.07 percent on other sites without social media. In this campaign, every content view was accompanied by MoneyGram branding and banners. Originally, the campaign was targeted to provide one million banner impressions, but the overwhelming response and popularity resulted in Muxlim.com's decision to deliver nearly 2.5 million impressions primarily during the six-week campaign while still maintaining the high CTR.

In this campaign, social media combinations brought extended value and visibility. Significantly more clicks (more than 300 percent) were made to MoneyGram banners and links directly connected to the advertiser when stories about something of significance to people were present. The thought, based on the success of other digital brand campaigns and studies on the use of social media in marketing, is that the stories gave people a reason to emotionally connect and share.

The true nature of harnessing the social web today is in using multiple media types. The MoneyGram campaign combined the use of Muxlim.com, Facebook, and Twitter, each having its own benefits for sharing and communication. Not only were messages originally posted and pushed to the community, but these tools were also used to listen and respond to users, creating further opportunities for sharing and interaction. Brands such as "Old Spice" are also successfully employing such methods today to communicate with and get feedback from their audiences.

It is understood that this campaign was only a beginning step. Volumes and views of the content and brand are temporary, without regular value-added engagement with the customer. MoneyGram is striving to create a long-term relationship with its customers so that its services become a top-of-mind choice when payment services are needed. In this case, social media has again proven it is an important, cost-effective part of the marketing mix as brands continue to engage with Muslim customers.

Sources: MoneyGram International and Muxlim.com.

Attack from Brand Competitors

There are always incumbent brands in any market, and Muslim markets are no exception. For example, in Turkey, Ülker foods has a very large range of food brands comparable in many ways to the Nestlé portfolio, and Indonesia has a similar giant in Indofood. Breaking a near monopoly situation in either of these countries isn't easy and only the giant non-Muslim brands could take them on. The alternative in this situation, apart from huge spending on brand to break into a market, is to look for areas of unsatisfied needs among consumers in the relevant categories.

To conclude this chapter, we will look at a brand that has overcome all of the above challenges and employed many of the strategies—Nestlé.

CASE STUDY 32: THE NESTLÉ APPROACH

Global Positioning and Local Relevance

According to Al-Harman and Low (2008), the global *halal* food market is estimated to be worth US$580 billion. Europe alone, which is predominantly non-Muslim, has a *halal* food industry worth US$66 billion. In 2008, Nestlé's revenue derived from its *halal* products was reportedly US$5.2 billion, close to 1 percent of the potential revenue from the global *halal* food market and almost 5 percent of Nestlé's sales for that year.

Recognizing the market potential derived from Muslim consumers, Nestlé has taken several key initiatives since 1992 to expand its offering and gain stronger traction in this market. By 2008, it had increased production capacity for *halal* food to over 50 factories in Islamic countries and 85 *halal*-certified factories worldwide. In Europe alone, 19 *halal*-certified factories produce products that cater to the Muslim community there. And Nestlé has established its Global Centre of Halal Excellence in a Muslim country—Malaysia.

This strategy is consistent with the statement by Frits van Dijk (executive vice president and zone director for Asia, Oceania, Africa, and Middle East) that Nestlé is set to increase its supply of ethnic and *halal* foods in Europe, having already established a strong presence in France, the UK, and Germany. In addition, Nestlé has established over 62 representative offices in the Islamic countries.

Nestlé has also developed *halal* products across 154 product lines. For example, some of the popular Nestlé product brands that are already *halal* certified include Milo, Maggi, Nido (milk), and Herta (snacks). One of the key factors in Nestlé's rapid progress is the input provided by the Halal Excellence Centre, which is located at Nestlé Malaysia and is tasked to transfer *halal* knowledge globally.

In 2009, Nestlé initiated a marketing campaign called "Taste of Home"—a *halal* campaign targeted at Muslims in Europe. The purpose of the campaign was to generate awareness and increase the visibility of Nestlé's *halal* products among Muslim consumers. The campaign carried strong "*halal*" branding and used visuals of *halal* dishes—such as chicken curry, noodles, and couscous—which could be prepared using the Nestlé "Taste of Home" range. The campaign was executed successfully during the month of Ramadan across 800 retail outlets in five European countries (Belgium, Germany, Netherlands, Italy, and Switzerland).

Nestlé has also made efforts to generate better communications concerning its commitment to *halal* food certification by clearly projecting the "*halal*-certified" logo on its products. With these logos, Nestlé intends to inform its Muslim consumers that their food products have been through a stringent evaluation process by the Islamic authorities of their respective countries. The following are some of the logos that Nestlé has used across different countries to communicate this attribute on its product packaging.

Frits van Dijk comments:

Nestlé is in the nutrition, health, and wellness business, and is one of the largest corporate brands in the world. Founded in 1866 in Switzerland, at the end of 2008 it had CHF109.9 billion in sales, over 280,000 employees, 456 factories in 84 countries, and 28 R&D centres.

The halal *code sits well with the Nestlé philosophy of sustainability from "crop to plate"—or, as many Muslims say, from farm to fork—and taking care of the emerging market consumers. Nestlé's halal adherence first started in the 1980s, but its first halal policy was established in 1992. The Nestlé Inter-Market Supply of Halal Food Products was developed in 1997 for the Nestlé Group, and Nestlé Malaysia is the Centre of Halal Excellence for the group.*

Although Nestlé's branding and marketing activity is principally in what it calls the "halal food culinary" category, with brands such as Maggi, it also features strongly in other categories such as creamers, coffee and beverages, infant nutrition and baby food, milks, breakfast cereals and cereal bars, and confectionery, with brands such as Tea Pot, Milo, Nescafé, Nespray, Corn Flakes, KitKat, and Smarties.

Sources: The quotations are taken from a talk given by Frits van Dijk, executive vice president, Nestlé SA, zone director for Asia, Oceania, Africa, and Middle East, entitled "Importance of *Halal* in Nestlé's Global Expansion," World Halal Forum Europe, The Hague, Netherlands, 2009; S. Al-Harman and P. Low, "The Way Forward," *Halal Journal*, 2008; www.nestle.com.my/Nestle+Insights/Corporate+Information/halalPolicy.htm; www.nestle-tasteofhome.com.

Summary

We have seen in this chapter that there are several challenges facing non-Islamic companies in building their brands in Muslim markets, but they are not insurmountable. This is mainly because, first, non-Islamic companies tend to have greater brand development and management skills than Islamic companies, and second, their brands are often already known—and in many cases liked—by Muslims.

The final chapter provides a general summary and a reminder about some of the main business strategies that brand and marketing managers should bear in mind when accessing and building share in Muslim markets.

Notes

1. "UK: Now Supermarket Giant Tesco Offers *Halal* Range for Barbeques," www.halalfocus.net, June 6, 2010.
2. *Sky News Online*, August 16, 2010.
3. *Ibid.*
4. www.colgate.com.sg/app/Colgate/SG/OC/Products/Toothpastes/ColgateHalal/FAQPage.cvsp.
5. Liz Gooch, "Advertisers Seek to Speak to Muslim Consumers," *The New York Times*, August 11, 2010.
6. *Ibid.*
7. http://articles.cnn.com/1998-11-21/us/9811_21_nike.islamic_1_nihad-awad-playgrounds-cair?_s=PM:US.
8. *The Independent*, June 25, 1997.

Summary of Power Brand Strategy Programs for Muslim Markets

In this book, we have examined the increasing purchasing power and untapped market potential of the world's 1.6 billion Muslim population, and explored the unified, universal, and sustainable emotional values that underpin the Islamic faith. We have seen how a number of Western brands have identified and seized the opportunities presented by this market and used flexible branding techniques to tailor their products and services for Muslim consumers. We have also analyzed the challenges involved in building Islamic brands, and identified what needs to be done to overcome them.

In this final chapter, we will summarize the strategies available to both Islamic and non-Islamic companies in building future global brands across both Muslim-majority and minority markets.

Strategies for Non-Muslim Brands

For the established international brands, the options are fairly clear. Non-Muslim, mainly Western brands, must realize that the primary driver in all Muslim markets isn't the product but its Islamic identity. It is not good enough, nor will it ever be, to view the Muslim global market from a geographic perspective, even though different Muslim markets do behave somewhat differently. It is necessary to view Muslim markets globally as a lifestyle market driven by enormous dedication to Islamic values and practices. Only by taking this view will brand managers find that global product management is possible. Given this position, here are some possible strategies they can adopt.

1. Ride on the Reputation and Positioning of Your Global Brand

Just as Nestlé has done, and what other companies are currently doing, use the power of your brand name to quickly penetrate the market. Of course, you need to ensure the acceptability of your products in terms of *halal* certification—which may be different in different countries—but overall trust is the reason people will buy your brand. Muslim consumers like global brands just as much as everyone else, but not necessarily at the expense of their shared values and principles. So, respect for and understanding of Islamic principles and practices are vital.

2. Develop New, *Shariah*-compliant Products

In connection with the above, even a powerful and well-known brand name may need substantial adjustment if the market is relatively new and still in the innovation stages of product development. Nestlé produces foods that are traditionally acceptable, and not much is fundamentally new or highly innovative in most food categories; however, for new, rising markets such as Islamic finance, it may be that substantially different product development and marketing are needed. HSBC has achieved this by opening an Islamic banking "window," as we saw earlier, and all its products have been created to satisfy the relevant *Shariah* law. Nevertheless, its global, trusted name gives HSBC a head start once the products are in place, and in many Muslim countries it has a leading market share.

3. Set up a New Islamic Business

If you really want to convince the market that you are serious, then set up a totally Islamic business, as Standard Chartered Bank has done. However, make sure that the trusted name is linked to the new name, as Standard Chartered has done with Standard Chartered Saadiq.

4. Go for the Luxury Market

In every country in the world there is an affluent segment that adores luxury brands, and this is true also for all Muslim markets, whether majority or minority in nature. In large economies such as India and Indonesia, while there are still a vast number of people who are poor, the middle classes are growing and the rich seem to be getting richer. In the Middle East, the luxury market knows no bounds. Look carefully for the gaps that other big brands have not yet filled.

5. Create Branded Islamic Services

Probably the world's most famous brand communications agency, Ogilvy & Mather Worldwide identified an opportunity to help Islamic brands grow. It created not a separate business, but a branded Islamic practice within its business called Ogilvy Noor. *"Noor"* means "light" or "enlightenment," and is thus a very suitable name for a brand-building and advertising business. This is a good example of another strategy, brand naming, where a brand name is created and tailored completely to Muslim markets and which is relevant to both Islamic and non-Islamic brands via the products and services it provides.

6. Add More Lifestyle Islamic-oriented Products to Your Portfolio

Companies such as the BBC and CNN have created programs for people in Muslim countries and those interested in Islamic affairs. Standard Chartered and HSBC have gained substantial market share in financial services, and Nestlé earns billions of dollars in revenue per year from its range of *halal* foods. Unilever caters to Muslim lifestyles with its Sunsilk shampoo for Muslim women called Lively Clean & Fresh, which helps remove excess oil from the scalp and hair—a common problem among wearers of *tudung* (headscarves). The company says the product is the first shampoo to speak directly to the lifestyle of a *tudung* wearer.

All these companies are enjoying brand success by demonstrating their commitment to changing what they do and what they offer to suit the needs and wants of Muslim consumers.

7. Use Your Country of Origin to Good Effect

People do care where products originate from and where they are made. The country-of-origin effect works well for those with a substantial reputation in certain categories, such as Germany in engineering, Japan in consumer electronics, and Switzerland in timepieces. Such a reputation brings trust and peace of mind about quality issues, which are critical to good branding and marketing.

8. Stay True to Your Values and Messaging

If your brand already has a strong international presence, it is likely that those brand values may carry through to Muslim markets, as they have done for brands such as Nike and Nokia. Walk through a few shopping malls in Muslim-majority countries and you will find the same global brands are projecting the same values and messages to consumers as they do in other markets.

9. Watch out for New and Growing Muslim Categories

Some categories of products and services that are growing are the obvious ones that are gaining much media exposure, such as social networking, media, and financial services; however, there are also other categories, such as personal care, cosmetics, and pharmaceuticals.

10. Capitalize on Technological Advantage and Offer Solutions

As Muslim businesses begin to get organized, they will need the services of technology partners and solutions providers. This is an opportunity for many technology-based brands interested in accessing the developing Muslim countries, as they are often trying to find the best solutions to help them become more efficient and effective. Look for the rising brands in each market, and by making it easier for them to build their businesses they, in return, will help you build yours. The rising stars in Muslim countries in the Internet and technology sectors may want to merge or be acquired, as was the case with Yahoo!'s acquisition of Maktoob.com.

Strategies for Muslim Brands ━━━━━━

Muslim brands have to be careful of how they approach their branding and marketing, if they have not already become successful. Here are a few tips distilled from the case studies included in this book.

1. Choose a Good and Relevant Brand Name

Brand names are very important and need careful attention in the branding process for both Muslim and non-Muslim brands, as mentioned above in connection with Ogilvy's "Noor." Other Islamic brands have shown that they, too, have given careful thought to this. MTC changed its name to Zain, meaning "beautiful," "good," or "wonderful" in Arabic; Fulla is named after a fragrant flower; and Ummah, the chocolate company, has a name that is world famous among Muslims as it refers to the Muslim populace.

2. Become Number One in Your Home Market

Very few brands of international stature have made it to the international and global stage without becoming number one in their home market. This applies to great brands such as Coca-Cola, Nike, Colgate, McDonald's, KFC, and so on. Once you have a following and you understand the world of consumers, it then begins to be easier to reach out to your near regional neighbors. This is the approach Ülker took.

3. Go Regional before You Try to Go Global

Usually, if you have gained the number one home market, you can then try regional marketing. Brands must be careful here, as the region can be very large; for example, half of the world's population lives in Asia. So, it makes sense to target immediate neighbors or those countries which have good relationships with yours, and which you understand in terms of how their consumers behave. For example, the obvious next step for Zain, which started in Kuwait, was to move into the MENA (Middle East North Africa) region.

4. Build Your Brand by Entering Muslim Markets First

Knowing the values and principles of *Shariah* law will help you to understand the market, even though the interpretation of some *Shariah* rules and *halal* accreditation procedures may be a little different in some Muslim countries. The point is that you are more likely to understand Muslims than non-Muslims in many categories, and may be more easily accepted.

You will feel more comfortable and can build your brand from this base. Muslim brands operating in Muslim-minority markets may have to accept that they may only be a niche player, but being number one in a niche market can be a great position to be in.

5. Adopt a Niche Market Position—Fill a Gap in the Market and Offer an Alternative

Following on from the above, it is often useful to look for a niche market position and stay away from directly competing with the big brands. There are always gaps in markets where the big brands haven't satisfied the needs of some segments of consumers. Such gaps provided opportunities for Fulla, the Muslim equivalent of the Barbie doll, the "Burquini" brand, and OnePure Beauty. Even the luxury markets are not out of reach for Muslim entrepreneurs.

6. Try to Leverage on Your Country of Origin

If your country has a good image and a reputation that has traveled well, then you may as well make the most of it. Take advantage of trade and export promotion grants that are increasingly available in Muslim countries.

7. Use Islamic Values of Universal Appeal and Relevance

As a Muslim company brand, use values that appeal not just to Muslims but to other non-Islamic audiences as well. For example, "truth," "honor," and "respect" are values projected by Saudi Arabia's Al Rajhi Bank, but few global citizens would disagree with those values, or indeed not be stirred emotionally by them to some extent. They are powerful motivators and attractors.

8. Stay True to Your Values, but Adapt Your Communications

The world is one big market, but it isn't. The Muslim population is one big market, but it isn't. These paradoxes are true—the Muslim market, as we have seen, is not homogeneous. So, when you create, develop, and manage your brand, choose values and propositions that are true to those of Islam, but manage your communications in different parts of the world to project them in ways that will attract the local population. Flexibility and adaptability are the keys to success. Flex the values to promote them in a way that local audiences can relate to. A good advertising agency should be able to help you do this.

9. Develop Your B2B Business and Brand

You know your market better than companies that are trying to gain entry into it, so use this expertise and help other brands enter your market. Be the catalyst, the expert, to whom all will turn. Many Western brands are very keen to work with brands from the Muslim world and create partnerships, especially where the Muslim firms need advice, guidance, data, and distribution. Most of all, they probably have little clue about your country's culture or the profiles of the market segments they seek, so these are the advantages you can offer. Muxlim.com did it; so can you.

10. Create a First Mover Point of Differentiation

Nothing works better than being innovative. Recall Johor Corporation, which got to where it is now by taking the *"waqf"* concept from the traditions of the Islamic faith, and looking for innovative ways of using it to build the business, the brand, and those of others completely differently.

11. Actively Seek out and Create Partnerships with Brands Looking to Enter Your Market

It is difficult to enter new and large markets, so look for a trusted brand to become your partner. Research in Motion (RIM, maker of the BlackBerry smartphone) wanted to enter Indonesia, a market of over 230 million people. It clearly needed to have a partner; it couldn't operate in such a huge telecommunications environment on its own, and that partner had to be a well-known local company. So, RIM created a partnership with PT Indosat. Now the BlackBerry brand is outselling global and former market leader Nokia in its category in Indonesia, and PT Indosat has another piece of business in a growing market.

The Future of Islamic Branding and Marketing

The next wave of branding will come from the Islamic world. As the world becomes one global market and deregulation continues, the pressure will increase for companies and governments to strengthen their brand positioning. I anticipate that there will be more government activity in this area. We are already witnessing Bahrain, Dubai, Hong Kong, London, Malaysia, Singapore, and others competing for "hub" status on a global or regional basis, and major brands competing in the private sector for both retail and wholesale markets. As Islamic finance continues to expand in double-digit figures annually, this embryonic market will attract many more players; and although branding and marketing activity is already quite high, I expect this to intensify over the next five to ten years.

Government-to-government branding and marketing will also grow, particularly as the more developed Muslim countries begin to see opportunities to help the poorer ones, with the production of *halal* medicines, vaccines, and pharmaceutical products. The strides forward now being taken by countries such as Brunei and Malaysia in the testing, accreditation, and standardization of such product categories will open up the global *halal* market significantly. Business-to-business marketing will also continue to flourish, as Islam has a centuries-old trading tradition and this is part of the DNA of many countries, especially those in the Gulf.

Arguably the most exciting area for Islamic branding and marketing in the foreseeable future is the lifestyle categories. The Western brands have already fully realized the potential here and are progressing with accreditation for many of their food, cosmetics, personal care, and other lifestyle product ranges. The challenge for brands from the Islamic world is to move quickly in order to secure a place at the table. The biggest requirement by Islamic brands that I can see isn't manufacturing competency or business know-how, but branding and marketing skills and techniques. This is an educational void that needs to be filled. The Islamic business world is now at a similar stage of development as Asia in the last decade of the 20th century. This manifested as a desperate pursuit of quality and efficiency, a mindset that thought branding and marketing was tactical advertising and promotion; and a focus on short-term thinking and profitability, as opposed to long-term thinking and brand investment. Branding wasn't seen as a legitimate strategic activity, and brands were viewed as intangible "marketing speak" that didn't justify monetary support. All in all, brand and marketing management were not seen as activities important to sustainable profitability and growth.

The scene is now changing in developing countries, and branding and marketing is beginning to lead the way in driving corporate strategy. Chief executives realize that brands are assets that can be worth multiples of the net tangible assets of a company, and that they need to treat branding and marketing appropriately, as investments that provide long-term sustainable value. Can Islamic countries and companies take this quantum leap in thinking? If they don't, then they will lose out on playing a significant part in the growth and development of the largest market in the world.

I am optimistic that they can, which will see the Islamic world at the center of the next wave of global branding .Nevertheless, in order to reach this stage, much more research and education is required. Appendix 1 outlines the Saïd Business School Project at the University of Oxford, which is currently looking at many of the areas discussed in this book. Appendix 2 contains a summary of proceedings from the recent Inaugural Oxford Global Islamic Branding and Marketing Forum undertaken as a part of this project in July 2010.

Appendix 1
The Oxford Research and Education Project on Islamic Branding and Marketing: Brief Project Overview

The Oxford Research and Education Project on Islamic Branding and Marketing ▬

This project started in October 2008 at Saïd Business School, Executive Education Centre, University of Oxford.

Saïd Business School, University of Oxford, is undertaking a project concerned with research and education in Islamic Branding and Marketing that would appeal to aspiring Islamic brand owners and managers in countries with Muslim-majority and minority populations, and to those in Western countries and corporations interested in doing business in Islamic markets.

Topics for Research ━━━━━━━━━━━━━━

The following is a list of possible topics already identified to be included in the Islamic Branding and Marketing Research and Education Project, although this will not exclude the introduction of other topics.

The Broader Perspective

Looking from a broader "big picture" perspective, it is important to understand what the project scope is, and as it involves the concept of "Islam" it is necessary to try and understand what this somewhat emotive word means by trying to answer questions such as:

- What does Islam have to do with branding and marketing?
- What is an "Islamic brand"? What is "Islamic marketing"?
- What are the "Islamic values" that impact on Islamic branding and marketing? Do they hold challenges or opportunities?
- Do the cultures, affiliations, and interpretations of Islam influence effective branding and marketing, and if so in what ways?

In trying to determine the answers to these (and other) questions, inevitably there will be historical influences that need to be taken into account, and so the project will also be looking at:

- The history of Islamic business and trade.
- The links between the origins and principles of Islam and modern-day business practice in Islamic countries and companies.
- The size and growth of Islamic markets (including populations, demographics, psychographics, global distribution of Muslims, segmentation statistics by industries, categories, etc).
- Specific research in order to establish patterns of consumer behavior and segmentation, relevant to Islamic branding and marketing, in industries such as financial services, lifestyle products, healthcare and medical products, women's products, and *halal* food and beverage products and services.

Islamic Country Brands

Closely connected with the above—through history and development—some countries are perceived to be more "Islamic" than others in their practices in the eyes of international consumers. All countries have a brand image composed of perceptions they may or may not like, and in an effort to improve their brand image and correct perception gaps by projecting a well thought-through strategic brand identity, some countries already are using tried-and-tested branding and marketing techniques. This dynamic situation may lead us into researching areas such as:

- The role of "national brands" in the branding and marketing of businesses, products, and services originated from that nation.
- A study of cultural differences in Islamic countries and how these pose challenges for branding and marketing.
- A study of the brand images of Islamic countries and products and how these are related to the "culture-of-origin" and "country-of-origin" effects.
- How country and company leadership influences the growth and success of Islamic businesses, and country images.
- The role of mergers, acquisitions, joint ventures, and strategic alliances in the growth of Islamic countries and companies.

"Experts" and "Partners"

As well as combining the resources of the Business School and the wider University, experts and interested parties from the private and public sector are encouraged to take part in the research and the building of case studies for educational purposes. We hope to deliver a truly multicultural learning experience for all.

The Outputs

One of the outputs of the project will be research findings that will be invaluable for Islamic and non-Islamic countries and companies interested in building brands and penetrating global markets.

Educational outputs will include case studies for learning purposes. These will examine successes and failures in Islamic branding and marketing in Muslim-majority and minority markets, and will include topics such as brand positioning strategies, cross-cultural and marketing communications strategies, and comparative studies with Western brands. The outputs are expected to be of value not only to Muslim companies, but also to Western companies wishing to further understand Muslim markets.

We invite you to join the Oxford network for the next stage of your development, and welcome discussions with all parties interested in becoming involved in the research and educational aspects of this project.

Dr. Paul Temporal
Associate Fellow and Project Director
Said Business School
University of Oxford
Egrove Park
Oxford OX1 5NY
United Kingdom

Appendix 2
The Inaugural Oxford Global Islamic Branding and Marketing Forum: Summary of Proceedings

July 26–27, 2010, Oxford, England

Saïd Business School, University
of Oxford

About the Forum

The Inaugural Oxford Global Islamic Branding and Marketing Forum brought together business and thought leaders to discuss and debate the opportunities and challenges of engaging the growing Muslim market. Held at the Saïd Business School, University of Oxford, on 26–27 July 2010, it was attended by over 230 delegates from across the globe.

Although the rise of industries characterized as *halal*, Islamic and *Shariah*-compliant have increasingly made headline news, this was the first forum of its kind focusing specifically on the branding and marketing aspects of addressing Muslim markets and consumers.

The Forum was structured to look at several different perspectives of Islamic branding and marketing. What do we mean by Muslim markets and brands? What are the challenges, how can they be overcome, and how to build customer loyalty? How are Muslims perceived today when it comes to religion, culture and branding, and what are the challenges of engaging Muslims in a multicultural global world? What can we learn from the development of the Islamic finance industry, and where next for this sector? What innovation can we hope for in the future, and what trends will shape the Muslim markets of the future?

Keynote addresses were delivered by global leaders such as Rt. Hon. Pehin Sri Haji Abdul Taib Mahmud, Chief Minister of Sarawak, Malaysia; Tan Sri Nor Mohamed Yakcop, Minister in the Prime Minister's Department, Malaysia; Miles Young, CEO, Ogilvy & Mather Worldwide; Shri K. Rahman Khan, Deputy Chairman of the Rajya Sabha and MP Indian National Congress; Tan Sri Dato' H. Muhammad-Ali, President and CEO, Johor Corporation; Roy Michel Haddad, Chairman and CEO, JWT Middle East and North Africa; Shaukat Aziz, Former Prime Minister of Pakistan; and HRH Raja Dr Nazrin Shah, Crown Prince of Perak, Malaysia.

Several key themes emerged, and these are elaborated on in the Executive Summary:

- The conference was the first of its kind in bringing together thought leaders, business pioneers and entrepreneurs to focus entirely on Islamic branding and marketing.
- Market definition and sizing, as well as consumer data and segmentation, show considerable variation due to the nascent nature of the industry.
- Muslim consumers, both globally and nationally, are not a homogeneous entity. Their diversity demographically, ethnographically and by gender must be recognised and understood.
- Islamic branding and marketing can be used to tackle wider global issues affecting Muslims at a political and international level.
- A positive change of attitude towards innovation, risk-taking and business aspiration is required to inspire and nurture Muslim entrepreneurs.
- Strong value propositions will be key to the success of Islamic brands.

Executive Summary ━━━━━━━━━━━

The conference was the first of its kind in bringing
together thought leaders, business pioneers and
entrepreneurs to focus entirely on Islamic branding
and marketing

According to the Pew Research Center, a comprehensive demographic study
of more than 200 countries finds that there are 1.57 billion Muslims of all
ages living in the world today, representing 23% of an estimated 2009 world
population of 6.8 billion. Not only is the Muslim population a significant
percentage of the global population, but AT Kearney also points out that
the market for *Shariah*-compliant products or services totals USD$2 trillion
annually and is growing rapidly. As Muslim countries develop, there is an
expressed need to develop and market their own brands to the rest of the
world. Additionally, there is substantial interest among non-Muslim companies in how to enter and penetrate this global market, which spans many
industries, including finance, food and beverage, cosmetics, healthcare,
pharmaceuticals, logistics, tourism, fashion, and others.

The Oxford Forum was the first to bring Muslim and non-Muslim leaders and companies from a variety of public and private sector organizations
together to discuss how to develop better trade and business relations and
to learn from each other about the markets involved and the techniques
required. Referring to the Islamic Branding and Marketing Research and
Education Project which organized the Forum, its Project Director, Dr Paul
Temporal, commented that: "The Forum is the Project's first significant
event at a time of rising interest."

Gay Haskins, Dean of Executive Education, welcomed everyone, and
Professor Andrew Hamilton, the Vice-Chancellor of Oxford University,
noted that "As the 'global village' increasingly takes shape at the start of the
21st century" Oxford University was a natural place to create a full understanding of Islam in the West, and that this innovative forum was part of a
centuries-long quest to deepen relations with the Muslim world.

Javed Husain, co-founder and director of the Media Reach agency, felt
that it was interesting that the debate about Islamic branding being hosted

by the Forum—the first of its kind—was being held in the West rather than the traditional Islamic lands of the East.

Miles Young, CEO of Ogilvy & Mather Worldwide, noted that the appreciation of this growing market is only slowly beginning to dawn on the commercial world: "It was when we sent out a mailer recently, describing Muslim consumers conservatively as the 'third one billion' that the bells started finally to ring in the global HQs of some of our clients. Yes, this is a market bigger than India or China is, and yet it receives a tiny fraction of the attention."

Market definition and sizing, as well as consumer data and segmentation, show considerable variation due to the nascent nature of the industry

Speakers throughout the conference were conscious of the variation in market sizing data that they quoted in their analysis. The Muslim global population was variously quoted as ranging from 1.57 billion to 1.9 billion, the global *halal* industry from USD$150 billion to anywhere up to USD$632 billion, and the Islamic finance industry between USD$1 trillion and USD$2 trillion. Not only were the numbers themselves different, it was clear that definitions of terms such as "*halal*," "*Shariah*-compliant" and "Islamic" were used with variation.

The analysis of both the size and the breakdown of the Muslim market was of evident concern in sizing the commercial opportunities available and the best way to tailor products and brands to meet those opportunities. As Sarah Joseph, editor of *emel* magazine, explained: "Investors should not be fooled into thinking the big numbers that were being quoted are one market—rather they comprise lots of markets with great variation." However, she noted more optimistically that "the unifying factor was that values do travel across sectors, whereas cultures do not".

For the industry to develop it was clear that more work on sizing and analysis would need to be undertaken. However, there was a challenge to source actual and reliable data. Professor Cedomir Nestorovic of the ESSEC Business School in Paris gave the example of France: "There are no real figures to size the market, and these will be difficult to obtain since 90 percent of *halal* food is sold in small shops."

There was general consensus on the key segments that were ripe for targeting. Dr. Temporal explained: "The *halal* industry focuses on five segments: Islamic lifestyle products, food and beverage, finance, education, and Internet and digital brands." Young noted the ranking of "the importance of *Shariah*-compliance increases with the body sensitivity of the product where food, dairy, beverages and oral care score highest, followed by fashion, personal care and 'regular' finance, and finally airlines, resorts, financial and insurance products. Some products are considered neutral of the *halal/haram* criteria, such as software."

Two of the world's leading global marketing and advertising agencies— Ogilvy & Mather Worldwide and JWT, the former using the Forum to highlight the launch of their specialist Islamic Branding agency Ogilvy Noor—presented their research into the Muslim market, along with their own consumer segmentation.

Research by Ogilvy Noor identified six consumer segments, of which three, when grouped together as "futurists", are of most interest to marketers. They are individualists who "choose" Islam. Their pride is intense, regardless of the extent to which they would be categorized as "devout." They believe in education and question intention. In particular, they challenge the use of *halal* to make sure it is not just a logo. Where information on *halal* status is not available, the company's reputation for *Shariah*-friendliness is key.

JWT commissioned the first commercial research into sizing the Muslim market. The aim was to identify the common values at the market's core in order to create relevance for the community at large with the ultimate goal of fine-tuning propositions across regions and countries. "Can we segment the Muslim world into groups that brands can be anchored on?" asked Roy Michel Haddad, Chairman and CEO, JWT Middle East and North Africa.

The Muslim consumer is not a homogeneous entity. Their diversity must be recognized and understood

Dr. Basil Mustafa, Nelson Mandela Fellow and Bursar, Oxford Centre for Islamic Studies, captured the mood of the Forum with the sentiment of diversity that was repeated by almost every speaker: "Muslims are a mosaic of views on *halal*, on culture, attitudes, economics, poverty and other demographics. This mosaic includes Muslims who live in both majority and minority Muslim countries." He warned that the "Islamic branding" discussion must avoid lazy stereotypes of monolithic Muslims or "Islam vs. West" dichotomies. Drilling deeper into the differences that are worth noting, Dr. Temporal mentioned "diverse locations, languages and dialects, cultural and lifestyle differences, degrees of religiosity, education, affluence and marketing sophistication".

Haddad went further still, stating that: "There is no single Muslim consumer, only a consumer to whom we have to respond, who has wants, needs and desires. Ramadan is the only time that the 'Muslim consumer' exists. Instead we must ask: can these consumers be reached based on their Islamic identity despite cultural and geographic differences?"

Young offered advice to Western marketers, who in his view face two big challenges when it comes to addressing the diversity of Muslim consumers: "First, most companies operate on a geographic basis, but the 'Islamic conscience' is something that is a more centralized concept. The best way to capture this is to move from localized management, to a centralized product management function to invest the Islamic brand into products from their very core. Second, Muslim consumers are not a segment that differs by one variable from the norm, such as the 'pink dollar'. Muslim consumers are an alternative norm where the starting point is Islamic identity, and everything else fits into it. Muslims' own belief in the significance of Islam in their lives is pervasive, and for them, this 'sincerity' is key in marketing practice."

It was not only Western marketers who needed to be conscious of this diversity, but also Muslims themselves, according to HE Shri K. Rahman Khan, Deputy Chairman of the Rajya Sabha and MP Indian National Congress. He spoke of this challenge when it came to the huge Indian Muslim population which is nonetheless classified as a minority: "The world Muslim community has generally ignored Indian Muslims even though they are the second largest Muslim population in the world. For example, the Organization of the Islamic Conference and Islamic Development Bank concentrate their activities on Muslim countries, so a small Muslim nation of two million will have a say in those forums, but a minority Muslim population like India's of over 200 million Muslims will have no say."

The Rt Hon Pehin Sri Haji Abdul Taib Mahmud, Chief Minister of Sarawak, Malaysia, had some further words of advice, cautioning that "the international community must be mindful" of the diversity and that "to take advantage of this the commercial world needs to develop regional trade as well as inter-regional trade. It needs to recognise that the halal market is growing and seek out Muslim consumers, whether the companies are Muslim-run or not."

Islamic branding and marketing can be used to tackle wider global issues affecting Muslims at a political and international level

Sir Iqbal Sacranie argued that the issue of Islamic branding affects both *halal* products, and Muslims and Muslim countries. Negative media coverage makes Muslims feel fearful and want to hide. In Sacranie's view one of the responsibilities of the Islamic branding industry is to address the wider issue of negativity.

The Rt. Hon. Taib Mahmud complimented the Forum on its role which he felt extended beyond just branding and marketing: "When it comes to Muslim nations issues are raised such as poverty, deprivation, terrorism, extremism and other forms of negative stereotyping, but by focusing on the economic angle, this inaugural Islamic Branding Forum offers a fresh way to tackle those issues," [he said,] noting that "an Islamic lifestyle does not mean an anti-Western or anti-modernity lifestyle".

As an example of how commerce could work towards addressing political problems, Dr. Mustafa described the rise of coffee as a consumer product as one model for building Islamic brands. In the 17th century it was first introduced to Europe from the Muslim world. Some Europeans were enamoured of it, others saw it as the sinful drink of infidels. Today coffee is a highly desirable commodity.

Effective Islamic branding and marketing would be borne by nurturing Islamic entrepreneurship, according to Tan Sri Dato' H Muhammad-Ali, CEO of Johor Corporation. Such entrepreneurship was ethically based, and community-centric and hence would tackle the lack of even wealth distribution, mass poverty and global conflicts. He went further to say that Islamic products and brands could be used to tackle general challenges wider than that of just Muslim consumers, addressing issues such as sustainability, financial crises, the rich/poor divide, and ethics in business.

HE Shaukat Aziz, former Prime Minister of Pakistan, elaborated on this by saying that: "At a global level, Islamic marketing and branding must be part of the work to tackle terrorism. Deprivation is the most likely root cause of terrorist acts—lack of income, justice, freedom, peace and harmony. Islam encourages peace, harmony and tolerance. Not terrorism!"

HRH Raja Dr. Nazrin Shah added optimistically that "Growing commercial opportunities can bind Muslims and non-Muslims in a common humanity even though till now religion has long been considered taboo in mass marketing." But he warned we should be cautious in how far we pursue segmentation on religious lines, if the Islamic brand proves a turn-off for non-Muslims. Caution must be exercised [in terms] of the inherent dangers of widespread use of faith-based brands which in the worst-case scenario could feed into Samuel P. Huntington's polarizing "clash of civilizations" thesis. He explained that political negativity could spill over into commercial negativity towards Muslim brands, making it difficult for Islamic products to penetrate Western markets. In his view, Muslim businesses already in the West were best-placed to counter such negativity.

A positive change of attitude towards innovation, risk-taking and business aspiration is required to inspire and nurture Muslim entrepreneurs

When it comes to developing world class products, Rafi-uddin Shikoh, CEO of DinarStandard, noted that none of today's global brands are from a Muslim country. He explained: "Innovation is being held back in Muslim companies by fear of failure, small thinking and a lack of critical thinking." Haddad added a lack of creativity to this list, which he felt stemmed from a poor understanding of Islamic culture. This lack of creativity was demonstrated through the stereotypical and shallow symbolism that exploited tired imagery like the crescent and the arch. It was time to "move beyond traditional expressions", he added.

One of the challenges, according to Tan Sri Muhammad-Ali, is that in South Asia business is seen by Muslims as a negative matter, something that is "worldly" and detracts from the spiritual. He coined the strapline "Business Jihad" to encourage Muslims to think of business as a religious duty and so work on changing perceptions. He emphasized that "Muslims are no less entrepreneurial; however, their businesses are not organised." For example, 95 percent of Middle East businesses are family owned. Though highly profitable only 6 percent lasted to the third generation, and only 2 percent beyond that.

He cautioned that for entrepreneurship to be Islamic it cannot just copy conventional models because of the risks of placing profit over people and being unsustainable. Conventional entrepreneurship was also exclusive to those with access to capital and networks and so the challenge for Islamic entrepreneurship is to find ways to encourage entrepreneurs from people with the lowest levels of capital and networks.

Mohamed El-Fatatry, CEO of Muxlim, said that "obtaining funding is challenging" as was finding "the right talent that has the passion for what you are doing." Khalid Sharif, CEO of Ummah Foods, noted that part of the attitude change required was an acknowledgement that while trillion dollar estimates were thrown around, there must be consciousness of the various political and economic problems facing Muslims such as poverty: "It is social improvement not greed that must be the driver for the development of the industry."

The Forum showcased two examples of innovation that brought community benefit: the Brunei Halal brand and the "Halal City" of Tanjung Manis, in Sarawak, Malaysia. Hajah Normah SH Jamil, Director of Agriculture and Agrifood, Ministry of Industry and Primary Resources in Brunei Darussalam, explained the philosophy of the former: "As a Muslim country, Brunei sees it [delivering *halal* food] as an obligation to Muslims" and its brand will "provide a platform for the development of local products and SMEs" and will open global doors for smaller corporations that "may not have the budget or leverage to otherwise gain access to international markets".

The Halal City is a green zone promoting sustainability and community development, two criteria that Datuk Hajjah Norah, Executive Chairman of Tanjung Manis Food and Industrial Park, explained were inherent to the *halal* brand. One of the programs had been to invest in farming tilapia fish. However, to improve sustainability and quality, investment was made in innovative processes so that the fish produced were not low-grade commodities, but high-level luxury products. As far as community upliftment was concerned, the Halal City was premised on corporate and aesthetic value "because it is crucial in an area like Sarawak that young people feel a strong pull to remain in their communities and not leave them. By making the Halal City attractive and investing these strong principles into it, there is the hope that they will feel strongly bound to their communities."

Strong value propositions will be key to the success of Islamic brands

"When it comes to Islamic branding and marketing, there are two challenges," explained Tan Sri Nor Mohamed Yakcop, Minister in the Prime Minister's Department, Malaysia. "First, is the need to develop a comprehensive range of products that are universally accepted by all Muslims. Second, value propositions are required that will appeal to non-Muslims" which would move the addressable market from 1.6 billion Muslims to the full global population. "Islamic branded products offer a better future for all, as they are based on the values of goodness and justice." But such products needed to be competitive and the substantive benefits had to be obvious. To achieve scalability, added Tan Sri, first a common *halal* brand needs to be established, and then "local and theological variation could be easily introduced." To achieve this, global standards would be helpful, and would require a global consensus in order to build the industry and avoid duplication.

Nestorovic explained that "bringing Muslim brands from Muslim countries would be challenging." Muslim brands need to think carefully about who their propositions are aimed at and whether the context is a majority or minority Muslim country. Muslim brands must choose whether to target Muslims or non-Muslims. For example, should a *halal* certification logo be placed on the product? In the case of France, it "already has a volatile environment when it comes to Islam, and this could exacerbate it. The best first step might be for such brands to be marketed to Muslims only," he advised.

Local propositions are increasingly popular as long as they deliver quality. John Timothy, International Corporate Affairs Manager, Tesco, explained that the "local approach is key. In Malaysia it will allow Tesco to become part of Malaysia's plan to export their *halal* products. In Turkey, the local approach is also used. To serve customers better the company has been broken into regional groups, and stores are localized for local taste."

Young explained that "Global brands are liked for their quality, innovation and heritage, but the sincerity of their *halal*-friendliness is doubted. Local brands are considered to have more insight and evoke pride, but raise concerns of quality and helpfulness. Global brands need to communicate their sincerity, local brands need to show quality, innovation and transparency."

He added that for any kind of Islamic value proposition the qualities it would need to demonstrate would include "honesty, respect, consideration, kindness, peacefulness, authenticity, purity, patience, discipline, transparency, modesty, community, dignity". The aim of an Islamic value proposition was "not to measure devoutness but to understand how devoutness, regardless of intensity, affects the lives of people as they work, play and consume".

An ethical approach to proposition development would reap rewards with non-Muslim as well as Muslim consumers, noted Afaq Khan, CEO Standard Chartered Saadiq. "Non-Muslim countries are also interested in Islamic finance as they want the most efficient use of capital, and to facilitate their own growth they need to engage with the commercial opportunity of Islamic finance in the Muslim world."

Muslim consumers needed education in Islamic value propositions. Khan gave the example that consumers were not always clear about what benefits Islamic finance brought them. Layla Mandi, CEO of OnePure, noted that for a proposition to be Islamic, it did not need to have the word "Islamic" in its name, offering her own example: "OnePure does not advertise that it is *halal* on the label, but is positioned in a premium space so its *halal* message can be explained clearly to consumers."

"The challenge is to educate consumers and to avoid the creation of technically *halal* products that miss the point," explained Joseph. "Much of the groundwork for these values has already been laid by the development of the ethical industry, the green movement, animal welfare and so on. The *halal* market is not the 'big ideal.' Instead we need to focus on the 'big ideal' of sustainable industry."

Saïd Business School

The Saïd Business School is one of Europe's youngest and most entrepreneurial business schools. An integral part of The University of Oxford, the School embodies the academic rigor and forward thinking that has made Oxford a world leader in education. The School is dedicated to developing a new generation of business leaders and entrepreneurs and conducting research not only into the nature of business, but also the connections between business and the wider world.

For more information, see:
www.sbs.oxford.edu/islamicmarketing
Saïd Business School
University of Oxford
Executive Education Centre
Egrove Park
Oxford OX1 5NY
United Kingdom

Index